THE AMERICAN DOG BOOK

BOOKS BY KURT UNKELBACH

Uncle Charlie's Poodle
Those Lovable Retrievers
Love on a Leash
The Pleasures of Dog Ownership (with Evie Unkelbach)
Albert Payson Terhune: The Master of Sunnybank
The Winning of Westminster
Murphy
How to Bring Up Your Pet Dog
The Dog in My Life
Ruffian: International Champion
The Dog Who Never Knew
Both Ends of the Leash: Selecting & Training Your Dog
How to Make Money in Dogs
How to Show Your Dog and Win
A Cat and His Dogs
Catnip: Selecting & Training Your Cat
Tiger Up a Tree: Knowing & Training Your Kitten
You're a Good Dog, Joe: Knowing & Training Your Puppy

THE AMERICAN DOG BOOK

BY KURT UNKELBACH

A Sunrise Book

E.P. DUTTON & COMPANY, INC. • NEW YORK

Published simultaneously in Canada by Clarke, Irwin & Company
Limited, Toronto and Vancouver
ISBN: 0-87690-201-8

Dutton-Sunrise, Inc., a subsidiary of E. P. Dutton & Co., Inc.

Library of Congress Cataloging in Publication Data

Unkelbach, Kurt.
  The American dog book.

  "A Sunrise book."
  1. Dogs. 2. Dog breeds. 3. Dogs—United States, Canada.
1. Title.
SF426.U54   636.7   75-42300

To Evie

Contents

Acknowledgment & Apologia

For the nature and scope of this book, the author depended upon what he has learned and not forgotten about dogs, as well as on scores of helpful dog lovers from both sides of the Atlantic. Breeders, exhibitors, trainers, handlers, researchers and historians—you know who you are, you also know that I am more unorganized than any three of you, and I want you to know that I am very grateful for every assist, whether it was a date that is not to be found in the record books, or breed data that has never before appeared in print.

Still, it wouldn't be fair to withhold special thanks from the secretaries and members of the many, cooperating breed clubs; and it might be immoral not to confess that the officers of the American Kennel Club and the Canadian Kennel Club supplied, confirmed, or clarified various and essential components of the text—upon request —if all that needs clarifying. And then there are those loyal dog lovers who rallied to our cause by contributing photos of their favorite breeds. They are credited on another page.

You will not find an Introduction on the next or any other page of this book. Reading dog lovers don't need one, and their dogs don't care.

K. U.
Walden Folly
Connecticut

The Topographical Dog

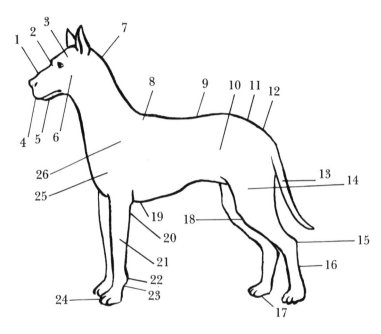

1 Muzzle	10 Loin	19 Brisket
2 Stop	11 Hips	20 Elbow
3 Skull	12 Rump (Croup)	21 Forearm
4 Lip	13 Tail (Stern)	22 Wrist (Carpus)
5 Flews	14 Upper Thigh	23 Pastern (Metacarpus)
6 Cheek	15 Hock	24 Toes (Digits)
7 Crest	16 Metatarsus	25 Point of Shoulder
8 Withers	17 Pad	26 Shoulder
9 Back	18 Knee (Stifle)	

THE AMERICAN DOG BOOK

I

The American Canine Scene

And where were you sixty minutes ago? It really doesn't matter, but between then and right now some two thousand pups were whelped in America. Most of the newcomers are planned pups, and those that survive early hazards will do more than replace those beloved, elderly beasts who have just barked their last hurrahs and those others who have just been cut down by traffic, research, humane societies, unappreciative owners, or disease. The new pups will add to the zooming canine population, which is now somewhere over the forty-million mark. Another twelve to fifteen million feral dogs are also on the scene, but they don't count as pets and family friends.

If we can rely on statistics, then one American out of every six owns a pet dog. But in this case, we can't rely on figures. Hundreds of thousands of people own more than one dog—from two or three to more than a hundred. Usually, multiple ownership denotes a dog fancier, a human type that has never been clearly defined by historians, psychiatrists, or wits. Like most dog owners, he is certainly a dog lover, but he considers himself a cut above the average lover. While dogs are generally his avocation, the hobby often becomes as important as—or more important than—vocation, family, and friends.

Whether or not this canine hobby includes breeding,* the fancier really believes that he is improving his favorite breed or breeds. He proves this to himself and perhaps a few other fanciers by engaging in one or more of the dog game's three popular sports: dog shows, Obedience trials, and field trials. Perhaps it would be best to define a

---

* For definitions of terms used in the pages that follow, see Chapter XII, "How to Speak with Authority in the Dog Game: A Glossary."

3

dog fancier as "an activist dog lover," since he does more with his dogs than pet, feed, love, and house them.

At this time in the history of *Canis familiaris* America is home to about a half-million, true-blue dog fanciers. These are the ones who will be around for years to come, and as a group they can be considered the very heart of the dog game. Then there are another half-million fanciers who for a variety of reasons become disenchanted after a few years and drop out of the dog game. The dropouts are never missed because each year they are replaced by new dog fanciers—in numbers to spare.

All the fanciers—the true blues, the dropouts before they drop, and the newcomers—are interested in one or more of the many pure breeds of dogs. The great majority of American dog fanciers (women outnumber men) are devoted to the established breeds recognized by the American Kennel Club and the Canadian Kennel Club. Other fanciers are involved with pure breeds that will surely be recognized at some future date, and still others are busy keeping old but now rare breeds from extinction.

No matter what one may think of dog fanciers, they are responsible for an amazing change in the public's attitude toward canines. A century ago the average dog lover was content to own and love any old dog, and that dog was usually a mongrel. It was held that the mongrel was more intelligent than the purebred, as well as more talented, more durable, and easier to keep. The American canine population amounted to fewer than two hundred thousand beasts, and if even 1 percent were purebreds, there was nobody around to make the claim.

Apparently, the first assessment of the American canine scene was made by one Nicholas Butler, an English exporter of durable goods who made an extensive tour of the United States in 1866, the better to acquaint himself with the New World's needs and to line up reliable importers. He was a dog lover, and among the impressions he jotted down when he returned to London was this one: "For every thoroughbred dog I saw in the United States, I saw a goodly many more of curs, perhaps as many as three hundred."

It is presumed that Mr. Butler knew a purebred ("thoroughbred") when he saw one, for almost all the pure breeds that he saw here had been originally imported from England. They were mostly sporting and hound breeds, generally owned by the more prosperous citizens.

In 1866 these owners were just beginning to stir, just beginning to come together to form the American dog fancy. It's hardly likely that any of them dreamed of the day (today) when the average dog lover would prefer a purebred over a mongrel. But these days seven out of every ten dogs are purebreds. The dog fancy has come a long way.

What really excited America's earliest fanciers was a phenomenon known as the dog show. Until this very page all texts on the subject have credited the English with this now popular spectacular, probably because most noted canine historians have been Englishmen. The truth is that the world's first dog show was dreamed up by King Rudolph II of Bohemia, a very unstable man. This melancholy ruler, beset by troubles on all sides, may have figured that nobody loved him more than his own hunting dogs. Whatever the inspiration, he invited his dearest friends to bring their dogs to his Royal Castle Gardens in Prague. The response to this invitation—or command— was a gathering of some five hundred beasts, including the king's own. This first show, staged in 1603, was a private gala. Rudolph's dogs did very well, and hardly anybody was surprised. The judge knew he was expendable. As far as Rudolph was concerned, the show was one of the most pleasant moments of his reign, although it may have put the skids under him. He was forced to abdicate in 1611.

Rudy's successor was King Matthias, who moved Bohemia's capital from Prague to Vienna and didn't give a thought to dog shows. Still, the memory of the private show must have lingered on in Prague, for it was there, in 1791, that the world's first public dog show was staged. There were many more dog lovers than dogs on hand. About 130 beasts of several breeds were involved in the competition, including St. Bernards, Dachshunds, Borzois, Great Pyrenees, and Poodles; all probably looked pretty much as they do today.

During the next half-century public shows were staged occasionally in other European lands, but none achieved the status of an annual event. Apparently, word of these early shows did not reach the British Isles, reason enough for England's dog fanciers to believe that they were staging the world's first dog show as dawn came to Newcastle-upon-Tyne one morn in 1859. This show was a spectacular success, and it spawned an increasing number of British shows, many of them annual events, in the following years. The most enthusiastic supporters of those shows were the breeders. In many breeds, the demand for pups outran the supply. The interest of British royalty in the shows was the frosting on the cake. From almost any point of view, dog shows were far more successful than the already established field trials.

In retrospect, there is a touch of irony about those early English shows. They were conceived by members of the field trial set, who were British gentlemen of wealth, leisure, and land. They owned dogs of the gundog breeds (later bastardized in America to "sporting breeds") and they were happiest when their dogs won at the trials. After a time, that wasn't enough, as in the phrase, "Your dog beat mine today, but mine is a better-looking dog." Presto, the dog show! There dogs were judged on the basis of good looks (breed conformation), and never mind how worthy they were in the field. Thus, the best lookers (in each breed) were the winners even if they were sometimes the stupidest beasts on hand. Human nature also played a hand: it didn't hurt a dog's chances if his owner was the son-in-law of the breed judge.

The sponsors of those early shows made up their own rules and regulations. As the years rolled along, breeds other than gundogs got into the act: old pure breeds, new pure breeds, and almost pure breeds. Confusion reigned. It didn't seem to matter. The British fell in love with the dog shows—and the purebreds. This love affair continues. Today, although England's purebred canine population is far less than half the size of America's, the English boast more dog shows and also host Cruft's, by far the world's largest annual dog show.

On this side of the Atlantic, the dog fancy didn't amount to much until the Civil War had become history. The purebreds on hand were imports—English, Irish, and French—or the descendants of earlier imports—mostly hound, sporting, and terrier breeds. Although better known for other achievements, George Washington was one of our earliest foxhound breeders. He was well remembered but not on hand for the very first American dog show in 1867.

Long before that year, of course, news of the English dog show fever had reached these shores, but our most ardent dog lovers had been too busy to organize similar events. At least one American had witnessed British dog shows during a visit with relatives. Grace Haskell, the wife of a prosperous farmer and sportsman with big landholdings in Virginia and Maryland, wasn't much as a dog lover, but she was a very good wife, and the gifts she brought home for husband James included a brace of young, adult Pointers.

James, of course, received a firsthand account of dog shows, spent a great deal of time thinking about them, and finally expressed his thoughts to friends who were also cattle, horse and dog breeders. In September of 1867 James and his friends hosted a dog show at one of the Haskell farms in Maryland. Presumably, that was America's first dog show. There's no record of an earlier one, and very little is known about this one beyond the fact that about one hundred dogs were present. As for the breeds, surely Pointers and English Fox-hounds were there, perhaps some terriers, and then a few beasts identi-fied only as herding dogs. As for the judging, it really had to be one man's opinion; breed standards were still things of the future.

The dog show fever did not catch on here as rapidly as it had in England. Over the next few years shows were more or less private affairs sponsored by and held for the benefit of serious breeders. In the spirit of the original Haskell show they were held for the purpose of comparison, to give one breeder the opportunity to compare his dogs with those of others in the same breed and thus judge how well his own breeding program was doing. What the breeders had in mind was improvement of the breed, not their own variety or its popularization. While the number of shows increased each year, all were small and dog lovers remained apathetic. As in England, the rules varied from show to show, and most of the breeders, exhibitors, and spectators were more than a little confused. Sporting breeds continued to domi-nate the entries.

Still, things were happening, all on the positive side for the future of the American dog fancy.

1873. Overseas, some of the deepest thinkers among dog lovers formed the Kennel Club in England. From that year onward English dog shows were governed by strict rules and regulations. This brought the breeding of purebred dogs under control in the British Isles and gave dog shows a heavy touch of respectability. In later years other lands would adopt the idea of a governing body for the dog fancy. If it had not been for the Kennel Club (England), God knows where the pure breeds of canines would be today.

1874. Fifteen dog shows were held in America. Of these, three reflected the Kennel Club influence and gave evidence that our dog fancy was drifting under control. In June the first benched show ever held in this country was sponsored by the Illinois State Sportsmen's Association and staged in Chicago. There were about two hundred dogs, the greatest number to date, and some three thousand spectators, another record. Everybody went home happy, since there were neither winning nor losing dogs. The judges did not rank the dogs, but they handed out commendations to the owners of superior beasts, all of them sporting dogs. Later that same month the New York State Sportsmen's Association held the second benched show at Oswego, N.Y. It was America's first great dog show failure; only three dogs were on hand. The first American show judged by Kennel Club rules was held at Mineola, New York, and was hailed by the press as a great success. Irish Setters, Gordon Setters, and Pointers dominated the breeds. There were also classes for "Setters of any Breed," meaning English, crosses, and dogs that looked like setters. This unbenched show took place in October. The next day, in Memphis, the Tennessee Sportsmen's Association sponsored America's first combined show and field trial. The rules for both were those of England's Kennel Club. The dogs were all Setters and Pointers. For the first time, (show) classes were held for pups. The year's other shows were less noteworthy.

1875. By that year the dog show fever started to spread a little. New, annual shows were added to the list, all sponsored by sportsmen's groups or newly organized, local kennel clubs. Detroit, Springfield (Massachusetts), Paris (Kentucky), Manchester (New Hampshire), Columbus (Ohio) and St. Louis (Missouri) joined the act. The year's total was about thirty shows, the most unusual at Memphis, where the event spanned four days: two for a dog show, followed by two for a field trial. And then there were dog shows that could hardly be classified as such, although they were so promoted. Country fairs and other celebrations staged them as added attractions and awarded prizes in such categories as biggest dog, smallest dog, funniest-looking dog, handsomest dog, dog with the longest tail, best-costumed dog, and so forth.

1876. *The American Kennel and Sporting Field*, by Arnold Burgess, was published by J. B. Ford of New York. This literary event had a profound influence on the future of the American dog fancy. The author, who died just before the book was published, had been the editor of *American Sportsman,* a popular magazine of the time. He had also written canine articles for other magazines and was a veteran dog lover and breeder. England had at the time a monopoly on canine authorities, but American dog lovers regarded Mr. Burgess as one of the greatest experts.

While his book was really devoted to the sporting breeds, it covered a wide range of subjects that were important to all dog owners and breeders: breeding, choosing a pup, care and management, training, feeding, pedigrees, and so forth. Throughout the book Burgess sprinkled personal opinions that turned scoffers of the dog fancy into supporters. A few Burgessisms:

> It is easy enough for individuals to claim for their animals superiority of blood and qualities, and if we have no thorough test for these there can be no way of proving or disproving the assertion. It must be remembered, too, that it is possible for a dog to be of pure lineage, yet dishonor it by cur-like qualities, and either vanity or lack of experience prevents the owner detecting this. Unprejudiced and positive tests are therefore greatly needed, and these can only be found in shows and trials under judges who have the common interest so keenly in view that they will allow neither friendship nor personal bias to control their awards.

Obviously, those words amount to a plea for breeders to mate only dogs of quality and for judges to walk the straight and narrow. Next, a blast at those who entered dogs of questionable pedigree, and a comment on the real purpose behind dog shows:

> To escape the baneful effects of such dogs being credited with the highest honors, and to carry out the principles for which we propose to inaugurate shows—namely, the encouragement of breeding superior, not inferior, stock—it must be made a *sine qua non* that every winner shall present an irreproachable pedigree. Experience fully sustains the aphorism that "blood will tell" and the best and most successful English breeders select dogs of the purest descent, even if not quite up to the mark on work, and the wisdom of the choice is shown in the great increase in the number of canine wonders which each year brings out.

And this, a call to arms for the founding of an American governing body along the lines of the Kennel Club of England:

> We have reached an important crisis in the history of our kennels, and the emergency can be met only by the establishment of adequate tribunals which will exercise the most rigid severity in judging, and the utmost impartiality in making their first awards.

These observations and others stirred America's dog fanciers, and a few of the more dedicated ones got together here and there in the hope of launching some sort of a control agency that could handle purebred registration and set down laws to govern dog shows and field trials. In the late 1870s and early 1880s several groups did get off the ground, but none survived. The National American Kennel Club (1878) came close, but it lacked both funds and believers and had to call it a day in 1883. As more local kennel clubs (all breeds) and regional specialty clubs (one breed) came into existence, shows and/or field trials continued to be run under different, arbitrary rules, sometimes guided by the Kennel Club's statutes, but more often not. While it would not be fair to say that the judging was dishonest right down the line, since all the judges were gentlemen of character, social standing, and accomplishment, it is true that they often knew more about good wines and cigars than they did about dogs.

Then, in 1884, just in the nick of time, ten sportsmen sat down to enjoy lunch in Philadelphia. A few were local citizens, but most had traveled far, and they had come together in the hope of providing guidelines for the American dog fancy. The meeting was productive, and a month later in Manhattan they announced the birth of the nonprofit American Kennel Club, designed to bring truth and light to the dog fancy—and rules and regulations, as well. The A.K.C. was a floating organization until 1887, when the first permanent headquarters were established in a room of 300 square feet on lower Broadway. In that same year the A.K.C. published its first Stud Book and designated it as Volume IV. This provided continuity for the three previous volumes published by the late National American Kennel Club.

At the start, membership was open to qualified dog fanciers, but they did not storm the doors. The membership rule was then changed from individuals to organizations with a consuming interest in pure-bred dogs, such as kennel clubs, specialty clubs, and other groups devoted to the interest of blooded beasts. At meetings each club was represented by a delegate, and each delegate was entitled to one vote. The then established clubs didn't storm the doors, but enough of them applied to keep the A.K.C. from floundering. The system of member clubs and delegates is still in effect, but not the bylaw that protected the male sex: until 1974 a delegate could only be a man. Today, female delegates are welcome. This is right and just, for there are far more women than men involved in the dog fancy. The courageous step was a big tribute to women's devotion—and a small tribute to Grace Haskell, who indirectly inspired our first dog show. When it came to equality of the sexes, the Canadian Kennel Club was miles ahead of the A.K.C. To date it has enjoyed the leadership of three women presidents.

In the early years, specialty clubs represented the majority membership and kept the A.K.C. afloat. Some of the first to come into the fold represented such breeds as the Irish Setter, St. Bernard, Boston Terrier, Beagle, Bulldog, French Bulldog, and Dachshund. Each was interested in a valid registration body that could also lend credence to a definitive breed standard. In the beginning, a breed standard amounted to one man's opinion. Of the few kennel clubs that joined in the early years, the most important (retrospectively) was the Westminster Kennel Club of New York City. This club's first show, a three-day event held in May of 1877 at Gilmore's Garden, had set all sorts of American records: the biggest to date in number of dogs (about 900), pure breeds (31), and spectators; the first to import a breed judge from abroad (England); the first to receive national coverage by newspapers and magazines. Queen Victoria, by then a dedicated Collie lover, entered (through her kennel manager) two Deerhounds that had been favorites of her late, beloved Albert and offered them for sale at $50,000 each. The British believed that all American streets were paved with gold.

By the time the A.K.C. came along, the general public had accepted Westminster as America's top dog show. Of course, it had a lot going for it: size, site, and media coverage. And no other kennel club could claim such a distinguished membership roster: captains of business and industry, leading sportsmen, prominent socialites, and old families. While Westminster is no longer our largest dog show, it remains the oldest and most prestigious, and February 1976 marked the club's hundredth staging of the annual event.

When Westminster joined the A.K.C. and agreed to abide by its rules and regulations, other important kennel clubs followed suit. The American Kennel Club was secure, and so was the dog fancy.

Meanwhile, the message of unity had reached Canada, where the Canadian Kennel Club was founded in 1888. Since 1889 the two national bodies have worked in harmony, and the differences in rules and regulations have been minimal. Most breeds recognized by the A.K.C., for example, are eligible for competition at C.K.C. dog shows, Obedience trials, and field trials, and Canadian dogs of those breeds have the same privileges at A.K.C. events. The only important difference is in membership: A.K.C. members are clubs (about 360), and C.K.C. members are individual dog fanciers (about 11,000).

Both governing bodies have had their ups and downs, but they have been on very solid footing over the past five decades. Without them, the dog game would still be chaotic, and the purebreds would not have achieved their present popularity. Unfortunately, two problems remain. They had their beginnings after World War II, when the real boom in purebreds began, and they continue to grow.

Puppy farms. This is a problem of abundance, directly related to the law of supply and demand. When more dog lovers started to look for purebred pups, pet stores were pleased to make those pups available. When respectable breeders refused to supply litters for the wholesale market, the retailers looked elsewhere. The solution was the puppy farm, an enterprise devoted to the mass production of pups —and never mind their quality. In 1950 there were an estimated two hundred puppy farms in America. Today there are about fourteen thousand, and there will be more next year. *Deplorable* is the kindest word one can use to describe conditions on the farms. All produce purebred pups in several breeds and ship them off by the litter at too early an age. Often a litter is shipped in an orange crate.

Thanks to the puppy farms, the number of pet shops has increased in dramatic fashion. Many of them, especially those in or near large cities, now deal only in purebred pups and dog supplies. Chains of pet shops have been established, and a dozen major syndicates offer local franchises. About nine thousand puppy shops, some in leading department stores, now rake in $400 million a year for this live merchandise of questionable quality. In the cases of the chains and franchises, litters of pups (some from abroad) are shipped to a holding facility, then distributed to the various retail outlets. There the pups are treated like any other merchandise. Smooth-talking salesmen often wear white jackets, and the name of the game is overpricing and rapid turnover. Convenience is a major reason for the astonishing success of the puppy outlets. It's easier to find puppy shops than legitimate breeders, and for a choice among twenty breeds one would have to visit that many breeders. Of equal importance to convenience is the innocence of the average dog lover. To the person who is buying a pup for the first time, one purebred pup is just as good as another. The high price tag on the cute puppy he selects is never a hardship—time payments ease the pain, although they won't ease the disappointment as the puppy matures into a substandard representative of his breed.

The money in poorly bred purebred pups is so good and the potential of guileless, new (seldom repeat) customers so great that it's a wonder the giant supermarket chains haven't gone in for selling puppies. Let's hope that they don't. The move would double the number of puppy farms, and America is already supporting too many.

To date, it hasn't been possible to slow the growth rate of those puppy farms, or factories. This remains something of a mystery. Most of the farms are found in the southern and midwestern states. All those states have health laws and anticruelty-to-animals laws. Despite the pleas of humane societies and concerned citizens, not a single state has enforced those laws in the puppy-farm area. Thus, the saddest kind of free enterprise is permitted to flourish.

Veterinarians. This problem is one of scarcity, and it becomes more serious with each passing year. The problem exists because of the continuing pet-population boom and the lack of new veterinary schools.

Between them, the United States and Canada can boast of only twenty-two such schools, no more than there were twenty years ago. In an average year these schools graduate no more than fifteen hundred new veterinarians. About two-thirds of them are immediately absorbed by major industries, research laboratories, and various federal bureaus. That leaves approximately five hundred new vets for private practice—not enough to make up for the annual retirement and deaths of experienced veterinarians. To compound the problem, an investment of about $50,000 is required these days for a new vet to open his own practice. Thus, the great majority of new veterinarians in the remaining category join the staffs of already existing small animal hospitals or become assistants to already established veterinarians.

As things stand now, we have about thirty-five thousand veterinarians engaged in private practice and dedicated to the welfare of America's pet population. While the total number of America's various pets is anybody's guess, the most popular pets—cats and dogs—now easily total one hundred million.

The distribution of practicing veterinarians further complicates the problem. Approximately one-third are located in or around big cities, where the demand for their services is great and fees are high. The other two-thirds are spread very thinly from coast to coast, and many of them cannot confine their concern to pets. Horses, cattle, and other livestock are also their responsibility. To say that our vets are very busy people would be an understatement.

Many universities have long been interested in establishing new veterinary schools. To do so means fighting miles of state and federal red tape and finding the necessary funding. Two new schools (one in New England) now have a chance of becoming realities and graduating their first classes in 1980. They would help ease the situation, although not by much, since there's every indication that the pet population will continue to grow. A score of new veterinary schools are needed right now, but there's no hope that the need will be fulfilled. Today's vet shortage is critical. Tomorrow's may well be chaotic.

This American problem is not unique. It is true in all the free countries of the world. Only Russia has the dog game under control: not everyone can own a dog, dog breeding is rigidly supervised, and veterinary service is free, where available.

American dog lovers would probably agree to the free treatment but not to the control of ownership and breeding. Short of the Russian method, the veterinary problem will not go away. It will be with us for a long time, possibly forever.

Over the past few years the American Kennel Club has registered better than a million new purebreds. Since only about 20 percent of the year's eligible pups will ever be registered, this indicates a minimum annual crop of five million purebred pups—give or take a hundred thousand. If you own a computer, the exact total can be reached by adding the number of pups in every litter recorded by the A.K.C. in a given year. And then there are another two million purebred pups who cannot be registered for the very simple reason that somebody neglected to register their sires and dams. They are the results of accidental breedings and such planned breedings as the popular "We did it for the education of our children, just this once." Nonetheless, the pups are purebreds.

The dog game is now far bigger than the average citizen (dog lover or dog hater) realizes. It plays an important role in our economy, to the tune of about eight billion dollars a year. Many major industries do not come close to that figure.

More than a billion of the total is spent on commercial dog foods and food supplements. Close to two billion is spent on canine research and veterinary services. Another billion-plus goes for purebred pups. The remaining billions are spent in a huge variety of ways that range from the rational (collars, leashes, kennel fencing) to the utterly ridiculous (perfumes, nail polish, fur coats).

Dog fanciers are the biggest spenders, and they feel compelled to spend, whether they can afford to or not. Consider a small, licensed outdoor dog show with an entry of 1,000 dogs. In advance of the show the fanciers pay a $10 entry fee per dog—for a total of $10,000. To get to the show, they travel anywhere from 10 miles to 2,500 miles; a ridiculously low estimate of combined travel expenses would be $10,000. At the show, at least 100 of the fanciers, now exhibitors, employ—for reasons best known to themselves—the services of professional handlers at a cost of about $50 per dog. And during the show, each fancier will spend about $20 on food and on the canine-owner-oriented items offered for sale at the booths: combs, brushes, other grooming aides, vitamins, ashtrays, books, stationery, magazines, paintings, photographs (of his dog), kennel fencing and gates, folding puppy pens, signs, toys, statuettes, and so forth. At show's end the fanciers collect their dogs and head for home (or the next day's dog show), to the tune of another $10,000. All those minimum figures come to a modest spending spree of $55,000—all of it from the pockets of the involved dog fanciers at the show.

Meanwhile, the sponsor of the show—a local kennel club—must shell out money for the services of a show superintendent (who actually stages and supervises the show, providing all the necessary equipment and labor), judges' expenses and fees, catalogs, advertising, rental of the show grounds, and other costs. A thrifty kennel club might get by on $5,000. At a small show over 2,000 spectators can be expected. All must buy tickets to see the show, some will buy show catalogs, and most will buy food and other items. If all are penny pinchers, they will still spend $5,000. Thus, a low spending figure for this small show represents $65,000.

On this same day at least four or five other dog shows will be held in America. Indoors or outdoors, ranging in size from a low of about seven hundred dogs to a high of about four thousand, the great majority are one-day affairs, and close to sixteen hundred such licensed annual shows were held in North America in 1974. A licensed show is one approved by and held under the strict rules and regulations of either the A.K.C. or the C.K.C., and only at a licensed show can a dog win the points that lead to the title of champion. The original intent of the dog show, to improve the breed, has now largely given way to: "My dog is better than your dog."

The average dog fancier does not rest between licensed dog shows. Somewhere nearby he can always find a match show, a canine event of a lower order but also limited to purebred dogs. Although the procedure is identical to that of the licensed show, a dog cannot win championship points, and the real *raison d'être* is to provide training and experience for the fancier and his new dream dog. After a few match shows it is presumed that the fancier will know if his dog has what it takes to win at the licensed shows. Those who hold to this popular presumption are continually disheartened. The losingest dogs at match shows often mature into the winningest dogs at licensed shows. And vice versa.

Match shows are also hosted by kennel clubs; a big one would have around five hundred dogs. Since overhead is minimal, the entry fee per dog is seldom over two dollars, and fanciers seldom travel more than a hundred miles, the cash expended for a match show is not impressive. In one package, all the match shows in a given year do not shake as many dollars loose as does a single big licensed show. Still, the lower-order shows are very important to the dog fancy. They keep veteran fanciers active, and they entice dog lovers, who rapidly become dog fanciers.

Without the dog show, the dog fancy would not fade away. But it would be hurt, and the overwhelming popularity of purebreds would, for the first time, diminish. However, there's absolutely no danger that the dog show will disappear. It is a way of life for too many people; they regard it as their favorite sport. This definition has always amused the multitudes, for the only contact found at a dog show is when a purebred dog bites a sincere breed judge, and the only bruises are found in the facial expressions of fanciers whose dogs have lost. The fanciers are right, nonetheless: the dog show is a sport. In the dictionary, a sport is defined as any amusement or pastime. There are other sports in the dog fancy, of course, and they will be treated in the pages ahead (see Chapter XI).

The image of the dog fancier as a big spender is reflected in a true story related to one of those other sports: the field trial. In the summer of 1966 I was enriched by $300 through the sale of a Labrador Retriever pup to Mr. A., a dog lover with a penchant for duck hunting. As an adult, this Lab more than proved his worth as a hunting companion, and friends of Mr. A. encouraged him to enter the dog in retriever field trials. He attended a few trials, just to get the hang of them, and decided that his dog was every bit as accomplished as the field trial champions that were running. When the Lab was three, Mr. A. entered him in a few field trials. Although the dog did not disgrace his master, he failed to place, and Mr. A. became discouraged. He was too new at the game to realize that he had a diamond in the rough.

Mr. X., a veteran member of the field trial set, had observed the dog in action and did realize his potential. His offer of $5,000 surprised Mr. A., who refused to sell. He loved his dog too much. Later, he accepted a final offer of $18,000. He didn't love the dog that much.

While Mr. A. was on the way to the bank, Mr. X. was on the phone making arrangements to place his new dog in the hands of a top professional trainer. Ten months later his Lab—by then a polished performer—was a sensational winner at the trials. Mr. X. has since recouped his investment. The dog's stud fee is a firm $1,000. Pups sired by him bring $500 to $1,500.

The $18,000 purchase price, the stud fee, and the puppy price tags are not unusual in the field trial world, although they would be extremely high for show dogs. The dog game's biggest spenders are found in the retriever field trial set. Lord knows how much money changes hands in this dog sport, but it has to be an impressive amount. A big spender in the field trial set makes a big spender in the dog show set look like a piker.

II

The All-American Breeds

There are several hundred pure breeds of canines in the world. Of these, fewer than one-third are recognized by the American Kennel Club and the Canadian Kennel Club. And of the recognized, only seven were developed from other breeds—known and unknown—in North America.

Of these All-Americans, five had their beginnings in the United States, one in Alaska (before statehood), and one in Nova Scotia. Today none are found among the very popular breeds. It is as if dog lovers have short memories.

Still, these seven breeds do constitute a portion of the American dog game's heritage. For that reason, they are honored on these pages before all of the other pure breeds.

Here they are:

ALASKAN MALAMUTE

The biggest and oldest of the Arctic sled dogs, his name derives from *Mahlemut,* the native Alaskan tribe responsible for his development in the long ago. Then (as now) the tribe dwelt along the shores of rugged Kotzebue Sound, partially within the embrace of the Arctic Circle. The people were as fond of dogs as children, although they used only the dogs for transportation and hauling freight. As a pack dog, a healthy specimen can carry up to fifty pounds and go for several hours without rest.

The breed was recognized by the A.K.C. in 1936, two dozen years before Alaska was recognized as a state. But the Malamute's beginnings were slow in both the United States and Canada, despite the world fame the breed achieved in 1933 for hauling the sleds of Admiral

Byrd's expedition to the South Pole. The myth that this beast's thick, double coat would make him unhappy in temperate climes persisted until after World War II. Since, his popularity has grown.

The Malamute is a member of the Spitz family. Thus, he is a cousin of the Samoyed and Siberian Husky, and also the Eskimo Dog, who is no longer recognized by the A.K.C. Other members of the family, all recognized by the A.K.C., are the Akita, Norwegian Elkhound, Keeshund, and Pomeranian.

This is a very tractable dog. He can take any climate, doesn't mind living outdoors, and is perfectly agreeable to living under the same roof with his human family. As with any powerful breed, the AM does require early training and constant discipline. The stronger the dog, the greater the need for him to know who is really the boss. If he is not abused, the AM makes a fine family pet. Still, a pack dog is not a pony, and undisciplined children should also be trained.

Breed Blueprint

For his size and strength, an adult AM is a fairly light eater, a fact that provides needless worry for many owners. A fat AM is exceptional

and is usually owned by an obese person who force-feeds him.

The big, broad head carries a slightly rounded skull that flattens toward the eyes, with a slight furrow between the eyes and only a suggestion of stop. The muzzle is broad and deep and slightly tapering. His big, almond shaped eyes are dark brown and look just right for the head. The wedge shaped ears, however, look a little small. They are medium set and carried upright. A scissors bite is proper. Beneath the coat the neck is arched.

His body looks very compact, although it's not really short-coupled. Shoulders carry a moderate slope, the chest is deep and broad, the legs are of heavy bone, and the feet are big, compact and arched. The AM topline slopes downwards from withers over very strong hindquarters. Angulation is moderate, and the medium set tail is carried in a curve (never a curl) over the back.

The double coat has a soft, wooly undercoat that's a little oily and runs from 1 to 2 inches in length. Over this, the harsh topcoat (guard coat) stands out. It's thickest around the neck, and varies in the same lengths as the undercoat. Proper coat colors range from light gray to almost black, with some white on underbelly and on parts of legs, feet and masking. The only permissible solid color is pure white. With that or any other coat, the nose must be black.

The ideal size for males is 25 inches and 85 pounds; for bitches, 23 inches and 75 pounds. These seem to be natural sizes for the breed, and the best show dogs seldom vary from them.

The AM does his maximum shedding during the summer months. Show judges who are aware of this fact seldom penalize for a poor coat at this time.

AMERICAN FOXHOUND

Great stamina and strong scenting power are the hallmarks of this breed, whose members are among the few purebreds who really prefer the company of other dogs to that of people. Since the great majority have always been kept in packs for the purpose of trailing the fox, they have been housed in kennels, and even today very few are kept as house pets. As a pet, the AF is generally regarded as a one-man dog.

Robert Brooke, an Englishman, brought the first pack of hounds to America in 1650. In addition to the dogs, Mr. Brooke was accompanied by his wife, ten children, and a modest army of servants. All settled in what is now Maryland, and there the master, his friends and his dogs introduced the noble sport of the fox hunt to these shores. The object of their attention was the native gray fox.

Over the next two centuries, other members of the landed gentry continued to import hounds from England, France and Ireland. George Washington was among the fox hunting enthusiasts, and dogs from both England and France were in his packs. Owning a pack of hounds was a social must for a southern gentleman of wealth, taste and property.

For a long time breeding was haphazard, with the best bred to the best, and bloodlines were relatively unimportant. The end results were hounds of many types, and from them have evolved the American Foxhound, Black and Tan Coonhound, and Walker Hound. This last breed remains unrecognized by the A.K.C.

The American Foxhound was really developed to meet the talents of the red fox, an eighteenth-century European import who proved much speedier and wilier than the gray, and also ran for longer

periods of time before going to ground. Once the red fox started populating the South, the need for a hound with more speed and endurance and louder music became obvious.

Breeders set themselves to the task and succeeded. Still, several types remained. Finally, the American Foxhound Club and the masters of several foxhound associations put their heads together and came up with a single standard that, while allowing unimportant variations, hews to a type.

Breed Blueprint

This dog is built for speed and endurance, and can run for hours. His intelligence matches his stamina, and nothing distracts him when he's on the trail.

The back is of moderate length, with chest deep (lung power) rather than broad. Sloping shoulders are clean and muscular, ribs are well sprung, and loin is broad.

The long skull is slightly domed (occiput), and the muzzle is long and square. Ears, set at eye level, reach almost to nose. Eye colors are brown or hazel. The bite is not specified, but it's usually scissors or even. The clean throat is free from folds.

Sound legs fore and aft, but never with bone so heavy that it results in cloddy movement. The moderately long tail is set high, carried gaily, and can have a slight curve.

The breed carries the usual hound coat: close and hard. Any coat color is okay, but usually it's a mix of white, black and tan. Males run from 22 to 25 inches, bitches from 21 to 24 inches. Weight is not specified, but a 24-inch dog in hard condition will average about 60 pounds.

AMERICAN WATER SPANIEL

In dogdom, one of the unsung tragedies of the Civil War was that it ended the dog breeding program of the Boykin family of Boykin, South Carolina. Over more than two decades, the family had developed a distinct breed whose fame as a hunting companion had spread throughout the South and Midwest. The dog was known as the Boykin Spaniel, and he was a dandy for flushing and fetching upland birds and for marking and retrieving downed waterfowl. While there are no records to prove the mix of breeds that produced the Boykin, a single photograph reveals that the Boykin was the spitting image of today's American Water Spaniel.

If the AWS is not the contemporary Boykin, then this is one of the pure breeds who lacks a definitive history. And if he really is the Boykin, that's all we know of his history, since nobody is aware of the breeds behind the Boykin. Either way, it is quite probable that both the Irish Water Spaniel and the Curly-Coated Retriever are among the ancestors of the AWS. He carries the instincts and the coat and color of both, and sometimes a pup comes along with the rat tail that is typical of the Irishman. While this mix is the best probability, it still doesn't explain the smaller AWS size. Did somebody add the blood of either the American or English Cocker Spaniel? We'll never know, but we can be sure of one thing: the breed was recognized by the A.K.C. in 1940. It has never achieved much popularity, and that's a pity. A fine, all-around dog.

Breed Blueprint

Since the AWS has never been overbred, the dog retains his natural instincts and is happiest in the field. He is intelligent, durable, and neither welcomes nor appreciates confinement. Not a good bet for the city.

A bit long in body, with sloping, muscular shoulders, a deep chest,

and strong loins. The well boned legs are long enough to give the dog his medium size.

The head is broad, moderate in length, and carries a full stop. Dark toned eyes (hazel, brown) are set well apart. For show purposes, light eyes (yellow) are a disqualification. Muzzle of medium length and square, and the bite is even. Tips of long, wide ears extend to the nose. Forehead and face carry short, smooth hairs.

The coat is closely curled and dense, solid liver or dark chocolate in the color, with a little white on toes or chest permitted. The medium length tail is usually carried a little low.

Height for both sexes runs from 15 to 18 inches and dictates weight: 28 to 45 pounds for males, 25-40 pounds for bitches. In any size the breed deserves greater popularity.

BLACK AND TAN COONHOUND

There are several coonhound breeds in our land, but the B&T is the only one recognized (1945) by the A.K.C. He is a cousin of the American Foxhound, and the American histories of the two breeds are much the same. However, the B&T looks more like a Bloodhound without wrinkles, for he carries Bloodhound blood in his veins.

This breed was developed to trail and tree the coon, otherwise known as the raccoon, the furry bandit who inhabits parts of Canada and all the states except Alaska and Hawaii. Thus, the majority of owners are usually coon hunters. A minority are big-game hunters who prefer bear and mountain lion to raccoon. A B&T has one of the best canine noses around, and can be trained to work the trail of any animal. However, he is not much of a scrapper, and prefers animals who eventually seek the safety of trees. To the hunter, the dogs' baying on the trail—and again when the quarry is treed—are known as music. A dog lover who is not a hound owner might call this sound something else.

The other coonhound breeds not yet recognized by the A.K.C., and not likely to be recognized, are the Redbone, Bluetick, Treeing Walker, English Coonhound, and Plott. While each of the breeds has admirers, the B&T has the most.

Breed Blueprint

As hounds go, this one doesn't break any speed records, but his superlative scenting power makes him an efficient trailer and he doesn't waste any time. Although he wears the typical short hound coat, he can take any kind of weather and terrain. He's a friendly beast who doesn't complain, but he'd probably like to if the city is his home. A hound who prefers confinement is not true to his breed.

His body features a strong, sloping neck, powerful shoulders, deep chest, well sprung ribs, and even topline. Forelegs straight, with elbows well let down and even. Standing, hind legs are well set back and show good angulation. The feet are compact, catlike. Moving, the dog shows both front reach and rear drive. Tail set a bit low and carried at almost a right angle when dog is in action.

A male's head is 9-10 inches in length, a bitch's an inch less. It carries a slight stop and is devoid of folds. The round eyes run from hazel to dark brown and are not deep-set. The ears are set low and back and extend beyond the black nose, and the bite is a slight scissors.

As the breed's name implies, the coat is predominately black. The tan is found over the eyes, and on sides of muzzle, chest, legs and breeching, and with black pencil markings on the toes. Any white is considered undesirable, and for show purposes, a dog with a white

patch (on chest or elsewhere on body) exceeding 1½ inches in diameter is disqualified. Light eyes, splay feet, and shyness are other faults.

Males stand 25 to 27 inches, and bitches 23 to 25. Weight is not specified, but a 25-incher will hit the scales at around 65 pounds.

BOSTON TERRIER

Of the All-Americans, this is the only breed ever to achieve great popularity. But that was a half-century ago, and the breed's rating has slipped ever since. The decline can be attributed to Mother Nature: the BT is difficult to breed. Since the cervix cannot accommodate the head of an unborn pup, most whelpings must be by Caesarean section. This procedure is both difficult and expensive, two things the average dog breeder tries to avoid.

The breed's history began this side of the Civil War, when pit fighting was considered something of a sport in and around Boston. To produce better fighters, sportsmen made numerous crosses of the English Bulldog and the Bull Terrier. The result of some of those crosses and an unknown amount of inbreeding was the Boston Terrier, and a member in good standing with the A.K.C. since 1893. At that time, almost all the breeders were Bostonians, and the beast was a fine pet, but a lousy battler.

Because of the difficulty in whelping, breeders have tended to go only with their best, and overall quality has remained high. Despite the Boston's warrior ancestry and thanks to this selective breeding, he remains a friendly fellow and is not as yappity as most terriers. And despite his name, he is found in the Non-Sporting Group, rather than the Terrier Group. If that's not unique, consider this: for show purposes, he comes in three sizes, or heavyweight, middleweight and lightweight.

Breed Blueprint

All three sizes look the same, and the overall appearance is more terrier than bulldog. A very compact build, with a short head, short tail, and distinctive markings.

The square head is flat on top, with the cheeks flat, the brow abrupt, and the stop well defined. The large, round eyes are set well apart and are dark in color. Ears are carried erect and are either cropped or natural. Muzzle is short and square, and free from wrinkles, and ends at a black nose. The bite can be even or sufficiently undershot to square the muzzle. The neck is held in a slight arc.

The Boston's chest has both depth and width, his ribs are deep and carried well back to the loins. The tail is set low (proper length is half the distance to the hocks) and can be straight or screw. Although quite short, it is not docked.

Forelegs hang true from shoulders, with even elbows and short pasterns. Hind legs show good angulation, with hocks let down. Compact feet are round and small, with well arched toes.

The short, smooth coat is brindle (preferred) or black, both with white markings, ideally on the muzzle, blaze over head, collar, breast, part or all of forelegs, and hind legs below hocks.

Now for those sizes, either sex: a heavyweight runs from 20 to a maximum of 25 pounds; a middleweight from 15 to just under 20 pounds; and a lightweight under 15 pounds. Heights are not specified, but a given dog in good condition is usually an inch or so under his poundage. Thus, a 22-pounder will stand 21 inches or a little less.

ROUP
FIRST
GILBERT PHOTO

Sometimes, Bostons throw solid black, liver, or black and tan pups. As dogs go, there's nothing wrong with them, but they can't be shown.

CHESAPEAKE BAY RETRIEVER

There may have been stranger beginnings for a breed, but try this one on for size anyway. When an English brig was wrecked off Maryland's shores in 1807, the American ship *Canton* sped to the rescue, and among those rescued were the captain, the crew, and two pups. A Maryland dog lover purchased both these pups: a dingy male named Sailor, and a solid black bitch named Canton. The origins of both were then and still remain unknown.

Before they achieved adulthood, Sailor and Canton were sold to different owners. It is not known if these two were ever mated, but Sailor did sire several litters and Canton presumably became the dam of others. Whatever the case, both are credited with being the earliest known ancestors of the modern Chessie. Along the way, the blood of at least Sailor was mixed with that of other pure breeds or mixed breeds, and presumably those other breeds were water lovers. One can only speculate about them, since there's no reliable documentation.

By 1885 a definite Chessie type had evolved. He was tough, able to retrieve in any weather, and the favorite of sportsmen and market hunters alike. The latter group used this breed to retrieve hundreds of waterfowl per day. Mass shooting, mass retrieving, and mass marketing.

Although he is one of the best of our retriever breeds, the Chessie's popularity has been held back by a couple of silly myths: that his oily double coat gives off an unpleasant odor in the house and that he is a stubborn, hard-to-train beast. Obviously, the myth spreaders have had no experience with the breed. A pity.

Breed Blueprint

The breed's hallmarks include a mad love for water, a willingness to work, and a never-say-die attitude. The Chessie looks like (and is) a powerful, determined dog, even when at ease and loafing.

The topline is a unique feature of the breed, in that it is optional. It can be level, or it can be slightly higher (seldom more than an

inch) over the back quarters than at the withers. Just one topline per given dog, of course.

Otherwise, the body is of medium length (almost short-coupled), and carries sloping shoulders, a deep and wide chest, and a round and deep barrel. The tail is heavy at the base, medium in length, and often moderately feathered. Legs carry good bone, and the webbed, hare-feet have good size.

The head is broad and round and features a medium stop, a rather short muzzle, and small ears set high. Yellowish eyes are set wide. The bite is not specified, but almost always it's even or a slight scissors.

The Chessie's coat is of extreme importance. It's a double coat, and never more than 1½ inches long. The coat colors are solid and vary from a deep brown to a faded tan. A small, white spot on the chest or toes is permissible, but never desired.

Males stand 23 to 26 inches, weigh 65 to 75 pounds. Bitches: 21 to 24 inches, 55 to 65 pounds.

For show purposes, a Chessie may not sport dewclaws on his hind legs, although they are okay up front. If dewclaws are present, they should be removed at a tender puppy age, the earlier the better.

NOVA SCOTIA DUCK TOLLING RETRIEVER

Of the All-American breeds, this is the only one not recognized by the A.K.C. Nor is there any possibility of recognition in the near or distant future. There are very few of these retrievers—and no breeders—in the United States. However, the breed is recognized by the Canadian Kennel Club. There the picture is brighter, but not by much. Estimating the current breed population at two hundred is probably overestimating.

The major reason for the dog's limited appeal is his rather obscure specialty in life, tolling. Unlike all of the other retrievers, this one was bred to run back and forth, playfully barking, on the banks of a body of water frequented by wildfowl. Eventually curiosity overcomes the ducks resting on the water, and they paddle closer for a better view of the dog's antics. When they are within gun range, the hunter, who has been waiting in ambush with his gun at the ready, stands and blasts away. The dog then retrieves the shot ducks.

It's fair to say that the dog acts in a foxlike manner, for the fox lures wildfowl within range of his jaws in the very same way. Nobody knows just when the NSDTR was developed or who his ancestors were, but there are many tales. The least credible one is that he represents a cross between the Golden Retriever (retrieving instinct) and the red fox (tolling instinct). Another holds that an old timer in Nova Scotia spent years trying to train one red fox after another as hunting companions. After innumerable failures he then crossed several breeds of water dogs and came up with the Tolling Retriever. Much more likely is the theory that the Golden, the Chesapeake Bay, and a spaniel or two are behind him. We'll never know.

Tolling dogs are not new to the world and were used in Europe for centuries. There the dogs, usually mixed breeds, performed the antics of a fox to lure wildfowl upstream and into nets. This netting sport did not cross the Atlantic.

Breed Blueprint

Although smaller and sturdier, this dog somewhat resembles a Golden. Nothing about him, except his retrieving instinct, suggests the Chesapeake. He's hard to find, but a good bet as a pet.

At first glance, the head does look something like a Golden's. The skull is broad (about 5 inches) and flat, with the occiput very slight and the stop gradual. The muzzle is also broad, and usually a touch longer than the skull; on a good head, the total length of skull and muzzle is 9 inches. Lower jaw is thinner than the upper, and the bite is a scissors. Nose is a little tapered at tip, and colored flesh or black. Golden brown eyes are set well apart, and medium-sized ears are set high and back; they are carried very slightly erect, with rounded tips falling forward.

The dog is reasonably short-coupled, with strong, sloping shoulders, very deep chest, and legs of heavy bone. The webbed feet are compact and arched, and carry strong, curved nails. Topline is level. To the rear, hindquarters are solid and square on top, with noticeable tuck-up and good angulation. The tail runs about 13 inches in length and is well feathered. It is set as an extension of the spine, and is carried low when the dog is not in action, but high and curled when he moves.

The Duck Toller wears a double coat. The undercoat is short and very soft. The topcoat is long, sleek and soft. It is wavy down the center of the back and straight elsewhere, and the hairs on face, legs and tips of ears are short. Proper coat color is fox red, just a touch lighter than an Irish Setter's. While white is not desired, a white patch on chest and belly is usual. Elsewhere, white is a disqualification.

The minimum size for males is 20½ inches and about 50 pounds. For bitches 18½ inches and about 35 pounds. There's no maximum size, but variances never amount to much. So long as bigger dogs are in balance, they are not penalized at shows.

As retrievers go, the Duck Toller is a little on the timid side. On the other hand, he's a docile beast and has a fine rep as a nonroamer and a nonfighter.

III

The A.K.C. Recognized Breeds

The American Kennel Club recognizes 121 pure breeds of canines. This grand total often confuses dog lovers, for the actual count of the breeds listed in any respectable text comes to 123. The discrepancy can be attributed to the fact that several breeds have varieties, the differences being in coat (Collie, Fox Terrier, Chihuahua) or coat colors (Cocker Spaniel, Bull Terrier), or size (Poodle, Beagle, Manchester Terrier), or coat and size (Dachshund). Under the skin, of course, the varieties of a breed are the same dog. And in two breeds, Poodle and Manchester Terrier, there are toy varieties. These two pint-sized versions are listed as separate breeds, an inconsistency that dog fanciers take in stride. It does help the judging at dog shows.

To facilitate common sense, breeds with an original similar purpose or nonpurpose in life are assigned to one of six different groups: sporting, hound, working, terrier, toy and non-sporting. Thus, the English Setter is in the *sporting* group, the Alaskan Malamute is at home in the *working* group, and the Basset Hound is never found in the *terrier* group, although the Scottish Terrier certainly is.

On to the groups. Please note that the number found in parentheses following each breed's name indicates the breed's current popularity in America. Also, in the interest of word conservation, most of the breeds own straight forelegs. The few exceptions will be noted. And (for those who may not know) a dog's height is measured from his withers to the ground.

Sporting Group

The breeds in this group are all hunters by nature. While they can be trained to trail and find game, they are essentially birdy dogs with keen scenting power and the brains to use their eyes at critical moments to mark the fall of and retrieve upland birds and/or waterfowl. The breeds can be further divided into three classes: pointing (upland), flushing (upland) and retriever (water).

POINTER (84)

There are many pointer breeds. All but one of them were developed on the Continent, and perhaps English Pointer would be a more apt name for this one. While earlier, Continental breeds must be behind the Pointer, the world still lacks proof and canine historians agree that his real development was British all the way.

The Pointer's looks and bearing justify his ranking among the aristocrats of dogdom. The beast was well known for his work in the field (abroad) as early as 1650. Oddly, he was first used to point hare. Another dog, usually a hound, was then unleashed to run down the hare. Decades later, when wing shooting became popular among the gentry, the Pointer forgot the hare and concentrated on birds. This has been his primary duty ever since.

A handsome fellow, he was the first of the sporting breeds to achieve popularity at dog shows, and was on hand at the very first one (1859) in Merry Old England. His admirers were anxious to prove that a sporting dog could also be a thing of beauty, and the Pointer did so well that the term *dual purpose* (meaning for field and show) was invented.

In a sense, and in the long run, the breed's good looks may have served as a disadvantage. Today, on this side of the Atlantic, few of the breed are used in the field. There are more show dogs, and many more dogs who serve only as pets. Still, even when several generations of the family tree haven't been used in the field, the Pointer retains one of the best noses in the business.

Breed Blueprint

Whether or not he's ever scented a pheasant, a proper Pointer looks like a dog with endurance and speed. A combination of power, grace, and alertness, he holds his head high in any situation, as if he's proud to be one of man's best friends.

The long, rectangular head sits atop a long, arched neck and carries a slightly rounded dome on the same plane as the muzzle. The stop is pronounced, and the round eyes should be of dark color—the darker the better. Ears are set at eye level and hang naturally to just below the lower jaw, and the tips are slightly pointed, never rounded. The bite is even or scissors.

Up front, the shoulders are long and sloping, with the blades close. The forelegs are of oval bone, and the elbows well let down directly under the withers. The chest is deep and moderately wide, and well sprung ribs reach down as low as the elbow-point. Feet are oval and long, and toes are arched.

The hindquarters reflect power, plus good angulation, slight tuck-up, and long thighs. Standing, the topline shows a slight slope from withers over croup. The croup falls off slightly to the base of tail. Straight and natural, the tail tapers to a fine point and reaches to the hock, or almost.

The coat is short, dense, and smooth to the touch, and a sheen is desirable. Coat colors are liver, lemon, black and orange, either as

solids or in combination with white. With liver or black, the nose is dark.

Males stand 25 to 28 inches, weigh from 55 to 75 pounds. Bitches: 23 to 26 inches, 45 to 65 pounds.

A beloved Pointer, either sex, who is timid or who wears straight shoulders, houndy ears, or a snippy muzzle is also an improper Pointer and should not be shown. The same applies to a courageous Pointer who moves like a crab or a drunken beast. Proper movement is smooth and straight ahead.

POINTER, GERMAN SHORTHAIRED (24)

Of the five pointing breeds who are members of the A.K.C. family, the GSP is by far the most popular. He has come along in steady fashion since his official recognition in 1930 and is living proof that a spoiled pet can also be great in the field and a winner at the shows. In many of the other sporting breeds, the same claim would be invalid.

The breed was developed about a century ago, or not so long ago that ancestral documentation should be vague. However, that's the case, and we are left with educated guesses. The most educated holds that the Spanish Pointer, Pointer, several Teutonic trailing hounds, and maybe the Bloodhound are behind the GSP. It is reasonable to assume that at least some of these were—and safe to believe that the result is a durable dog who (unlike some sporting breeds) doesn't mind getting his feet wet. In Europe, he's used on bird, fowl, and small game. In America, he's used mostly on bird, sometimes on duck, and rarely on small game.

The GSP is a friendly dog and makes an excellent pet. One of his traits is making noise on any occasion. The way law and order has been going, the trait has endeared him to many owners.

Breed Blueprint

This is a medium-sized dog with loads of energy and a love for action. Admirers will rave all day about his looks, power, and intelligence.

His head has a clean look: fairly broad, arched on sides and a little rounded on top. There's a slight pitch from the brown nose to the forehead, where the stop is very slight. The dark brown eyes are

of medium size, and the broad, long ears are set above eye level and hang close. The jaws have a true scissors bite.

The back is short, with a slight slope from withers to the set of tail. The latter is set high, must be docked, and is never carried bent over back. Still rearward, there are broad hips, good angulation, and apparent tuck-up.

A good dog has sloping shoulders (blades quite close at the withers) and a deep chest to the elbows. Moderate is the word for the spring of ribs. The arched feet are compact and either round or spoonshaped, and carry heavy nails and a hard pad.

The coat is short and thick and feels hard to the touch. It is shorter, softer and thinner on ears and head. There are several proper coat colors: liver, liver with white spots and ticked, liver and white ticked, and roan-liver. The permissible white is grayish, not chalk white.

Males stand from 23 to 25 inches, weigh from 55 to 70 pounds. Bitches: 21 to 23 inches, 45 to 60 pounds.

About that docked tail: it's about two-fifths nature's intention. Where specified (this and any other breed), a docked tail is only a must for show purposes. Docking is man's attempt to improve the looks of a given breed. The same goes for cropped ears. Of course the involved breeds were never consulted about these matters, but they have survived. Several states now outlaw both practices on the grounds of cruelty to animals, but the law is rarely enforced.

A pup hardly notices a docking, but cropping does cause pain for more than a week. For those who wonder if the operations will continue to be fashionable, the answer is yes. It would appear that only a federal law could put an end to docking and cropping.

POINTER, GERMAN WIREHAIRED (64)

The breed is a little younger than and in debt to the German Short-haired Pointer, an immediate ancestor. The Wirehaired Pointing Griffon, the Pudelpointer, and the Stichelhaar are also behind this wirehaired sporting dog.

The breed gained A.K.C. recognition in 1959, a fact that does not answer an oft'-asked question: why did the Germans, since they already had the GSP, bother with developing a wirehaired pointer?

Well, the general idea of avid sportsmen of the time was to develop a dog of uncommon ruggedness, a beast who could go all

day in the coldest water, over the roughest terrain, and through impossible cover with a minimum of damage to himself. Thus, the dog's coat was designed as armor anywhere, any time, in any weather.

This is a fine family dog. He's loyal to those he knows best, but he isn't much of a mixer and is often regarded as aloof. His undercoat is a sure bet to shed in summer.

Breed Blueprint

Beneath their coats, this fellow and a GSP are pretty much the same dog. Even the coat colors are the same.

The GWP wears a double coat. The outercoat is harsh, wiry and straight, lies quite flat, and runs up to two inches in length. The undercoat is very dense. Bushy eyebrows, a short beard, and whiskers decorate the face.

The feet are also a little different. They are round and always webbed.

To the eye, body length looks a little different from the GSP's but it isn't. The GWP is a little longer than he is tall, the ratio being about 10 to 9.

Males stand 24 to 26 inches at the withers. Less for bitches, but never under 22 inches. Weights are not specified, but a 25-inch dog will hit about 60 pounds.

RETRIEVER, CHESAPEAKE BAY (48)

See page 28.

RETRIEVER, CURLY-COATED (116)

This is the very oldest of the recognized retrievers. There's no way of knowing just what other breeds are behind him, but it is known that he's been around since 1790. Designed for water, he's also a honey on upland birds (currently New Zealand's popular dog on quail, the most abundant game bird). This makes him more popular and populous elsewhere than he has ever been in his native England. Currently, we have about ten breeders in America, and all are hoping that the dog's virtues will become better known.

A good reason for his lack of popularity in his native land is that his existence was something of a secret for about two centuries.

Those who knew a good hunting dog when they saw one kept the breed under their hats; most were gamekeepers and poachers. The former required fast, durable, and efficient dogs; the latter needed dogs with the same virtues, plus the asset of working quietly. The Curly had that asset—and still has. He is also one of the best jumpers in the canine world.

Curlies were relatively unknown in the United States before 1930. Then a few were imported from England and earned excellent reputations in the early retriever field trials. That should have been enough to catch the public's fancy, but the Labrador Retriever was coming along strong at the same time and soon dominated the retriever category. Interest for the Curly waned and was not revived until the 1950s. Even today the breed deserves much greater popularity in the sporting set.

Breed Blueprint

The Curly is the tallest of the retrievers. He is a water lover, and his long legs work to his advantage in swamps and marshes. One of the easiest dogs to train, and one of the handsomest when his coat is right. In general: a charmer.

His long, well proportioned head carries an almost flat skull, and long, strong jaws that are free of snipiness. Wide nostrils and a black nose are musts. Bite is even, eyes are black or brown, and the low set ears are small and lie close to head. The ears and tail are covered with tight curls.

Despite those long legs, the body is short-coupled. The shoulders are deep (slope), as is the chest. Forelegs are set well under the body and hind legs carry low hocks and moderate stifle. Feet must be round and compact, with arched toes. The quarters are very strong.

The dog's tail is moderately short—when pulled down, never beyond hock—and is carried straight (as an extension of topline) and tapers from base to tip.

The coat colors are solid black or solid liver. The coat is one big mass of crisp, tight curls. It never needs brushing or combing, and those curls are never more than ¾ inch in diameter.

While the breed standard does not specify sizes, breeders aim for males that stand 25 to 27 inches at the withers and run from 70 to 80 pounds. Bitches are 2 inches shorter and 10 pounds lighter.

To keep those coat curls tight, one merely wets both hands and massages the coat with a circular motion. And if the coat should grow too long, a little clipping is the remedy.

RETRIEVER, FLAT-COATED (108)

As with so many of our pure breeds, this one's family tree has never been nailed down. The dog has been around for more than a century, and during that time many wise men have been sure that his

ancestors included the Rough Collie, Irish and Gordon Setters, and Labrador. Still, proof has always been lacking.

This retriever first gained attention as a show dog in England in 1860. Within a decade, Mr. Flat became England's most popular retriever, and he retained that status until World War I. For two decades (1870–90), he was also extremely popular in the U.S. When breed popularity peaked in America, there were more Flat-Coats present than there are today in the world.

Following World War II, breed interest was so low that the A.K.C. came close to dropping the Flat-Coat from the roster. It didn't happen, some interest did develop, and today America is home to about a dozen breeders. The beast's numbers are building, more are being seen at the shows, and chances of reviving the Flat-Coat's popularity look excellent. A fine worker, a great pet.

Breed Blueprint

A good example of what happens when a beast has only a few breeders to his name: they concentrate on producing superior pups. Buyers are few, and all demand quality. In a very popular breed, such as the German Shepherd Dog, bum pups sell as fast as quality pups, and breeders often become careless.

The head is long and nicely molded, the skull is flat and broad, and the stop is slight, and the long, strong jaws carry either a level or scissors bite. The ears, on the small side, lie close to the head. Eyes are of medium size and dark brown or hazel in color.

The dog is a little longer in body than the other retrievers, and his topline is either level or shows a slight slope from withers to tail set. The shoulders slope, the blades are close, and the chest is deep and fairly broad. To the rear, the tuck-up is slight, the angulation moderate. The straight, natural tail is carried at back level.

The proper rib structure is a bit unusual. Fore ribs are fairly flat, show a gradual spring, and are arched over the center of body, and are lighter from there to the quarters. Overall, a rather streamlined retriever with legs of good, round bone and feet of moderate size with toes held close and arched.

The coat is dense, reasonably fine to the touch, and lies flat. In full coat, the dog's limbs are feathered. Coat colors are solid black and solid liver. A yellow coat pops up now and then, but it's not acceptable for show.

The standard calls for a medium sized dog running 60 to 70 pounds. Size is not specified, but an average male runs about 24 inches, and an average bitch a couple of inches less. Breeders are now working for another inch or so in height for both sexes.

RETRIEVER, GOLDEN (14)

Rated by many as one of the world's most beautiful breeds, the Golden is proof that beauty and brains can go together. He's a dandy at home and in the field, but has now reached a critical point of zooming popularity and marketability. Will the vast majority of breeders go for easy sales or for quality?

The Golden has been around for more than a century in England, and for most of that time his admirers have been willing to believe that he began as a cross of the Bloodhound and the Russian Tracker, a huge sheepdog who no longer runs around in Russia or anywhere else. But less than a decade ago, documents came to light that proved one Lord Tweedmouth had actually developed the breed. The good lord blended the Bloodhound, Irish Setter, the now extinct Tweed Water Spaniel, and perhaps a black retriever or two.

The Golden took a long time getting established in North America. He was brought to British Columbia in the early years of this century by retired British army officers, then spread from San Francisco to Alaska. Since he was used mostly on dry land, his talents as a water dog were generally unknown until the late thirties when he made his mark in retriever trials. From that day to this, his popularity has been building, although these days he's seen more at home and at the shows than in the field. All along, he has had to fight the myth that he prefers warm, calm water and dislikes icy, wild water.

Breed Blueprint

A good all-around beast, he's friendly and eager to please when loafing, hard-working and confident when in the field. An owner has to resist the temptation to spoil him.

The Golden's head features a broad, slightly arched skull, a deep, wide foreface, and a noticeable stop. The eyes are medium sized and set well apart, never lighter in color than coat, and dark brown is preferred. The ears are rather short and hang close to head, the rounded tips falling just below jaw. Ear set is just above eye level at the forward edge, just below at the rear edge—thus, a backward drop. The bite must be a scissors.

The body is almost short-coupled, with a 12:11 ratio of length to height. Shoulders slope, legs are of good bone, chest is deep, and the feet are medium, round and compact. The rib cage is long and well sprung, but never barrel shaped. The dog carries an even topline and a slightly sloping croup. The powerful hindquarters show good angulation, hocks well let down, and often a very slight tuck-up. The tail has a medium set, reaches to hocks, and is carried in an upward curve.

The Golden has a double coat. Topcoat runs over two inches and lies flat, and it can be either straight or a little wavy. Both it and the shorter undercoat are very dense. Feathering is usual. Coat color can be any shade of "lustrous golden," meaning anything from a tinted cream to a rich mahogany.

Males stand 23 to 24 inches, and weigh from 65 to 75 pounds. Bitches run 21½ to 22½ inches, 60 to 70 pounds. On height, the standard permits a variance of one inch, either way, both sexes. Thus, a bitch is sometimes a little larger than a dog.

For show purposes, both the wrong bite and the wrong size are disqualifications. So is triciasis. While such disqualifications may seem like making mountains out of molehills, they do help any breed in the long run. They amount to culling.

RETRIEVER, LABRADOR (8)

In America and everywhere else in the world where sporting dogs dwell, the Lab is far and away the most popular of the retriever breeds. For pet, show, field, and just about everything else, a good Lab is hard to beat. The trick is to find a good one. The breed is suffering from too much popularity over too long a period of time, and quality has been sliding downhill for at least a decade. The bums now vastly outnumber the worthies.

The Labrador is a cousin of the Newfoundland; both trace their ancestry to the now extinct St. John's dog, a talented retriever and the favorite beast of fishing fleets that sailed from Newfoundland to England two hundred years ago. The St. John came in a variety of sizes, and in England the big ones (as time marched along) became

Newfs, while the smaller, speedier ones were developed as water dogs and became Labradors. A short century later, in 1903, nine years after the first Lab had reached these shores, the Kennel Club of England recognized the Labrador as a pure breed.

In America the Lab's many virtues remained pretty much a secret until the early 1930s, the dawn of licensed retriever field trials. The Lab dominated those trials (and he still does) and was on his way to fame, popularity, and finally, too damn much popularity. As long as he remains the superdog at the trials—and it looks as if he will for a long time—his popularity will not wane.

Breed Blueprint

The Lab is a medium sized, compact dog with power, spirit, and a weatherproof, carefree coat. He is famous for his soft mouth—jaws that do not damage what they hold, be it a duck or a fresh egg. All those qualities if he is bred right.

Overall, a good Lab's head is clean cut and free from fleshy cheeks. The skull is wide, and a slight stop prevents a bovine look. The jaws are long and powerful and always free from snipiness. Eyes are medium sized, never narrow-set, and preferably brown or black. The ears are set a little low and back, and hang moderately close to the head. They are of medium size, never houndy. The bite can be either even or slightly scissored.

The dog is truly short-coupled, or (compared to the Golden) 12:12. Up front, his shoulders slope, his chest is broad and wide, legs have good bone, and feet are compact with toes arched. The neck is of medium length, and should not (despite its substance) look like it belongs on a bull.

A Lab's topline is even over well sprung ribs, wide loins, and powerful hindquarters that show good angulation. The tapering tail is very wide at its base, never extends beyond the hock, and is carried gaily but not curved over back. Lab lovers call it an otter tail, and it does resemble an otter's rudder; however, the otter is not known to be behind the Lab.

The dog wears a double coat. The topcoat is short, dense, reasonably hard, and free from wave. The undercoat is shorter, wooly, and just as dense, and lighter in tone than the topcoat. Coat colors are black, yellow (any shade from cream to fox-red), and chocolate. Coat colors are solid, although on blacks and chocolates, a "small white spot" on chest is permissible for show. Nobody knows how big a small spot can be. It's every judge for himself.

Males: 22½ to 24½ inches, 60 to 75 pounds. Bitches: 21½ to 23½ inches, 55 to 70 pounds.

Twenty years ago, black was the popular color, and a chocolate Lab was a rarity. Today, there are more yellows than blacks, and the chocolates are no longer unusual. Unfortunately, a chocolate with a good, dark eye is unusual.

SETTER, ENGLISH (52)

This could be the oldest gundog breed in the world. The ES is known to go back to the fourteenth century, but the dogs behind him will always remain unknown and open to conjecture. As we know the ES today, he is the joint accomplishment of two British breeders, both this side of 1850: Edward Laverack (inbreeder, and author of the first breed book, *The Setter*, 1873) and R. P. Llewellin (outbreeder). The former had beauty on his mind, and the latter talent in the

field. By 1874 the ES was very popular in England, and the first two American representatives of the breed were hunting in New Jersey. Here, the breed's popularity zoomed over the next few decades. Today, an ES lover is considered negligent if he comes within a hundred miles of Pittsburgh and doesn't visit the Carnegie Museum. There, in all his stuffed glory, one of the breed's early greats is on display. Long ago he responded to the name Count.

The ES is a beautiful, affectionate dog, now far more popular as a pet than a gundog. He is a very social animal, and requires the constant company of people or other dogs. Thus, he's unhappy as the only dog in an outdoor kennel. And he is not a dog for a lazy owner; he does require plenty of exercise and his coat, one of his main attractions, needs daily grooming to stay in proper condition. A good bet for the hunter who also wants a pet for his children.

But since generations of these setters have been bred only for looks and show, the wise hunter will find his pup in a litter bred from field stock.

Breed Blueprint

Beyond visual beauty, the dog is famous for his sweet disposition, brain power, and (if bred right) yen for action in the field. Like all other medium sized sporting breeds, he's not designed for the city.

An ES head is long and lean, the skull oval with a definite stop. The muzzle is long and square, and the bite either level or scissors. Eyes of dark brown, with moderate length ears set at eye level. The head sits on a long, lean, arched neck.

The body carries sloping shoulders, with blades close at the withers. The chest is deep, but of moderate width, and the rib cage is carried well back. Legs are of flat bone, and the feet are compact with well arched toes. The topline slopes down from the withers, and the straight, tapering tail is set as an extension of the back. The hips are set wide, and the hind legs carry long thighs and good angulation.

The dog's long coat lies flat, and there's some feathering on the forelegs, breeches, and tail. There are many proper coat colors: black, white and tan; blue belton; lemon and white, and lemon belton; orange and white, and orange belton; liver and white, and liver belton; and solid white. For those who wonder, belton is an intermingling of white hairs with a predominate color.

Males stand around 25 inches and 65 pounds. Bitches are around 24 inches and a few pounds less.

The ES standard calls for a body of moderate length. It's a little longer than a retriever's.

SETTER, GORDON (60)

One of Scotland's major contributions to dogdom, the Gordon is older than the ES and takes his name from one of his major developers, the Fourth Duke of Gordon, and his successor, the Fifth Duke, who went to his ultimate reward in 1835. By then, the Gordon's rep in the field was well known, and the first dogs of the breed arrived in America in 1842. Daniel Webster was among the first importers.

Although never as popular in this country as the ES, the Gordon was favored by many sportsmen. But interest waned when field trials came along. Instinctively, the dog quartered (ranged in close) and this put him at a disadvantage when compared with the other setter breeds. By the end of World War II, the Gordon was headed for the long list of extinct breeds. Oddly, he was saved by the show set and not by the sporting fraternity. These days, his popularity for both show and field is on the upswing, and in another decade his numbers may challenge those of the ES.

The Gordon is sturdier than the other setter breeds. Although still inclined to range close, he can be trained to cover more ground,

and is once again in the forefront at the trials. Of the setters, the average Gordon makes the best in the field for the occasional hunter. Not as gregarious as the ES, but a great one-family dog.

Breed Blueprint

The GS is regarded as handsome rather than beautiful, durable rather than speedy. Gentle with children, suspicious with strangers, and happiest in the great outdoors.

His heavy head is deeper than it is broad, with a rounded skull and a clearly defined stop. The muzzle is long (but never pointed), the flews clean, and the nose is broad and black. The dark brown eyes are oval, and the ear set is on a line with the eyes. The bite is scissored or level. The neck is long, lean and arched, and without throatiness.

Overall, a Gordon's body is pretty much the same as the ES, with these notable exceptions: heavier bone, sturdier, and closer to short-coupled.

The coat is always black with tan markings. It's long, soft to the touch, and shining, and can be straight or wavy. As for those tan (rich chestnut or mahogany) markings, here's where they should be located: 1) as spots over eyes (maximum: ¾ inch in diameter); 2) on sides of muzzle, but as a stripe never reaching to top; 3) on throat; 4) two clear spots on chest; 5) inside of hind legs; 6) forelegs, pasterns to toes; 7) around vent. A very small white spot on chest is permitted and so is black penciling on toes.

Males go 24 to 27 inches, 55 to 80 pounds. Bitches run 23 to 26 inches, 45 to 70 pounds.

Absence of any of those tan markings hurt a dog's chances at shows, but not his feelings. Solid red and predominately tan pups often pop up in litters, even though litter mates may be properly marked.

SETTER, IRISH (3)

With the exception of English and Gordon Setter admirers, the Irish is generally accepted as the most beautiful of the setters. He is also much too popular for his own good, and show and pet stock (majority) look quite different from field stock (minority). The latter are usually smaller, sturdier, less refined, and resemble the Irish dog of the good old days.

The Irish is younger than the Gordon, who could be one of the breeds behind him, although that's not certain. The Bloodhound (for scent), the old Spanish Pointer, and some unknown spaniels could be behind the IS, too, but don't bet on it. Although credited to Ireland, English breeders also had a hand in this setter's development, and were particularly effective in changing the original white and red coat colors to a solid red. Still, Ireland's Cecil Moore is credited with breeding the first great Irish Setters, and one of them, Palmerston, was such a big winner at dog shows that just about everybody forgot that the breed was originally designed for the field.

The first dogs of the breed arrived in America a century ago. Known then as the Irish Red Setter, he quickly earned a fine reputation in the field. Within a decade, the English Setter pattern was repeated, and the emphasis on breeding show dogs began. America's love affair with the IS is far from over, and he stands a good chance of topping all other breeds in popularity at some time in the future.

Obviously, Big Red makes a fine pet, or he wouldn't be so popular. Compared with the other two setters, he develops more slowly and often requires a longer period of training.

Breed Blueprint
The biggest of the setters and a true aristocrat in looks, he has a

sweet, rollicking personality that belies his swiftness in the field. He moves in a graceful, powerful manner, although one would never guess that at the shows. There, he is gaited on a lead so tight that his front feet barely touch the ground, and his head is up in the sky. One wonders why.

The IS's head is long and lean, or at least twice the length of the width between the ears. The skull is slightly domed and shows both distinct occiput and stop. The muzzle is moderately deep and square, and the bite is either scissors or even. The dark to medium brown eyes are somewhat almond shaped. The long ears are set well back and low, never above the level of the eyes, and when extended they reach almost to the nose. The long, arched neck is free from throatiness.

On scale, this dog is built pretty much along the lines of the English Setter. The major differences are in coat and size.

The coat is of moderate length and lies flat and carries long, silky feathering on ears, forelegs, thighs, belly and brisket, tail, and between close, arched toes. Coat color is solid mahogany or rich chestnut red, with no traces of black. However, a proper coat can carry small touches of white on the chest, as well as a narrow center streak of white on the skull.

The IS stands taller than the average ES; males are 27 inches and 70 pounds; bitches 25 inches and 60 pounds. An inch either way for both sexes is okay. Overall, the Irish has a streamlined look and carries less poundage than other breeds of his size.

The average dog bred from generations of field stock runs 2 to 3 inches under the above specifications and carries 5 to 10 pounds less. In show circles this fellow is often disparaged as a "swamp setter," since he really doesn't fit the breed standard. Still, he fulfills the original intention for the breed, and he keeps his owner happy.

SPANIEL, AMERICAN WATER (92)

See page 22.

SPANIEL, BRITTANY (17)

It can be argued that this dog is not aptly named, for he is quite unlike any other member of the spaniel family and, in fact, acts more like an offshoot of the pointer family tree. Although the Britt has been bred for more than a century and his true ancestors may never be known, it's fair to call him a twentieth-century breed. As we know it today, Britt type was set in France somewhere between 1900 and 1910, and this beast is a canine-come-lately to America (1931). Here, his hunting instinct has been preserved, and his current popularity can be credited to his work in the field rather than his success at shows.

If he is a spaniel, then the Britt is the only one naturally distinguished by the lack of a tail. He comes either tailless or with a short stub tail that is set high and usually runs up to four inches in length. If longer, it can be docked back to four inches (for show purposes). A given litter of pups usually contains a few tailless wonders and a few with stubs.

The dog earned his early rep on woodcock, but he's also adept on all other upland game birds. Unlike the other spaniel breeds, he

ranges far and wide and freezes on point when he locates game. With a little training, he also makes a fine water dog. Thus, the Britt is a triple-threat beast: pointer, retriever, and pet. A few have been used as guide dogs for the blind, a field now dominated by Golden and Labrador Retrievers. Overall, the Britt is still being bred right, and his popularity is destined to grow.

Breed Blueprint

A natural for anyone who thinks a pointer or a setter has too much size as a home resident. The Britt has a dual personality: fearless in the field, he wilts if he's treated harshly at home.

His rounded skull is a touch longer (about 4¾ inches) than wide (4⅜), and the muzzle runs about two-thirds that length. The stop is there, but it's sloping or gradual, not decisive. The occiput is there, too, but is only apparent to the touch. Eyes are well set in the head and darker eye colors are preferred. The ears are set high (above eye level) and are slightly rounded at tips; they are short for a spaniel; extended, they reach midpoint of muzzle. Bite is a true scissors. The neck is of medium length and free from throatiness. The Britt is one of the few breeds who cannot own (for show) a black nose. A nose of that color is a disqualification. A proper nose is colored fawn, tan, light brown or deep pink.

The body is short-coupled, and the topline slopes slightly from withers to rump. Sloping shoulders, well sprung ribs, a deep chest and good angulation are all typical of the breed. Legs carry good (but not heavy) bone, and feet are small for a spaniel, shaped half-hare, half-feline. Toes close and well arched.

The coat is a little coarser than the one found on other spaniels. The hair is dense, can be flat or wavy, but never curly. Feathering is light. The right coat colors are dark orange and white, or liver and white, and a little ticking is okay. Any black in the coat is a disqualification.

Height (both sexes) runs from 17½ to 20½ inches. For show, any lower or higher measurement is a disqualification. A 19-incher will tip the scales at about 35 pounds.

About those parenthetical skull measurements: they fit a 19½ inch dog. And the skull is never so rounded that it creates an apple head. Overall, the breed's standard indicates that the Brittany set is a very particular one. And why not? It's the best way to maintain quality.

SPANIEL, CLUMBER (113)

Like the Brittany, the Clumber was developed in France and is also an unusual spaniel. Absolutely nothing is known about his ancestors, although some canine authorities urge that the Saint Bernard is one of them. Since the Saint is known to have arrived on the scene more recently than the Clumber, the facts of life do not sustain those authorities.

It is known that the breed reached England about 1840, and that a few Clumbers were in America just after the Civil War. The dog was really designed to find and flush small game when said game was very abundant; he's a slow, close-ranging, careful worker. From 1900 to 1950, his numbers were in steady decline. A few breeders in England kept him from fading away, and now a few more in America are helping to guarantee his future. He's no longer rare, but most dog lovers

have never seen him, or don't recognize him when they do see him.

The dog's name may come from Clumber Park, home of the Duke of Newcastle, an early breeder. And then there are those who say that the dog moves in a slow and clumsy manner. Whatever the true source of his name, the Clumber is an ideal companion for the man who doesn't like to hunt in a hurry. The dog also makes a fine, affectionate, unperturbed pet, and an excellent subject for dinner party conversation.

Breed Blueprint

A long, low, heavy-set dog with plenty of endurance and the will to please. The friendly beast looks more serious than he really is as he moves along at a slow, steady gait.

The Clumber's head is massive with a flat top, rounded brow, distinct stop, median furrow between the eyes, and a big occiput. The muzzle shows power, is almost square, and carries overhanging lips; the jaws are broad and deep, and the bite is scissors. His large, hazel eyes are deep set and show haw. Long ears are set low; they are very broad at the base, and the front edge is rolled and carries modest feathering. The long, powerful neck carries a ruff and looks shorter than it is.

Up front the shoulders are immense, and the chest is wide and deep. The forelegs are short and of heavy bone; the feet are big, compact, and round, with hair between the toes. The Clumber's even topline runs down a long, broad back with a very slight arch over the loin. There's no tuck-up. The hind legs carry a little less bone than the forelegs and show moderate angulation, with hocks let down. The short (docked) tail is set at spine level and is usually carried low.

The dense coat is silky, straight, and moderately long, with abundant feathering everywhere except below the hocks. Proper coat colors are lemon and white or orange and white. Usually, the coat is predominately white, with even markings on the head, solid lemon or orange ears, and ticking on the muzzle and legs.

Males run from 55 to 65 pounds, bitches from 35 to 50 pounds. The standard does not specify height for either sex, but a 55-pounder in hard condition will stand about 18 inches.

SPANIEL, AMERICAN COCKER (9)

It will never happen, but this dog, the smallest member of the spaniel family and of the sporting group, might as well move over to the non-sporting classification. Today few American cockers are used in the field. Many are show dogs, and many, many more serve out their lives as pure pets. The sad truth is that the hunting instincts of the ACS have not survived his great popularity. Indeed, he is the only sporting dog ever to have topped all breeds in American popularity (1940–56). His rush to the top was not unexpected. In just three years in the middle of the depression, one commercial breeder sold over thirty-five thousand pups at fifty dollars a head.

The breed is a spinoff of the English Cocker Spaniel, who was the result of spaniel breedings that dated back through the centuries. The original English version is credited to a mighty stud dog named Obo, who set the type. Obo was whelped in 1879, and a couple of years later a son of his, Obo II, arrived in America. In time, Obo II became the daddy of the ACS. For reasons unknown, he stamped a type that

was a little different than his sire's. Thus, the ACS can be regarded as the son of the ECS.

These days, it's easy to find American Cocker pups, but not so easy to locate pups of quality. The best bets will be line bred and from show stock.

Breed Blueprint

A good ACS makes a wonderful pet, loves people, and is very adaptable. In the field (if he's not a dud), he quarters in close and flushes, but often must be trained to retrieve.

His head carries a rounded skull, with a smooth forehead and distinct stop, and a broad and deep muzzle. The jaws are squared, and the bite is scissors. The eyes round and full, and their color depends on coat color (see below), and the long, lobular ears, set at lower eye level, extend to the tip of the nose, carry feathering, and hang close.

The body is short-coupled, with a deep chest reaching to the well let down elbows. The legs are of good bone, and the feet are round and compact. The topline slopes downward from the withers, and the short (docked) tail is set as an extension. Ribs are well sprung, hips are wide, and the angulation is good. Overall, a compact body.

The coat is short and fine on the head. On the body, it's a double coat. The one not seen, or the undercoat, is short and fine, but not too dense. The medium length topcoat is silky, and lies flat or a touch wavy. The breed's three varieties are denoted by coat colors, and they are noted here with proper eye color in parentheses:

Black, with a little white on chest and throat okay (dark brown, black).

Ascob (any solid color other than black) with white permissible as above (black, dark brown, and dark hazel in reds). And then there's the black and tan, rated as an Ascob. The jet black coat carries no more than 10% tan, and the tan appears only in a clear spot above each eye, on sides of muzzle, on cheeks, the undersides of ears, on all feet and legs, and under the tail.

Parti-Colors are dogs with coats of at least two definite colors with even markings, but the primary color can amount to no more than 90% (no lighter than hazel for light shaded coats, and the darker the better for all coats).

The ideal heights are 15 inches for males, and 14 inches for bitches, but ½ inch more (both sexes) is permissible for show. Weights aren't specified, but a 15-incher will run a little heavier than 25 pounds.

This should be a merry dog. A good one is great with children. A bum one is more trouble than a spoiled child.

SPANIEL, ENGLISH COCKER (69)

As noted, the ECS is the daddy of the ACS, and daddy has been a recognized breed (England) since 1892. And just as the American Cocker had his beginnings as a smaller version of the English Cocker, the latter started off as a small edition of the English Springer Spaniel, the next in line on these pages.

The word *cocker* comes from the second syllable of *woodcock*. The undersized Springer excelled at finding and flushing that game bird; hence, English Cocker. In the land of his coming, he has long been the favorite of the spaniel family. He has never challenged the American Cocker on this side of the Atlantic, and the best reason for

that can be credited to confusion. Interbreeding of these two similar dogs was quite common, and various sized beasts popped up in the same litters. Frequently, an oversized ACS was entered as an ECS at the shows, and a small ECS would be entered in ACS classes. The confusion was eliminated by the Canadian Kennel Club (1940) and the American Kennel Club (1947). Today, an English Cocker is really an ECS, and the same is true of the ACS.

While a comparison between two similar breeds is risky, it's fair to say that the average English Cocker represents more quality. There are far fewer breeders, the importing of top stock has continued, and the dog has retained his field instincts. He's a bright, faithful beast, seldom looks for trouble, and makes a worthy pet.

Breed Blueprint

The big difference between this dog and the American Cocker is his greater size. It's not much, but it gives him a cleaner look and gives him an advantage in beauty. One wonders why he isn't much more popular.

His head is quite like that of an English Springer. The skull is arched and slightly flat on top, its length is the same as the square muzzle, and there's a definite stop. The medium sized eyes are slightly oval, and set well apart, and color depends on coat color (see below). The long, lobular ears set low and close to the head, and extend to the nose. The bite is even.

The compact body is short-coupled, with sloping shoulders, chest to elbows, and good spring of ribs. Legs are of good bone all the way, and feet are firm, round and catlike. Topline slopes down gradually from withers, with short, docked tail as extension. Strong quarters and good angulation.

The coat is short and fine on the head. The body carries some undercoating, or enough for protection. The medium length topcoat is silky, either flat or wavy, with feathering. Proper coat colors (with accompanying, proper eye colors in parentheses) are:

Solids, black and tans, roans and parti-colors. A solid with white feet and chest is a solid, not a parti-color. In parti-colors, no one color dominates, and the colors are evenly distributed. Aside from proper black and tan, and white as above, the coat colors are black, red, blue, orange, lemon (dark brown) and liver (hazel, but the darker the better); light parti-colors (same as liver).

Males: 16 to 17 inches, 28 to 34 pounds. Bitches: 15 to 16 inches, 26 to 34 pounds.

Those are ideal specifications, but deviations are not disqualifications. Conformation and balance are considered more important than size and weight.

SPANIEL, ENGLISH SPRINGER (25)

The Springer has been around for several centuries, and the general belief is that he is the forebear of most other breeds of land spaniels. He was developed before man invented the shotgun, and small game was very plentiful. He was used for finding and springing game into the net, or into the view of the falcon or the hound. Then, after the introduction of the shotgun and wing shooting, it was discovered that the smallest of the Springers were more adept in the difficult cover beloved by woodcock. The British breeders who concentrated on the smaller size came up with the dog we now know as the English Cocker.

Thus, there is no doubt about it: the English Springer is the daddy of the English Cocker, who is the daddy of the American Cocker, who is the daddy of no other breed.

The Springer, a true dog for the sportsman, ranks third among the spaniel breeds in America and his popularity is on the upswing. As land spaniels go, he doesn't mind getting his feet wet and is used on duck, as well as upland birds and small game. He's a durable dog, would rather work than loaf, and is fairly easy to train. His short, docked tail is seldom still, an indication that he's ready for anything. If the Springer has a weakness, he hasn't advertised it.

Breed Blueprint

Too active to be considered an ideal pet for the city, this dog benefits from exercise and should have room to run. The size difference in field and show stock has been pretty much eliminated, and most of the beasts now fit their standard.

The Springer head is impressive, but not heavy. His skull is broad, slightly rounded, and flat on top. Skull and muzzle length are equal, with widths in harmony, and the stop is moderate. Eyes are round, fairly deep set, and hazel to dark brown in color. Long, wide ears are set at eye level, hang close, and extend to the tip of nose. The bite can be either even or a close scissors.

The body is short-coupled, with sloping shoulders and a deep chest. The legs carry strong bone, and the compact feet are either round or oval, and well arched. Topline carries a gentle slope from withers to tail, with tail set following natural line of the croup. Hips are broad, angulation is moderate, and tuck-up is very slight.

This breed's coat is of medium length, dense, fine in texture, and flat or wavy, with moderate feathering. Proper colors: liver or black with white markings; the same plus tan markings (tri-colors); blue or liver roan; or predominately white with tan, black or liver markings. The hair is short and fine on head, front of forelegs, and below hocks on front of hind legs. Coat determines nose color: liver or black, in harmony with coat.

Ideal heights: 20 inches for males, 19 inches for bitches. In sound condition, a beast carries about $2\frac{1}{2}$ pounds per inch. If built right, a dog with those specifications will move in long, easy strides at reasonable but not world record speed.

SPANIEL, FIELD (118)

This breed and the English Cocker are first cousins. They have the same origins and came along at the same time but developed into different beasts. While Cocker breeders had a compact dog in mind, Field breeders were looking for a longer, lower beast, and every breeder differed in concept. As far as type goes, the Field was not really defined until after World War II. The dog has never been popular in America (or anywhere else), and in an average year only two or three litters are whelped on this side of the Atlantic.

The dog now breeds true to type, and quality is very high. Field-wise, he's on a par with the Springer and a cut above the best Cockers. He's intelligent, fond of humans, and is A-rated as a pet. His chances of becoming better known and more abundant rest in the hands of his few owners. He needs exposure, and being entered at dog shows would solve that problem. As things stand now, this is a secret breed on the verge of becoming a rare one.

Breed Blueprint
As merry as a good Cocker and just as companionable, but with a better nose and more endurance in the field. It's never easy to find a pup—but always worth the search.

The Field Spaniel's head and neck carry more length than the Cocker's. The well developed skull has a distinct occiput and a moderate stop. The muzzle is long and lean, never snipy or square, and the bite can be even or scissors. There's a choice of color for the medium size eyes: hazel, brown, or almost black, depending on coat color. Ears are low set, moderately long and wide, hang close, and have moderate feathering.

The body is reasonably compact, or a bit longer than tall. Sloping shoulders, a deep chest, moderately sprung ribs and a level topline are all features of the breed. The legs are of flat bone, and the feet are round and thick. The topline is level, and the loins can be straight or arched. Angulation is moderate, and the docked tail is carried low.

The dense, silky coat is either flat or slightly wavy, never curly, and feathering on the chest, behind the legs, and under the belly is moderate. Proper coat colors are black, liver, golden liver, mahogany red, roan, or any of these colors with tan over the eyes and on the cheeks, feet, and pasterns. White on the coat is permissible but not desirable.

A good Field Spaniel (either sex) stands about 18 inches and weighs from 35 to 50 pounds. If that sounds vague, try this: if he looks well balanced, the dog is carrying the proper number of pounds.

SPANIEL, IRISH WATER (106)

For as long as dogs have been important to man, there have been two classes of spaniels: land and water. The IWS is a water spaniel who believes he is a retriever, and a wise owner doesn't argue with him. At first glance, his most distinctive feature is his natural rat tail. The tail is his and his alone, and no other spaniel or retriever can make that claim.

The IWS had his beginnings in the early years of the eighteenth century. Two distinguishable types evolved, and they were known as North Country and South Country. Around 1820 a Dublin gentleman, one Justin McCarthy, got into the breeding act, and by 1850 he had developed the South Country into the IWS as we know him today. Unfortunately, he did not keep records, but there's reason to believe that he infused the blood of both the Poodle and the Portuguese Water Dog (once almost extinct, now making a comeback).

True or not, McCarthy's IWS gained immediate favor (post 1850) in both Ireland and England. When market hunting flourished in America and ducks and geese were plentiful (1870–90), there were more dogs of the breed here than there are today.

This dog is the tallest of the spaniels. Although a great worker in the field, he has a reputation as a clown and doesn't take life too seriously. His popularity had waned, but it's now on the rise. A fine, all-around dog.

Breed Blueprint

In addition to the unique rat (whip) tail, the dog sports a topknot of long, loose curls. His face is naturally smooth coated and does not require clipping.

The dog's big skull is high domed and carries a prominent occiput. The muzzle is long, deep and square, and the bite is even. Hazel colored eyes are of medium size and lack eyebrows. That topknot shows a well defined peak between the eyes. The long, lobular ears are set low, hang close, and (extended forward) almost reach the end of the liver nose. The ears carry abundant curls that extend a couple of inches beyond tips. The neck is long and arching.

The IWS body is of medium length, with sloping shoulders, deep chest, and well sprung ribs. The legs are well boned, and the large feet carry webbing between the toes. The topline is either level or shows a gradual slope upward from withers over quarters. Thus, the dog's powerful rear can be higher than the withers, but no more than an inch. Hips are wide, angulation is moderate, and the tail is set low and carried level with back. At its base, the rat tail carries a couple of inches of short curls, and from there to the tip it is covered with short, smooth hair. The tail tapers, and is short of the hock when extended.

The breed carries a double coat: the undercoat is short and dense, and the topcoat is an abundance of tight, crisp curls. The only proper color is solid liver, and any white on the coat is considered objectionable.

Males stand 22 to 24 inches and weigh 55 to 65 pounds. Bitches are 21 to 23 inches, 45 to 58 pounds.

For many years, the myth has persisted that this dog and the Chesapeake Bay wear coats that create an objectionable odor in the house. Completely invalid nonsense!

SPANIEL, SUSSEX (121)

Developed from a blend of early land spaniels, this low-slung dog has been on the scene for more than a century. Never really popular, he has been on the verge of extinction several times—so close that inbreeding was necessary to keep him going. Today, thanks to a small but devoted set of breeders in both England and America, he's still with us. The contemporary Sussex does not have the size and bulk of the original, but he is far more congenial, and owes some of his substance to a fairly recent cross (several decades ago) with the Clumber Spaniel.

The Sussex is the only spaniel who talks while he works. When he scents small game, be it four-footed or winged, he gives voice. He also sounds off at home when dinner is late. Like the Clumber, he has a great nose but lacks speed. Unlike the Clumber, he has a rolling gait, similar to that of a veteran sailor on dry land. A fine pet, but it's not easy to find a pup.

Breed Blueprint

His coat color is a rich golden liver, or gold over liver. The liver hairs, either flat or slightly waved, have yellow tips that provide a golden sheen. No other breed wears this coat.

The skull is moderately long and wide, with a full (never pointed) occiput, a full stop and heavy brows. The muzzle is short (about 3 inches) and square, the lips are pendulous, and the bite can be even or scissors. The hazel eyes are big and show a little haw, and the nose is liver. Thick, large, lobular ears are set at eye level. While the neck is arched, it's so short that the dog carries his head just a little above the topline.

The shoulders slope, the chest is deep and wide, the legs are of strong bone, and the feet are big and round. The back is long, and the hindquarters are sturdy and carry moderate angulation. The low set tail is docked (3–5 inches) and carried at back level.

That yellow-tipped coat is always abundant, and feathering is on the moderate side.

Weights (either sex) run from 35 to 45 pounds. The Sussex set hasn't specified heights, but an average American male runs 16 inches, and a bitch about 15 inches. Overall, the dog is on the longish side, appears very chesty up front, and has more power than speed.

SPANIEL, WELSH SPRINGER (111)

This dog is often referred to as a first cousin or a spinoff of the English Springer, but both references are just so much gibberish. The Welsh was developed much earlier than the ESS and represents a combination of land and water spaniels. Before 1902 he was considered a Cocker: Welsh Cocker Spaniel. He is sized between the Cockers and the ESS and has more style and staying power than any of them.

Although well known in England, the Welsh has never really caught on in America, perhaps because the ESS has more size and supposedly requires less training, a rumor without foundation. The Welsh is easier to train than a docile wife. He has endurance to spare and a great record for longevity. He richly deserves popularity.

Breed Blueprint

Experienced owners insist that this dog needs early field training, when a pup is about six months old. Delay in training means a so-so, rather than a superior hunting companion.

The Welsh head is of moderate length, with a slightly domed skull and a well defined stop. The medium-sized eyes are hazel or darker, and the low-set ears hang close, narrowing toward the tips. The medium-long muzzle is straight and fairly square, and the bite is even or scissors. The neck is long, muscular, and clean.

Short-coupling characterizes the sturdy body, which features sloping shoulders, a deep chest, and well-sprung ribs. The legs are of good bone, the padded feet round and thick. The topline is level, the hindquarters strong and wide, and angulation moderate. The docked tail (⅔ of its natural length) is set low and carried even with the topline.

The flat, dense coat is remarkably water-resistant. It's silky in texture, and always carries two colors: a dark, rich red and white. In any litter, a curly coat can appear, but it's a no-no.

Oddly, the breed standard does not specify size. An average male stands about 19 inches, weighs some 45 pounds. Bitches: a little shorter, a little lighter.

VIZSLA (49)

Deep in his heart, the Vizsla is really a short-ranging pointer of Hungarian extraction. Thanks to his keen nose, he's also good at tracking and in water he's a fine retriever. Thus, a triple threat beast who goes back at least a century, was almost wiped out (1918), made a strong comeback between wars, then dwindled again when the Russians occupied Hungary (1945). Fortunately, some of the Hungarians who fled managed to take their dogs with them and the Vizsla is still with us. He gained A.K.C. recognition in 1960 and has been moving up in the popularity polls.

Although Vizslas are now found in several countries (including Russia), the dogs are more abundant in America than anywhere else, with more than five hundred litters whelped every year. That figure indicates that they're becoming more and more popular as pets.

As sporting dogs go, this one is speedy, streamlined, and very light of foot.

Breed Blueprint

A gentle, friendly dog with plenty of endurance for the field. Today's best pups are found in field-bred lines.

The lean head sits atop a moderately long, arched neck. The medium-wide skull carries a slight furrow and a fair stop. The color of the medium-sized eyes harmonizes with the coat, but yellow is out. The long, thin ears are set low, hang close, and are rounded at the tips. The tapering muzzle squares off at its end and is longer than the skull, and the bite is scissors. A good nose is always brown.

At first glance the dog looks a little leggy, but he's actually short-coupled and streamlined. The shoulders slope, and the chest is deep, reaching the elbows, and fairly broad. Legs of good bone and compact, catlike feet are essentials for the breed. Angulation is moderate, and there's a slight tuck-up beneath the loin. The docked tail—$\frac{2}{3}$ of its natural length—is thickest at its root and is set just below the level of the back.

The very short coat is smooth, dense, and close-lying. Solid coat colors are a rusty gold or a sandy yellow, the darker the better. Small white spots on the chest or feet are permissible.

Males stand 22 to 24 inches, bitches 21 to 23 inches. For show, a deviation of more than 2 inches, under or over, is a disqualification. A 22-inch dog will carry about 60 pounds.

WEIMARANER (38)

Various hounds and pointers are believed to be behind this German native, developed some 150 years ago to track an assortment of wild game that ranged from deer and boar to wolves and bears. By 1896 breed type had been set, and the Weimaraner was being used as a pointer and a retriever. Until the Second World War his breeding was tightly controlled in Germany.

The first American arrivals (1929) made their home in Rhode Island. A few other imports arrived during the thirties, and an unusual breed story started to unfold. Determined to maintain breed quality, the dog's early breeders formed the Weimaraner Club of America (1941). To buy a pup, one had first to join the club and then swear on a stack of Bibles to abide by certain rules and regulations. This had worked in Germany, but in America, where the A.K.C. granted breed recognition in 1943, the plan was destined to get out of hand. All went well until after the Second World War, when the devoted members of the club decided to popularize the breed. A publicity campaign was launched and succeeded, and soon (despite the very high prices) there weren't enough pups around to meet the demand. The press and the magazines joined the act, and since *Weimaraner* proved difficult to pronounce (it's Vy-mah-rah-ner), the public referred to him as the Gray Ghost or Miracle Dog. Since many people believe anything they read in a favorite publication, half the dog lovers in America believed that this dog could do just about everything, including climbing trees and flying. By the time the furor faded away, scores of indiscriminate breeders with dollar signs in their eyes were mass-producing pups, and prices tumbled. So did overall quality.

Today the dog is used mostly on upland birds (pointer manner), and with a little training he's more than adequate on water. He's a fine family dog and appreciates warmth and comfort. As a kennel dog, he's a complainer.

Breed Blueprint

The dog's quite thin coat is the reason why he appreciates warmth when he's not in action. Since he's as neat as a cat, a dog in good condition rarely needs grooming.

His head is moderately long, and so is his clean-cut neck. The skull carries a prominent occiput, slight furrow and a fair stop. Both the skull and the muzzle are the same length, and the bite is a scissors. Eyes are set well apart and are colored light amber, gray, or blue-gray. The lobular ears are set high, and are reasonably long; extended, they are a couple of inches short of nose point. Nose is always gray. Overall, skin is tightly drawn.

The body is reasonably compact and streamlined, characterized by sloping shoulders, long well sprung ribs, chest to elbows, good leg bone, and compact, arched feet. Toes are always webbed, and nails are gray or amber. For show, dewclaws must be removed.

The topline shows a slight slope downward from the withers. Angulation is good, and tuck-up is moderate. The docked tail (6 inches) is usually on the light side, not particularly thick at root.

The dog's coat is short, smooth and sleek. Proper colors are solid shades ranging from mouse-gray to silver-gray, often lighter on the head and ears. A small, white marking on chest is permissible, but not elsewhere on the body. Long coats and blue or black coats are disqualifications for show.

Males: 25 to 27 inches. Bitches: 23 to 25 inches. A 1-inch deviation (over or under) is allowable. A 26-inch dog will hit the scales at 70 to 75 pounds.

WIREHAIRED POINTING GRIFFON (102)

An American resident since 1900 but still not well known here, this dog owes his very existence to one man: Edward Korthals. This native of Holland, inspired by Mendel's findings and with money to spare, decided to develop his own pointing breed. In a remarkably short period (1874–85) he used a judicious blend of setters, pointers, and spaniels and came up with Korthals Griffon. The dog is still known by that name in France, but he has become the WPG elsewhere in the world.

The major reason why the dog has not become popular in this country is that he remains true to his breed—and to Korthals's intentions. In the field the WPG ranges close (spaniel fashion) and is never in a hurry. Korthals may have set a speed record as a breeder, but he was a leisurely hunter, and the dog he developed fit his style like a glove.

The WPG will work on water, but he prefers dry land. He's friendly and makes a good pet, and the quality of the average American pup is first-rate. We now have about three dozen breeders.

Breed Blueprint

Ideal for the leisurely sportsman who hates to groom. Grooming the unkempt topcoat can actually damage the soft undercoat of this intelligent, people-loving beast.

The WPG's long head is furnished with a harsh coat, plus mustache and eyebrows. The skull is long and lean, the yellow or light brown eyes are large and full, and the medium-sized ears are set high, carry light hair, and hang flat, although tips can carry slight curve. The square muzzle supports an even or scissors bite.

The body is sturdy and compact for a pointer and the forelegs appear a little short. All the legs carry good bone and are furnished with short hair (wire up front) and feet that are round, firm, and reasonably small. The shoulders slope, the ribs are rounded and

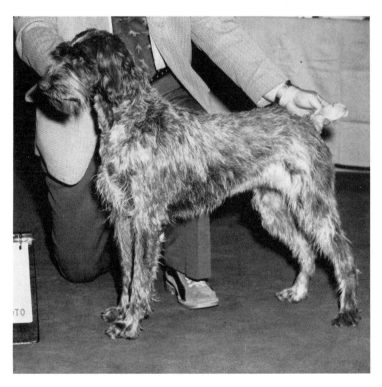

carried well back, and the topline is even. Thighs are long, angulation is moderate, and tuck-up is slight. The docked tail ($\frac{1}{3}$ of its natural length) is covered by a hard coat without plume and is carried gaily or level.

This is a double coat. The undercoat is short and soft, and the topcoat is of moderate length and harsh to the touch. Proper colors: steel gray with chestnut splashes; gray white with ditto; chestnut; and dirty white mixed with chestnut.

Males stand $21\frac{1}{2}$ to $23\frac{1}{2}$ inches. Bitches: $19\frac{1}{2}$ to $21\frac{1}{2}$ inches. Weights are not specified, but 22 inches of dog will go about 55 pounds.

In this breed, black is an evil color on both coat and nose. The sniffer should always be brown.

Hound Group

The hound breeds come in various shapes and sizes. Man developed them all for hunting purposes, and they are classified as either tracking hounds or gazehounds. The trackers are endowed with strong noses, and they find and follow the trail of wild game to its natural conclusion, or to the current location of the trailmaker (in the ground, up a tree). The gazehounds, all of them speedsters, use their remarkable vision to spot game and then either run it down or bring it to bay. While attending to business, the tracker makes a great deal of noise and thus, quite unintentionally, keeps his owner notified about his progress and location.

AFGHAN HOUND (28)

One of the world's very oldest canine breeds, this gazehound was running around Central Asia some three thousand years ago, and there have been claims that a pair of Afghans were passengers on Noah's Ark. Although known in Britain since 1894 and in the United States since 1910, serious breeding did not get underway in either country until the 1920s. The dog became an immediate success in England, but it took him a little longer to become popular in America, and A.K.C. recognition did not come until 1938. Two decades later his popularity started to zoom.

This hound is rarely used in the field now, and he serves mostly as a pet and show dog. His prominent hips, set wide apart, are designed to give him speed, the ability to turn on a dime, and leaping power. The Afghan can take a six-foot fence with the greatest of ease.

Obviously, this ancient breed was not designed for city life. The Afghan is happiest when he has room for running and jumping, and confinement is not his cup of tea. While most texts describe him as dignified, aloof, and inscrutable, most breed lovers agree that he's a friendly, often clownish beast and makes a fine family pet. He's not much of a barker, and his howl is an eerie wail. Since breed quality remains high, puppy price tags are usually high, even ridiculously high in pet stores.

Breed Blueprint

The dog's thick, silky coat never requires trimming or clipping, but daily grooming is a must; otherwise, dead hairs form mats and the dog's beauty goes down the drain. Not a breed for the casual owner.

The head is long and very refined, with the skull and muzzle in balance. There's no stop, and the nasal bone falls away in front of

the eyes. A slightly Roman nose, and a prominent occiput is hidden by a silky topknot. All reasons why the now obsolete term *monkey-faced dog* was invented. The eyes are almond shaped (almost triangular) and dark in color, the long ears are set at eye level and extend almost to the tip of the nose, and the nose is always black. The bite is level, and the neck is long and arched.

The body is reasonably short-coupled. The shoulders slope, and the chest is deep. The forelegs carry length between the elbows and pasterns. The big feet are arched and covered with long, silky hair. The topline is fairly level from the shoulders to the loin, then falls away toward the stern. The hips are high and wide, tuck-up good, and angulation strong. The tail is set low but carried high, curling into a small ring at the tip.

The thick, silky coat is short on the neck and saddle, longer and very abundant elsewhere, with plenty of feathering on the ears and feet. All coat colors or combinations of colors are permissible, but white markings, especially on the head, are undesirable.

Males stand 27 inches and weigh 60 pounds. Bitches are 25 inches and 50 pounds. For both sexes, an inch over or under the standard is okay, as are a couple of pounds either way. The Afghan is always on the lean side if he's in the pink of condition.

BASENJI (47)

One of the world's oldest breeds, this native of Central Africa is famous as the only naturally barkless dog. He's not mute, however, and he converses in a singsong manner that's often described as something between a chortle and a yodel. His family tree remains a mystery, as does his presence in the hound group. He looks and acts more like a terrier, and in the field his talents come closer to a sporting dog's than a hound's. By reputation the Basenji is a fine tracking dog, although he is not used for this purpose in the Western World.

Breeding did not begin until the late thirties in either England or America, and the A.K.C. did not grant recognition until 1943. Since the Basenji is relatively small and quiet, requires minimal grooming, and is as fastidious as the average cat, the dog is ideal for the small house, small apartment, and small car. A good one is easy to train and gets along well with children who are not tail pullers. Most of the show dogs, including all the big winners, are also family pets.

The Basenji is a spirited fellow who dotes on affection and deserves far more popularity than he's achieved.

Breed Blueprint

This dog moves in a very unhoundish manner. His gait is smart and resembles that of a show trotter. Otherwise, he doesn't resemble a horse, although that's his favorite animal.

The Basenji head sports a flat skull, of medium width, tapering toward the eyes, and a bit longer than the tapering muzzle. Pup or adult, a properly bred dog carries deep set wrinkles on the forehead and sides of the muzzle. Dark hazel, almond-shaped eyes and small, pointed, erect ears (set well forward) are proper. The bite is scissors. The arched neck is long and full at the base.

This is a short-coupled but lightly built dog, and he seems to be a little high on leg. The chest is deep, the ribs well sprung but in proportion, and the topline level. The legs carry clean, fine bone, and the small feet are compact and arched. The hindquarters are strong, with well-let-down hocks, long second thighs, and moderate angulation. The high-set tail is curled tightly over either side of rump.

The coat is short and silky, and the skin under it is always loose. Proper coat colors are deep chestnut red, black, or black and tan, all with white feet, chest, and tail tip. A white blaze, collar, and legs are fairly common and okay. The big faults in this breed are coarseness of head and the wrong bite.

Males stand 17 inches and weigh 24 pounds. Bitches are 16 inches and 22 pounds.

BASSET HOUND (21)

The contemporary Basset is about a century old and represents a type developed from an earlier version in France. According to undocumented but popular belief, the earlier one began as something of a freak and was really a short-legged St. Hubert Hound, found in otherwise normal litters of that long extinct breed. Thus, the original Basset came along as a short St. Hubert, eventually outlived his parent breed, and (once in England) enjoyed an infusion of Bloodhound blood. From a comparison of heads, that's easy to believe.

This mournful-looking hound has one of the best noses in the business. He is a tracker, and his long and low body is designed for work in heavy cover. In the old days he was used by the numbers (in a pack), and purists still hunt him that way today. For the most part, the Beagle has taken over the Basset's role as a single.

The low-slung beast achieved his first popularity through the show route in England, along about 1880. The first American litter (from imported British stock) was whelped in 1902 (Virginia), but it was several decades before the breed caught the public's fancy. As both pet and show dog, the Basset is amazingly popular today. There are many large kennels devoted to the breed, and they greatly outnumber our hunting packs.

Once on the trail, the Basset moves along at surprising speed. Still, his greatest speed is in growth. A pup grows in a hurry and achieves most of his size by eight months. He makes an agreeable pet, but usually requires a firm hand. And despite his looks, he does need running room. Hence, not an ideal city dog, although pet stores argue differently.

Breed Blueprint
When not on the trail, this beast should move along at a slow, steady pace that is never clumsy. A good one has a many-furrowed brow and much heavier bone than other breeds of his size.

The big head carries a skull and a muzzle of equal length. The occiput is prominent, but the stop is moderate. The muzzle is deep, heavy, and always free from snipiness, and the bite is even or scissors. The dark brown eyes are set deep and show haw. The low set ears are very long and extend beyond the nose, which is darkly pigmented (black preferred), with wide set nostrils. The neck is powerful and arched. Tight head skin is a fault.

The Basset's long body carries sloping shoulders, an even topline, well sprung ribs, very deep chest, and legs of heavy bone (and wrinkled skin). The huge feet are round and deep; forefeet are straight on, or can be slightly turned out.

To the rear, the hindquarters are very full and rounded, and just about the same width as the shoulders. Hocks are well let down, angulation is good, and feet are straight on. The natural tail is set high and carried gaily.

The coat is short, smooth, hard and dense, and the skin under it is loose. Any hound coloration is acceptable: white, black and tan, with the tan running from any shade of brown to a deep liver. Distribution of markings is unimportant.

The height (both sexes) should not exceed 14 inches. For show, anything over 15 inches is a disqualification. The standard does not specify weight, but 14 inches can mean as much as 45 pounds.

BEAGLE (4)

The merry Beagle has been running around Europe and England for more than five centuries, but during the first four he came in several sizes and shapes, including a pint-sized edition that was eight inches at the withers. An entire pack of the little fellows was tossed into a couple of panniers (saddle baskets), carried to the fields, and released to find and chase the many hares. Most of the credit for today's Beagle must go to American sportsmen who imported packs from England (1860–90) and bred them for size and type. Since then this dog has reigned supreme as America's most popular hound, so abundant that quality pups carry the lowest price tags among the purebreds. There are now about five million Beagles in the United States and Canada.

This is the average hunter's favorite dog for tracking rabbit and other small game and for flushing upland birds. Wealthy sportsmen keep hundreds of beagle packs and there are many more field trials for the breed per year than for all other breeds put together. Very easy to train, his size and economy price contribute to his continuing popularity as a house pet as well.

Breed Blueprint

This dog's sad face belies his cocky, playful disposition. An excellent bet for a child—or for an adult buying his first purebred.

The head is neat for a hound: fairly long, broad, and full, slightly domed at the occiput, with a moderate stop. The big, soft eyes are set well apart and may be brown or hazel in color. The long ears are set low, hang close, extend just short of the nose tip, and are rounded at the tips. A medium-long, straight, square muzzle and an even bite are characteristic. The neck is medium length, arched and clean.

The body is short-coupled, with sloping shoulders, a deep, wide chest, well sprung ribs, and a level topline. The legs are of good bone, and the feet are round and compact. The short, muscular back carries a broad, slightly arched loin. The hips and thighs are strong, and angulation is moderate. The natural tail is set high, carried gaily (never curved over the back) and appears a little short.

This dog has a close, hard coat of medium length, and any hound color is appropriate.

For show and field trial purposes the breed comes in two sizes: 13 inches and under (usually—for show—no less than 10 inches) and 13 to 15 inches. Those sizes are for both sexes. The standard does not specify weights, but in the pink of condition, a beagle runs about 2 pounds per inch. For family purposes size is immaterial.

BLACK AND TAN COONHOUND (94)

See page 24.

BLOODHOUND (55)

This big, forlorn-looking beast has the very best nose in the canine world and—thanks to his name—one of the worst public images. The blood in his name does not mean that he's bloodthirsty. Rather, it means that he's blooded, or that his heritage is as creditable as that of a thoroughbred horse.

One of the oldest of the hounds, he has been tracking game and people for over a thousand years in Europe, at least half of that time in England, and since about 1850 in America. Modern type was set in America, and he is now far more popular here than anywhere else in the world. Today this big hound is used mostly by the police for tracking and finding wanted or lost humans. His function does not include treeing, attack, or holding at bay.

Although affectionate and friendly, the big beast's size and large appetite have restricted his popularity as a pet. Pretty much a one-man or one-family dog, easy to train, and not recommended for city living.

Breed Blueprint

As with other big breeds, bloat (distended abdomen and twisted stomach) can be a problem. For that reason, water is withheld for at least two hours after feeding. A hound glove makes grooming an easy task.

The big head is narrow and long—at least 12 inches on a male and 11 inches on a bitch—with occiput prominent and stop moderate. The skull and muzzle are of equal length. Ranging from hazel to yellow, the deep-set eyes show plenty of haw. The low-set ears are extremely long and are thin and soft to the touch. The muzzle is deep and square, carrying even width throughout, and the bite may be even or scissors. The nostrils are wide and open, the lips square and deep, with hanging flews. The long neck is arched and throaty, with loose skin apparent. The head skin is also loose and falls into folds when the head is lowered.

The body carries sloping shoulders, a deep chest, well sprung ribs, and a level topline. The legs are of heavy bone, the feet big and deep. The back and loins are very strong, and angulation is moderate. The long, tapering tail is set high and carried up but not over the back.

A Bloodhound coat is short, dense, and hard. Colors are black and tan, red and tan, and tawny. A small amount of white is okay on the chest, feet, and tip of the tail.

Males stand 25 to 27 inches and weigh 90 to 110 pounds. Bitches are 23 to 25 inches, 80 to 100 pounds. Breeders and many show judges prefer the maximum sizes as long as all parts are in proportion. An adult requires about three pounds of food per day.

BORZOI (51)

Known as the Russian Wolfhound until 1936, the Borzoi (pronounced Bowr-zoy) has been an American resident since about 1890, although it took another couple of decades before serious breeding got underway. This sight hound is a speedster who, a few centuries ago—if one believes rumors—was the pride and joy of wolf-hunting Russian nobility. The Russians weren't talking very much, but the average dog fancier is willing to believe that the breed derives from a mix of the thin-coated Greyhound and a heavy-coated Russian herding dog.

With the decline of both the wolf and Russian aristocracy, the dog became popular with the upper classes at the shows and in the home, first in England, then in America. In both countries, the trouble with the breed can be traced to the breeders. Since Borzoi pups continue to bring high prices, about half the breeders are devoted to pro-

duction profit, and that's no way to maintain quality and type. Fortunately, the other breeders know what they're doing, so a careful buyer can find a pup who will mature into a dog who looks and loves like a Borzoi. For the new owner the problem is finding the right breeder. A veteran judge or professional handler will know several.

This dog looks good in the city, but that's the last place he should be. If he's to stay in condition he needs running room. And that's why, as a pet, he's found on so many estates, and often in numbers. Confinement is not his cup of tea.

Breed Blueprint

Among the big breeds this one isn't the best bet as a child's playmate. He is gentle, but he's also reserved and on the cool side, and he might even consider himself superior to Junior. A true aristocrat.

His head is on the elegant side: slightly domed, long and narrow, with only a hint of a stop. The dark, slanting eyes sport dark rims, and the nose is black. The small, fine ears are set well back, with the tips almost touching occiput when the dog is in repose. The muzzle is long and deep, with something of a Roman nose, and the bite is even or scissors. The short, clean neck is a little arched.

A Borzoi's sloping shoulders are very close at the withers. The chest is deep, as is the slightly sprung rib cage. The legs carry good, flat bone, and the harefeet are well arched, with toes close. The topline carries a little curve over the loins, and the long, powerful hindquarters show good angulation. The Borzoi is always wider in the hindquarters than the shoulders. This gives him strong drive and plenty of reach up front without interference from the hind legs. The long tail is carried low, in a curve that reaches below the hocks.

The long, silky coat can be flat, wavy, or a little on the curly side. It's short and smooth on head, ears and fronts of legs. Feathering is long at the rear, moderate up front. Any coat color or color combination is okay but white usually predominates.

Males stand at least 28 inches and range from 75 to 105 pounds. Bitches are at least 26 inches and weigh 15 to 20 pounds less than males. For show, smaller sizes are not a disqualification, but such dogs must be exceptional to win. The best breeders concentrate on producing the big ones.

DACHSHUND (5)

The Doxie comes in three coats and two sizes. In any coat or size he is descended from a larger, sixteenth-century beast, fondly remembered (through art) as the Badger Dog. The long extinct BD of Germany was developed to trail and go to ground after the badger, and that's really a terrier trick. In German the word *dachshund* means "badger dog," an interesting fact that Prince Albert never could get across to his beloved wife, Queen Victoria. She went wild over the longish (and by then little) dogs, and to her and her subjects *hund* sounded like "hound." So blame Victoria for turning the Doxie into a hound, and credit her for the dog's original popularity in England, circa 1860. By then the dog was also in America.

Here most of the early imports were from Germany. They all wore smooth coats and were used in packs on rabbits and sometimes on fox. By 1880 Doxie popularity in America was assured. By 1940 he placed in the first ten in the breed popularity poll and has been there ever since. Today strictly a show and pet dog, he is not used for hunting.

Except for the certainty that the smooth coat came first, the long coat next and finally the wire, no two canine historians are agreed as to coat evolution. There's plenty of speculation about crosses with other breeds to achieve the long and wire coats, but the real truth will always be in the dark.

Although popular all over the world as a house pet, the dog who runs like a sausage with short legs is not ideal for sedentary or short-tempered people. The little beast is as curious and active as a terrier, he dotes on attention and play, and he's noisy when strangers approach. Every good Doxie wants and demands companionship.

Breed Blueprint

The three varieties are classified by coat, and each variety comes in two sizes, Standard and Miniature. No matter the dog's coat or weight, his quality is measured by one breed standard:

The head is long and tapering. The slightly arched skull slopes gradually (without any stop) into the fine and slightly arched muzzle. The bite is a scissors, and the medium-sized, oval eyes are always dark in color. The longish, rounded ears are set very high and forward edges hang close. A proper neck is long, clean and slightly arched.

A Doxie's long body is carried on very short legs. Still, the body is substantial rather than slim, and there's no awkwardness in gait. The shoulders slope, the chest is deep, and the breastbone is prominent. The feet are compact, arched, and turned a little out up front. The topline is level, the rib cage full and oval, and there's a little tuck-up and strong angulation at the rear. The natural tail is set as continuation of the spine, and is never carried much above the back.

Coat colors are solid (usually red, but red yellow, yellow, and brindle are okay), two-colored (black, chocolate, gray, or white, each with tan markings), and dappled (brown, gray, or white with darker, irregular patches of gray, brown, red yellow or black).

Varieties. (1) Smooth: short, dense, shining coat; (2) Longhaired: long, silky coat with abundant feathering; (3) Wirehaired: short, rough, hard coat, with bushy eyebrows and beard.

Divisions. (1) Standard: 10 to 20 pounds, (2) Miniature: under 10 pounds.

Sometimes, a year old Mini who is just under 10 pounds will

continue to mature and add a few ounces. The moment he hits or goes over 10 pounds he becomes a Standard, albeit on the small side. However, if he is not used for show or breeding, it is legal for his owner to continue to refer to his dog as a Mini.

FOXHOUND, AMERICAN (112)

See page 20.

FOXHOUND, ENGLISH (120)

In England this dog dates back to the thirteenth century, when stag hunting was in fashion and a large, swift hound was needed to stay in the chase. The EF amounts to a smaller, even speedier version of those unknown, early beasts. Nobody paid much attention to type until about 1800. By then foxes were more abundant and fashionable than stags.

The EF has been in America since about 1730, and he was imported in large numbers a century later, when hunt clubs got underway. Nobody knows if he's the real daddy of the American Foxhound, but certainly he's one of the forebears. Today the two breeds are very similar in all ways—so much so, that many hunt club

packs amount to mixes of the two. Otherwise, pure AF packs out-number pure EF packs by a ratio of eight to one.

Like the AF, this hound isn't much of a pet. Pups are okay, but mature dogs prefer their own kind to people. Thus, it's best to keep the EF in numbers and in a kennel.

Breed Blueprint

To avoid needless repetition, and since differences are minor, check the AF blueprint (Chapter II), but note the following:

The EF head has a more pronounced stop. Usually, the long ears are cropped back to 1½ inch and are rounded at tips. Extended (after cropping), they fall short of the nose. The muzzle is wider, and the bite is even.

Overall, the EF is a dog of more substance. His chest is wider, and he carries up to 10 pounds more weight. Both angulation and tuck-up are slight.

The standard does not specify heights or weights, but average males stand 24 to 25 inches and weigh 65 to 70 pounds; average bitches run 22 to 23 inches and weigh 55 to 60 pounds.

GREYHOUND (95)

This is another of the world's oldest breeds—old enough to have been a favorite of royalty in the glory days of ancient Egypt and to be mentioned in the Bible, so old that he's behind such other breeds as the Afghan, Borzoi, and Saluki. The dog has come down through the ages in great shape, chasing and overtaking just about every speedy wild animal that man has desired for his dinner table. He has been thwarted in recent times by the mechanical rabbit, and the Greyhound and his artificial prey have made dog racing a popular spectator sport in several states.

These days the big gazehound is rarely used for hunting. If he's not a professional racer, then he's a show dog or pet or both. Although an American resident since about 1880, he has never achieved high status as a pet. There's no valid reason for this sad state of affairs, for he's a clean dog, easy to groom and train, and he eats no more than any other dog his size. What may hold him back are his need for plenty of exercise and his inherent aloofness. The Greyhound believes that he's one of dogdom's aristocrats; he is not a loner—but he's not a good mixer, either—and he resents city life.

Breed Blueprint

The dog's top speed is something to behold. His hind legs reach beyond his forelegs when he's at a full gallop. At a trot the word *graceful* best describes his action. Either way, he moves in a hurry.

The Greyhound's long, narrow, wedge shaped head carries a very modest stop. The eyes are always dark. The ears, on the small side for a hound, are set high and back, hang close, and are semi-pricked when at attention. The muzzle is long and clean, and the bite is even. The long, clean neck is arched.

Although the body looks long, it's reasonably short-coupled, carrying sloping shoulders and a deep chest. The legs are of good bone, and the feet are hare and tight, more like a hare's than a cat's. The topline shows a little slope downward from the withers, and the hindquarters are wide and powerful, with good tuck-up and angulation. The long, low set tail is broad at the base and tapers to a point, curving slightly upward at the tip.

The coat is very short, smooth, and dense. Any coat color is okay.

Males weigh 65 to 70 pounds, bitches 60 to 65 pounds. The breed standard does not specify heights, but an average male stands about 30 inches, an average bitch about 28 inches.

There are four other breeds of true Greyhounds in the world: Chortray, Hungarian, South Russian, and Tasy. They are neither present in America nor recognized by the A.K.C. or C.K.C.

HARRIER (114)

This dog has been around in England for over six centuries and in America since Colonial times. His chief claim to fame is that he is the first trailing hound to be developed for hare, rather than for fox. There are numerous theories about the breeds behind him, but sober canine historians agree that he is really a small edition of the English Foxhound. Although the two breeds do differ in a few ways, this theory seems reasonable.

The proper way to hunt the Harrier is by the pack. Today there are only a few breeders in the world and there have never been more than six at any given time in America. Of the few pure Harrier packs in the world, not one is in this country.

Although Harrier pups are always hard to find, they are easier to train than most hounds and make fine house pets. An ideal choice for a man who wants a rabbit dog who is a little slower than a Foxhound and a little bigger than a Beagle. The best way to view a Harrier is to find a breeder and visit his kennel. The dog is seldom seen at dog shows.

Breed Blueprint

In appearance this dog is the English Foxhound all over again, but with the following differences:

The head always carries a dish face (concave nasal bone), and the ears are never cropped. And on the feet, the toes turn slightly inward.

Both sexes stand 19 to 21 inches, although bitches can be a bit under. Weight is not specified, but the average Harrier runs 40 to 45 pounds.

IRISH WOLFHOUND (54)

The giant of dogdom and still another of the world's oldest breeds, this dog was too proficient for his own good and was racing toward extinction in the early years of the nineteenth century. By then the object of his talents—trailing and bringing down the Irish wolf—was extinct.

By 1860 the breed was down to a few survivors, and nobody in Ireland cared. Luckily, however, one man in Scotland did care. Captain G. A. Granham, British army, purchased some of the survivors, none of them noble specimens, and through careful breeding and ('tis rumored) judicious outcrossing with other big breeds, saved and revived the IW as we know him today. The Granham restoration spanned more than two decades.

The IW is still used to hunt big game here and there, but not in America, where he's used for pet and show. His popularity is amazing for such a big dog. He is an affectionate, loyal beast, and despite his size, can get by with a modest amount of daily exercise. Nor is he

awkward in the house; somehow he learns to move about without knocking down furniture and small children. Of all the big breeds, he is the best suited to city life. On the other hand, he is not the best pet for the economy-minded. To put it mildly, his appetite is very hearty.

Breed Blueprint

Most IW lovers own two or three of the beasts, a fact that speaks well for his pet potential. While easy to train, he can't be forced, and the training requires patience.

The long head carries a moderately broad skull and a slight stop. The eyes are always dark, and the small ears are set high and carried in Greyhound manner. The muzzle is long and slightly pointed, the bite even or scissors. The neck is long, muscular, and clean.

The IW body features sloping shoulders, a deep, wide chest, legs of good bone, and moderately large, round feet that are compact and well arched. The back is a little on the long side, with muscular hindquarters, noticeable tuck-up, and good angulation. The long tail has moderate thickness, shows a slight curve, and should be well covered with hair.

The coat is rough and hard on the body, legs, and head, very long and wiry over the eyes and on the underjaw. Proper coat colors are gray, brindle, red, black, pure white, fawn, and any other color that appears on the Scottish Deerhound coat.

Minimum size for males is 32 inches and 120 pounds, for bitches, 30 inches and 105 pounds. That's for show, when the dog is 18 months or older. While the dog sometimes comes a little smaller, even bigger dogs (a few inches and pounds over the standard) are preferred by the purists.

NORWEGIAN ELKHOUND (31)

Norway's gift to the dog fancy is the most versatile—and maybe the oldest—hound in the world. As any breed fancier will tell you at the drop of a hat, this dog was around as early as 4000 B.C., and there are skeletons under glass to prove that claim. Since the Elkhound's true ancestry will never be known—canine historians were unknown until recent centuries—it is safe to believe that this beast developed

naturally and that man had little or no influence on his design.

By nature, the NE trails, finds, and holds at bay, and his excited barks attract the hunter to the site. Over the span of many centuries the dog was used mostly on bear. But around 1860, as Norway was becoming bearless, the dog's attention was directed to the more abundant elk. The Elkhound, then, is really the former Bearhound.

Since his recognition by the A.K.C. in 1935, the dog has been constantly edging upward in popularity. In America he has been used as a White House pet (Herbert Hoover) and on all sorts of wild game, from rabbit and raccoon to deer and mountain lion. A few have been used as retrievers, and many have been trained to herd livestock. The Elkhound has also been a big winner at shows over the past two decades.

A carefully bred Elkhound makes a fine family pet. Unfortunately, irresponsible breeders have put the emphasis on looks rather than temperament, making it necessary for the wise puppy buyer to go only to established breeders. There he can usually view both the pup's parents and grandparents and judge for himself as to inherited disposition.

Breed Blueprint

When wet, the coat does not carry a doggy odor. When dry, a simple, daily brushing keeps it in condition. The dog matures slowly and usually requires more than average training discipline.

The Elkhound's wedge-shaped head is devoid of loose skin. It is broad between the ears, slightly rounded front and back, and carries a moderate stop. The oval eyes are dark brown and should never protrude. The high-set ears, wide at the base and tapering to a point, are always carried erect. The medium long muzzle tapers evenly but not to a point, and the bite is scissors. The medium long neck has no looseness of skin.

The body is very compact, with moderately sloping shoulders, a deep, broad chest, and well sprung ribs. The legs are of strong bone, and the feet are small, tight, and oblong in shape. The back is very short and straight, tuck-up and angulation very slight. The short tail is set high and is carried a little to one side, in a tight curl over the rump.

The Elkhound has a double coat, with the undercoat light, soft, and wooly and the topcoat thick, hard, and smooth-lying. The hair is short and even on the head and fronts of the legs, and longer elsewhere. The coat color is always gray with black tips on the long hairs, and it is lighter gray on chest, stomach, legs, and underside of the tail. White markings are not nice.

The ideal size for males is 20½ inches and 55 pounds; for bitches, it's 19¼ inches and 48 pounds. For show, a solid color other than gray disqualifies.

It's very easy to put too much weight on this dog, so feeding must be watched. Obesity shortens longevity. One easy way to control an adult's pounds is to give him two meals a day—the first meal is always the same size, and the second is changed weekly until the dog stays at the proper weight.

OTTER HOUND (117)

Developed in England in the thirteenth century from other, unknown breeds, this is one of the earliest purebreds, used for the purpose of hunting the otter. Down through the centuries this shaggy hound hunted in packs and earned a fine reputation for a keen nose, so sensitive that it could pick up otter scent on land, on water, and even (it is claimed) underwater. In modern times water pollution has reduced the numbers of both the fish and otter, and pure OH packs are just memories.

The dog has been in America since the beginning of the century and has been shown since 1907—but never in large numbers. Today the OH population in the United States is larger than in any other country; however, the fact is more impressive than the figure, about 500. On this side of the Atlantic the dog has not been used for otter hunting, but a few have been used on fox. The beast's future depends upon his acceptance as a pet, something that can only be achieved through vigorous promotion—and that hasn't happened yet. As a pet, he's quiet and gentle and makes a fine one-family dog. But he does not like to be pushed around and isn't the best bet for aggressive small fry. Okay for city living, although his coat is a magnet for soot.

Breed Blueprint

This is the dog for the man who has everything but is troubled by otters. Shave this beast and he resembles a short Bloodhound, who just could be one of his ancestors.

The big head is fairly narrow for its size and runs from 11 to 12 inches in length (occiput to tip of nose). The skull is slightly domed,

the stop is moderate, and the long, square muzzle carries a scissors bite. The dark eyes are set deep, with just a touch of haw, and the low set ears are long, pendulous, and hang close. The nose can be black or liver, depending on the coat color. The neck looks short (because of the coat), but is really of medium length.

The short-coupled body features sloping shoulders, a deep and broad chest, legs of heavy bone, and feet that are big, round and webbed toed (unusual for a hound). The topline is level, ribs are well sprung, and the hindquarters are powerful and carry moderate angulation. The tail is long and must reach at least to the hock. At rest, the tail is carried down. In action, it is carried up in sickle fashion but not over the back.

The OH wears a double coat—with the usual short and wooly undercoat and the rough, hard outercoat averaging from 3 to 6 inches in length. Any coat color is acceptable, although liver and white is rarely seen.

Males stand 24 to 27 inches and weigh from 75 to 115 pounds. Bitches are 22 to 26 inches, 65 to 100 pounds.

The dog is short-coupled, but it's okay for a bitch to be a little long in the body—maybe one of the authors of the breed standard owned some long bitches.

RHODESIAN RIDGEBACK (68)

It is held that the RR was designed by Mother Nature and not by man. Originally a wild dog, he was domesticated in South Africa as early as the seventeenth century and was used as both guard and hunting dog. Then, in the nineteenth century, the beast came into his own as a lion tracker. As such, he first became famous in Rhodesia, and there—in this century—selective breeding of the RR got underway.

This beast looks more like a sporting dog than a hound and takes the Ridgeback part of his name from the ridge of hairs running along the spinal column from withers to hips, and growing toward the head, that is, in the opposite direction from the rest of the coat. No other pure breed carries this unique feature.

The dog is fairly new on this side of the Atlantic and has only carried A.K.C. credentials since 1959. Since it's illegal to hunt lions at zoos, wild-animal farms, and circuses, the RR now serves chiefly as a pet and is sure to become more popular with dog lovers looking for a big, good-natured, reasonably quiet beast. Too big and strong for Jack and Jill to handle, but a good bet for adults.

Breed Blueprint

As big dogs go, the RR is easy to train, requires minimal grooming, and fits into family life if the children aren't brats. He still retains a good nose, so owners shouldn't leave unguarded roasts on the dinner table.

The head sports a broad, flat skull, a fairly well defined stop, an absence of wrinkles, and a long and deep muzzle with an even bite. The color of the round eyes should harmonize with coat color, and the medium size ears are set high, hang close, and taper to a rounded point. Nose is either black or brown, again harmonizing with coat color. The strong and clean neck is of medium length.

The RR body is a little on the long side, with sloping shoulders, a deep and fairly wide chest, legs of heavy bone, and feet that are round, compact and arched. The topline is level and runs over a moderately sprung rib cage and strong, slightly arched loins. Tuck-up is slight and angulation is fair. The tail has a medium set, gradually tapers toward the end, and is carried with a slight upward curve. It's never curled.

The dog's coat is very short, dense, and sleek, but not to the point of being silky. Proper coat colors run from light wheaten to red, with a little white on the chest and toes okay.

Males stand 25 to 27 inches, weigh up to 75 pounds. Bitches are 24 to 26 inches and up to 65 pounds.

The hallmark of the RR, of course, is that unique ridge. Viewed from above, it extends to the hips from immediately behind the withers, where two crowns, one on either side, meet and form more or less the shape of a bulb. From this, its broadest point, the ridge tapers down to a point over and between the hips. The more symmetrical the ridge, the better the coat—and the better the dog's chances in the breed ring.

SALUKI (72)

Another of the world's venerable breeds, this gazehound just might be the oldest member of the famous Greyhound family. His admirers think so, anyway, and it is a fact that he closely resembles mummified remains and stone carvings that date back to 6000 B.C. At any rate, it seems evident that he's a native of some Arab land (Syria?) and that he took a long time getting to England (1830), and an even

longer time reaching America (1920). He's been an official member of the A.K.C. family since 1927.

In olden times the Saluki was used to chase just about everything, including the very speedy gazelle. In modern times the swift beast is mostly a pet and show dog, although in other lands where falconry is still popular, he is occasionally used as half the hunting team. The falcon, on high, locates the game; the dog is released and runs it down.

The Saluki is a beautiful sight as he walks down Park Avenue with the butler, but he's really not designed for city life. One of the great joys of ownership is watching him move. His walk is springy, his trot is a prance, and his run is sheer grace—even over rough ground. The beast makes a gentle, affectionate family pet, although he can be aloof with strangers.

There are two varieties, distinguished only by coat: Feathered and Smooth.

Breed Blueprint

The Saluki's delicate looks are deceptive. Given plenty of running room during puppyhood, he develops into a rugged beast with plenty of stamina. A little daily grooming with a soft brush keeps the coat in shape. The dog's one eccentricity is his phobia of water—he likes to drink it but hates to swim in it.

The head is long and narrow; the level skull is widest between the ears and carries a very slight stop. The large, oval eyes are dark brown to hazel in color, and the long, silky ears are set high and hang close. A black or liver nose is proper. The muzzle is parallel to the skull, and the bite is even. A long neck is a must.

The Saluki carries sloping shoulders, a deep but fairly narrow chest, and moderately sprung ribs. The long legs are of medium bone, and the feet look much bigger than they really are because of hair between the long, well arched toes. The back is fairly broad, with a little arch over the loins, and the hips are set very wide apart, with good tuck-up and moderate angulation. The long tail is set low and carries a natural curve.

The coat is always smooth, soft, and silky. As for the varieties: the Feathered Saluki carries slight silky feathering on the legs and thighs, and very noticeable feather on the underside of the tail; the Smooth lacks all feathering. Proper coat colors are white, fawn, gold, red, grizzle (bluish-gray) and tan, black and tan, and tricolor (white, black, and tan).

Males stand 23 to 28 inches and bitches—"considerably smaller"— 20 to 25 inches. The standard doesn't specify proper weights, but a dog who stands 25 inches will run about 65 pounds.

To a veteran Saluki fancier, the Feathered variety is the superior one. He thinks a Smooth looks a little naked. Dogs and breed judges, however, don't give a damn.

SCOTTISH DEERHOUND (103)

Any deer's worst enemy is this shaggy version of the Greyhound. He depends more on his nose than his vision, and unlike most trailing hounds, he not only finds his prey but brings it down. While his true ancestry remains a matter of debate, dogs like him were chasing deer around England many centuries ago, and he has been breeding true to type for 200 years. To their credit, breeders have never tried to refine this beast, and he can be considered a canine antique. He looks much the same today as he did in 1776.

In America, where he arrived about 1876, he hasn't been used on deer for a long time. Here hunting deer with dogs is immoral and

also rather illegal. Still, since the Deerhound is easy to train, he has been used with great success on other game.

This dog has never enjoyed great popularity in America, and chances are that he never will. Although he makes a fine pet and craves human companionship, his giant size is against him for the city or the house with a small yard. Puppy quality remains high.

Breed Blueprint

A great choice for the dog lover who has the open spaces for a big pet but has to watch the food budget. The adult Deerhound gets by on about half the food required by other big breeds in his size range. Reason unknown. And if Junior must have a big dog, this one is a fine choice.

The Deerhound's long head is broadest between the ears, tapers a little to the eyes, and from there the muzzle tapers to a point. The flat skull shows a slight rise over the eyes, but not enough to qualify as a stop. The eyes are dark brown to hazel, and the ears are set high, folded back, and are sometimes carried semierect when the dog is excited. The bite is even. A proper beast sports both mustache and beard, and black or dark ears with short hair. The neck is long and very strong.

Shoulders carry good slope and blades are close. Otherwise, strip away his rough coat and this is the Greyhound, but with more size and bone.

The coat is 3 to 4 inches long and is harsh, wiry and dense, but softer on the head, belly, and breast. A slight fringe of hair, not enough to be termed feathering, is found on the inner sides of each leg. Coat colors, a matter of personal preference, run from the popular dark blue-gray to dark and light grays and brindles, yellows and reds. With any coat, dark ears and muzzles are virtues. Any white on coat is a sin, the lesser sin being a white tip on tail.

Males stand 30 to 32 inches, and bitches are from 28 inches upwards. As for weights, 85 to 110 pounds is the range for males, and 75 to 95 pounds for bitches.

For show, and no matter the quality of the beast, a white blaze on head or a white collar (or both) are disqualifications. Something for puppy buyers to remember. But if the pup is just going to be a pet, forget it.

WHIPPET (62)

As canine breeds go, this is a relatively new one, no more than a century old. The Whippet was developed (bred down in size) from the Greyhound. The original intent was to produce a pocket size version of daddy for the British commoner's popular new sport of dog racing. In due time, the intent was realized, and Whippet racing was on its way. The fever spread from England to Europe, and finally to America. These days, dog racing—with Whippets as the racers—continues to be very popular abroad. Here, the Greyhound pretty well dominates the sport.

This little speedster has been clocked at forty miles per hour, and although doing the 100 yard dash in under ten seconds is still a notable achievement for a human, the beast does it in a breeze. No other dog of the Whippet's height or poundage can match his speed.

En route to glory as a racing star, the Whippet won the hearts of dog lovers and soon proved his worth as a family pet. He's affectionate, clean in his habits, rarely needs grooming, and barks so in-

frequently that he sometimes startles himself when he does. As a show dog, he's one of the easiest to handle in the ring. Like the Greyhound, he's a sight hound.

Breed Blueprint
The Whippet develops more slowly than most hounds and doesn't reach full maturity until about two years of age. By then, his show quality is apparent, and he's either a sure winner or a dud. Either way, he's still a winning pet.

His bite is scissors. In all other respects—except size—he very closely resembles the Greyhound.

Males stand 19 to 22 inches and bitches 18 to 21 inches. For show, ½ inch either way is okay. Weight can be calculated at about 1 pound per inch, so a 20-inch dog will weigh close to 20 pounds.

For show, disqualifications are improper size, blue or china-colored eyes, eyes not of the same color, and undershot or severely overshot bite.

Working Group

All the working dog breeds were originally fashioned to assist man in his labors. As such, in peace and war they once constituted the world's largest, skilled, unpaid work force. These canines served in numerous capacities, often replacing humans and usually doing a better job. These days, while some members of each breed are still at their appointed tasks and some have been assigned to new duties (such as detecting caches of dope at ports), the great majority serve as pets. In America the popular belief holds that any pup of a given breed inherits the talents of the breed's ordained duty. The truth is that the pup inherits no more than physical conformation and latent instinct that must be whetted. As the son of a mason must be taught to lay brick, so the St. Bernard pup must be trained to carry a small cask of rum and find the lost mountain climber. Without training, the dog would lose his way.

AKITA (61)

Three varieties of Inu are native to Japan, and the best of the educated guessers believe that they are members of the famous Spitz family. Of the three, the Shishi Inu, or Akita, is the largest and is probably the forebear of the other two varieties (Shika and Shiba). Long ago the dog's ownership was restricted to nobility, but later the Akita became the popular hunting dog for those who liked to dine on deer, bear, and wild boar. In modern times he has become the favorite canine of both the police and army in Japan, where his fame as a working dog is based on his guard work. Arriving in America after the Second World War, he's come along fast as a pet, and he won A.K.C. recognition in 1973 as the newest addition to our working breeds.

This big beast is one of the strongest in his size range. Although this does not negate his virtues as a family pet, a pup is best trained by an adult and in the breed ring he should be handled by that adult. The Akita is friendly enough with small fry but seems to require and respect a firm hand.

And then there's the matter of finding the right pup. Traditionally, the introduction of a new breed to America attracts a number of individuals without prior experience in canines. Tempted by the thought of getting in early on a sure thing, the inept ones start breeding right and left, with no thought to blood lines, conformation, or temperament. This did happen to the Akita. Fortunately, the breed's best friends formed a national breed club. The best pups around are those bred by the members of that club.

Breed Blueprint

Adult Akitas sometimes need a little watching with strange dogs of the same sex. Otherwise, no problems with the good ones.

A proper Akita's head is big, broad, and (viewed from above) forms a blunt triangle. The skull is flat and broad, the stop well defined, the muzzle broad and full, the jaws square (never snipy) with a scissors or level bite. The nose is black. The dark brown eyes are small, triangular, and deep set, and the triangular ears are rounded at the tips and carried erect and a little forward. The neck is thick and strong.

Although the body looks compact, it's a little long, the ratio of length to height being 10:9 for males and 11:9 for bitches. The shoulders carry moderate slope, the chest is deep and wide, the legs are of heavy bone, and the feet are small and catlike. The level topline runs over well sprung ribs, and the strong hindquarters show moderate tuck-up and angulation. The big tail is set high and curls over the back.

The Akita wears a double coat, with the undercoat short, dense, and soft and the topcoat straight and harsh and running to 2 inches in length over the body. The topcoat stands a bit off the body, and is shortest on the head, legs and ears, longest on the tail. Any color is okay, and undercoat may be different than topcoat.

Males stand 26 to 28 inches, and bitches go from 24 to 26 inches. Weight is in proportion to body and 26 inches would mean about 95 pounds. For show, a male under 25 inches and a bitch under 23 inches are out of the running.

The curl of the Akita tail varies from beast to beast, and runs from three-quarters to full to double. It must dip to or below the level of the back. A few other things to watch out for: drop or broken ears, nose color (always black, although liver is permissible with a solid white coat), and noticeable undershot or overshot bite.

ALASKAN MALAMUTE (34)

See page 18.

BELGIAN MALINOIS (119)

This is one of three varieties of the same breed of sheepdog. All three are now on the American scene, and since 1959 the A.K.C. has recognized each as a separate breed: the Malinois, the Sheepdog, and the Tervuren. In conformation and in ancestry, all three are identical. They differ only in coat.

The chances are that none of these sheepdogs would be around today if a few dog fanciers hadn't rushed to the rescue. Down through the centuries the canines were used in Belgium (and France and Holland) to herd sheep, guard them from wolves, and escort them to market. Since the breeding of sheepdogs amounted to the mating of a top worker to a top worker of the opposite sex, the dogs came in an astounding number of sizes, shapes, and coats. About a century ago, sheepdog unemployment began and their numbers declined; the open

ranges were now fenced, the European wolf was no more, and the railways had arrived.

On the other hand, dog shows were becoming popular, and Belgium had its quota of dog fanciers. Among them were serious breeders who decided that one type of sheepdog was enough, and through their efforts a dog with a standard conformation evolved. By 1880, this Belgian sheepdog was breeding true, insofar as conformation went. What the breeders couldn't get together on was coat. In a given region, one coat was favored over the others. One of the coats that prevailed is worn by the Malinois, who takes his name from the area around the Belgian town of Malines, also known as Mechlin. While a pup still isn't easy to find in America, quality is very high and the beast makes a fine pet. Like his cousins, he retains his natural instincts and some families train him as a guardian and herder of small children.

Breed Blueprint
A strong, active, handsome dog and a cinch to train. For those with a deep appreciation of canine beauty, a male is usually better-looking than a bitch, even if they're litter mates. Often the female body is a little longer, making her a little short of elegant.

The clean-cut head features a flat skull that's equal in length and width and carries a moderate stop. The muzzle, of the same length as skull, tapers to nose, but is never snipy. An even or scissors bite is okay. The medium-sized eyes are always almond shaped and must be brown, the darker the better. The triangular ears are set at mid-eye level and back, and are carried erect. Pigmentation (lips, nose) is black.

A male's body must be short-coupled, but a bitch's, as noted, may be a little long. Either sex carries long, sloping shoulders, a deep but not overly broad chest, legs of strong, oval bone, with feet with elongated, arched toes. Up top, the withers are set a little high, and the topline shows a slope from withers to back, and from there on, it's level. The hindquarters are broad and well muscled, with a little tuck-up and moderate angulation. At rest, the tail is carried down to hocks, but when the dog is in action, it's carried up and shows a curl toward the tip.

This is a double coat: a very dense undercoat, with the topcoat short and straight. It's shortest on the head, ears, and lower legs, and longest on the neck, tail, and backs of the thighs. Proper coat colors run from a rich fawn to mahogany, with a black overlay. In addition, a black mask and black ears are musts. A small white spot on chest and white toe tips are okay, but white is undesirable elsewhere.

Males stand 24 to 26 inches, and bitches go 22 to 24 inches. The standard does not specify weights, but 24 inches means about 60 pounds.

Malinois disqualifications for show include hanging ears, a stump or cropped tail, and dogs deviating by more than $1\frac{1}{2}$ inches over or under specified heights.

The dog's motion is free and easy, and he can turn on a dime. Also, he has a couple of unique actions: he does not believe that the shortest distance between two points is a straight line, and (on his own) he tends to circle from A to B; with the greatest of ease, he breaks from a fast trot to single tracking (all four feet hit the same line under his center of gravity).

BELGIAN SHEEPDOG (80)

For the story behind the breed, see Belgian Malinois (above). This is the same dog, but he wears a different coat.

Another confusing fact about the BS is his name. Originally, and when he arrived in America (1907), he was B. Groenendael, named after the town in Belgium where he was first bred. Here, it was simpler to call him BS, because that's what he really is: a Belgian sheepdog. Years later, when his cousins arrived, the A.K.C. granted him exclusive rights to BS.

Breed Blueprint

Same as for the Belgian Malinois, except for the coat. Thus:

The BS wears a double coat, with the topcoat long, straight, and dense. It is shortest on the head, outer sides of ears, and lower parts of legs and is longest on the neck (collar), the back of the forearms, on the tail, and as a trimming for the hindquarters.

The proper coat color is black. It can be solid black, or mostly black with certain white limitations: white as a small patch on chest, between pads, on tips of hind toes, and as frosting (gray or white) on chin and muzzle. For show, white tips on the front toes are considered a fault, but not a disqualification.

BELGIAN TERVUREN (82)

Again, same dog, different coat. Tervuren, where the dog was developed, is also a town in Belgium. The BT was the second of the Belgian sheepdogs to arrive in America, about 1940.

Breed Blueprint

For conformation, see Belgian Malinois. As with other Belgians, the undercoat is very dense. The topcoat is long, straight, and abundant, medium-harsh to the touch. It's shortest on the head, ears, and lower parts of the legs and longest around the neck, on the back of forelegs, on the breeches and tail. Coat colors range from rich fawn to russet mahogany, all shades with a black overlay. On adult males in particular, the black is very pronounced over the shoulders, back, and ribs. The face mask is black; the ears are predominately black, and the tail tip is usually black. White is okay as a small patch on the chest and toe tips. Frost on chin or muzzle is normal.

There are many breeds of sheepdog in the world, and most are easy to identify. Insofar as instant recognition goes, however, the three

current Belgian breeds continue to confuse both dog lovers and fanciers. In general:

(1) A beast wearing a short coat is a B. Malinois. The coat is never solid black.
(2) If he wears a long, solid black coat, the beast is a B. Sheepdog.
(3) A long coat that's not solid black is worn by a B. Tervuren.

BERNESE MOUNTAIN DOG (97)

Two mysteries surround this lovable beast: where *did* he come from, and why isn't he more popular in America. The story is that the Roman legions brought the BMD to Switzerland some two thousand years ago. 'Tis said that the Romans used him as a guard dog, but this beast is much too good natured for guard duty. Whatever his intended purpose in life, the Swiss used him as a draught animal, for hauling carts to and fro. The name *Bernese* comes from the Swiss town of Bern, where he made his last stand (in 1890) and was then saved from extinction by dog fanciers.

Although this dog has been in America for about half a century, he has never caught the public's fancy and has been standing by while many less deserving breeds soared in pet popularity. A pity, since the BMD makes an excellent family pet: he's friendly, affectionate, loyal, and hardy, and he's not apt to walk off with a stranger. He now has a score of American breeders—more than ever before—and quality pups are not difficult to find. Since theirs is a common cause, these breeders, united, might be able to enhance Bernese popularity. Exhibiting more of the dogs at shows would help.

Breed Blueprint

A fine choice for the person who wants a big breed and hasn't been able to make up his mind. As purebreds in this size range go, a sound BMD pup is relatively easy to find. He's easy to train and doesn't require heavy exercise.

The BMD head features a flat skull, a well-defined stop, and a strong, deep muzzle. The medium-sized eyes are a dark hazel-brown and the short, V-shaped ears are set high and hang close. The bite is even or scissors.

The body is compact, almost short-coupled. The shoulders carry moderate slope, the chest is deep and broad, and the rib cage is well

sprung. The legs are of good bone, with round, compact feet. The topline is level, the hindquarters powerful, and angulation good. The thick, furry tail is carried up gaily, but never curled or over the back.

A Bernese coat is long, soft, silky, and a little wavy. Coat colors are jet black with russet-brown or deep tan markings. These markings appear on all four legs, as a spot just above each foreleg, as spots over eyes, and as borders on either side of white chest. If the big patch of white on the chest is star-shaped, so much the better. Not necessary, but nice, is white on the feet, tip of the tail, and as a blaze on the foreface.

Males stand 23 to 27½ inches and bitches 21 to 26 inches. An average dog of 25 inches will run 65 pounds.

For those who like the BMD but would prefer a bigger dog along the same lines, try his cousin, the Greater Swiss Mountain Dog. The latter is not yet a recognized breed in America, but he's around and winning new friends.

BOUVIER DES FLANDRES (71)

A twentieth-century miracle, the Bouvier was really developed this side of 1900 and barely survived the First World War. Dogs similar to him, but in all sizes, shapes, and coats, had been trotting around for centuries in Flanders, where they were famous as farm dogs and cattle herders. Not until 1912 did Belgian and French dog fanciers get together and decide what this beast should look like. Then, shortly after the standardized version was breeding true, the war came along. Fortunately, a few Bouviers survived, and the breed was on its way again. The beast we know today owes his very existence to the dog fancy.

This bearded cattle dog has been in America since 1930, but he had to wait a couple of decades before he started attracting attention. Here, he has been a pet and show dog, but in Europe he is frequently used for police and military duties. The beast doesn't mind in the least, of course, but few of his owners can pronounce his breed name. Properly, it trips off the tongue as "Boo-vyay duh Flawn-druh."

The dog's popularity continues to be on the slow but sure side, but it is not likely to boom until the majority of the breeders achieve consistency in temperament and conformation. While a good Bouvier makes a fine pet, finding the right pup continues to be a matter of finding the right breeder. Males make better pets; bitches are often scrappy, especially with canines of their own sex. Male or female, this is not a dog for careless or impatient people.

Breed Blueprint
The Bouvier wears cropped ears and a docked tail. Since even a good one can be stubborn, early training and a firm hand help.

The head carries a flat skull that's a little longer than the deep, wide muzzle, and the stop is scant. The nut-brown eyes are oval in shape. The high-set ears are cropped in a triangular form and carried erect, and the nose is black. The proper bite is scissors. The full, rounded neck is usually carried upright.

The compact body carries long, sloping shoulders, a deep chest, and legs of moderate bone with round, tight, arched feet. The slightly arched topline runs over a strong rib cage, and squarish, powerful hindquarters. The back is short and the angulation is slight. The high set tail is docked (about 4 inches) and carried erect.

This is a double coat. The undercoat is soft and quite fine, and the unkempt top coat must be harsh, rough and wiry. The hair is

short and almost smooth over the skull, longest over the brows (eyebrows) and muzzle (mustache and beard), very thick and rough on the legs, and short on the feet. Proper colors run from fawn to black, also salt and pepper, or gray and brindle. A white star on chest is okay.

Males stand from 23½ to 27½ inches, and 22¾ inches is the minimum for bitches. A 25-inch beast goes about 70 pounds.

BOXER (26)

Another dog man developed in Germany within the last century, he is the result of careful breeding by a small group of dog fanciers who apparently felt the need for a new breed. While they certainly succeeded, they forgot to keep records, and we'll never know the breeds behind the Boxer. There are many theories about his ancestry—and just as many about his name. *Boxer* doesn't happen to be a little town in Germany, nor is it a Germanic word. Nonetheless, he is a true native of Germany, not of China, and has never been linked to the Boxer Rebellion. Many dog lovers insist that the Boxer derives his

name from the way he uses his front paws in play, in the manner of a pugilist. However, not all Boxers do this, and many dogs of other breeds do.

The Boxer was not designed as a worker, and he owes his presence in the working group to a few breed members that performed for the German military during the First World War. Since those days, a few have been used for police, guide, and guard work.

The first imports from Germany reached the United States around 1900. The beast did not attract much attention until the thirties, when he started winning big in important American dog shows. Leading dog fanciers got behind him, the general public followed suit, and by 1950 the Boxer boom was in full swing. Today the breed is one of the most popular in the world—proof enough that he has pet virtues by the bushel.

Breed Blueprint

Alert, playful, companionable, and easy to groom. A good bet, too, as an innocent watchdog: his looks, not his antics, turn strangers away.

The Boxer's head is clean and devoid of deep wrinkles, with the skull slightly arched, the occiput modest, and the stop quite distinct. The eyes are dark brown, the high set ears are cropped long and carried erect, and the tip of the black nose is always higher than its root. The powerful muzzle is squarish and the bite is undershot. The neck is arched and free of dewlap.

The short-coupled body features long, sloping shoulders, chest to elbows, ribs carried well back, and level topline (although the favored show stance gives it a downward slope from the withers). Legs are of good bone, with compact, arched feet. The toes are always a little longer on the hind feet than up front. The strong hindquarters show good angulation and a slight tuck-up, and the docked tail is set high and carried upward.

A good Boxer coat is short, shiny, smooth, and tight to the body. Fawn or brindle are the only proper coat colors. Fawn shades run from light tan to mahogany, with the deeper colors preferred; brindle should have clearly defined black stripes on a fawn background. White is limited to ⅓ the ground color (fawn or brindle) but is off limits on the back of the torso. The dark mask on the muzzle, a feature of the breed, can carry white, as long as it does not detract from the alert expression. A genetic oddity of the breed is that even the best litters sometimes include one or more pure white pups. Although a solid white Boxer makes a perfectly good pet, the breed standard treats him as a reject. He cannot be shown, and no breeder in his right mind will employ a white beast's reproductive talents. Nonetheless, pet stores charge extremely high prices for such pups. (The foregoing also applies to the German Shepherd Dog.)

Males stand $22\frac{1}{2}$ inches to 25 inches, bitches 21 to $23\frac{1}{2}$ inches. For show, a male can't go under his minimum and a bitch can't go over her maximum. Proper weight is about 3 pounds per inch.

BRIARD (96)

A native of France, this beast has been around since the fifteenth century. So one can only wonder about his true ancestry. The belief is that he was developed for guard duties, and the fact is that over the last century he's gained more fame as an all-around farm dog, with herding as his specialty. His many talents are really appreciated by the French, and he remains their favorite among the working breeds. Very popular as a farm dog, pet, and show dog—a worthy performer with the military and the police.

The Briard has been bred—and thus known—in America for more than fifty years, but he's still a stranger to most dog lovers and has been standing by while other shaggy breeds have won popularity. Maybe his day in the sun is just around the corner. His few, devoted American breeders hope so. They have maintained excellent quality, and most (unlike the French breeders) have had the good sense to permit the beast to wear his natural ears. This has not detracted from the dog's remarkably acute sense of hearing.

The Briard's coat is also remarkable. While it lacks an undercoat and is not oily, it sheds water like a duck and dries quickly. Thus, an ideal companion for those who love to walk in the rain. The average dog lacks wanderlust, is very quiet for his size, and is light on his feet in a cluttered room. Give him an A for pet qualities.

Breed Blueprint

Often a slow learner, he requires a calm, patient owner. Fortunately, he has the memory of an elephant, so constant discipline (once he's trained) is not necessary.

His head is large and long, with skull and muzzle of equal length, forehead slightly rounded, and stop well defined. The eyes, beneath long eyebrows, are dark and large, the high set, medium-long ears hang reasonably close, and the square nose is always black. The muzzle is of medium width, never narrow or snipy, and the bite is even.

This is a short-coupled dog, although it's okay for bitches to run a trifle long. A good Briard carries sloping shoulders and a deep, broad chest. The legs are of heavy bone, and the strong, round feet carry close toes and black nails. A peculiarity of the breed: two dewclaws on each hind leg. For show, those dewclaws are musts. A level topline, steep croup, strong hindquarters with good angulation, and a well feathered natural tail are characteristic. The tail reaches the hocks and is carried low, ending in a crook.

The coat is long, slightly wavy, stiff, and strong. The hair is longest and heaviest on top of head, ears, and eyebrows. Any solid color except white is okay, with dark colors preferred and shadings permitted. White hairs intermingled with the color are okay, but white spots are not.

Males stand 23 to 27 inches, bitches 22 to 25½ inches. For show, dogs below those minimums are disqualified. On the average, 25 inches means 70 pounds of appetite.

As for those ears: the breed standard permits either natural or cropped ears. If cropped, they should stand erect. Cropped ears do not add beauty; often they splay outward resembling wings on the head.

BULLMASTIFF (78)

This beast is often confused with the Mastiff, who is one of his ancestors and has much more size. Mr. B. dates back to about 1860, and he was developed from the Mastiff and the Bulldog for both guard and (on command) attack duties. He's a native of England, and there, for a short time, he was also popular in the strange sport of dog-man fighting. The dog was muzzled, and the man was armed with a club. Almost always the Bullmastiff was an easy winner. The beast crossed the Atlantic in 1898, but the sport did not.

Always a massive animal, this dog has been refined over the years, mostly in the temperament department. By the time of his recognition here (1933), he had become a rather docile animal, and his friends predicted great popularity as a pet and show dog. This hasn't happened yet, but every year a few more people discover his pet potential and spread the word. If not exercised, he tends to pile on the fat, but a long daily walk is sufficient to keep him in shape. Because of his size and strength, this beast is a better pet for adults than small children.

Breed Blueprint

A big, playful dog who doesn't know his own strength, so it's wise to discourage such friendly action as jumping up on people. A pup should be kept in lean condition; trouble results from soft bones carrying too much weight.

The big head carries a broad skull with a flat forehead and a modest stop. Medium-sized eyes are always dark, V-shaped ears are set very high and hang close, and the big nose must be black. The short, broad muzzle is one third of the skull length, with a level or slightly undershot bite.

The powerful, compact body carries slightly sloping shoulders, a deep, wide chest, and a strong rib cage. The legs are of good bone, with medium-sized, deep feet with black nails. The topline is level over a short back, slightly arched loins, and well developed hindquarters. Angulation is moderate. The high set tail, thick at the base and tapering to the hocks, may be straight or a little curved but is never carried up and over.

The coat is short and dense. Colors are red, fawn, or brindle, with a small white spot on the chest permitted. The mask and ears are darker than the body.

Males stand 25 to 27 inches and weigh 110 to 130 pounds; bitches are 24 to 26 inches, 100 to 120 pounds. For show, maximum sizes are preferred.

COLLIE (11)

This very popular dog comes in two varieties, differing only in coat type: Rough (better known) and Smooth. The Collie's ancestry will always remain unknown, but it is known that he was developed in Scotland in the eighteenth century for the purpose of herding sheep in mountainous country. His pet possibilities were not highly regarded until Queen Victoria visited her first dog show (1860), fell in love with the Rough, and bought several. Her example was the next best thing to a royal command. British dog lovers went wild over the Collie, and puppy prices went sky-high. The best pups then sold for $2,000 and more. By 1880 wealthy Americans had imported pups, and Collie popularity in this land was on its way. Within a decade the beast was a very popular show dog. But in this country, as his popularity increased, his price decreased. In the twenties, when the Collie's

popularity sagged a bit, Calvin Coolidge and novelist Albert Payson Terhune came along to provide stimulus.

The Rough variety has always been the more popular. Whether or not breeders and dog fanciers have improved the breed is open to question. The beast has been so refined, especially in the head, that he no longer looks like the one who captured the heart of Queen Victoria. Nor is he the sturdy dog who once chased sheep over rough terrain. Still, the contemporary Collie makes a fine family pet. The problem—and it's a big one—is finding the right pup. Undependable breeders are all over the lot; the best ones can be found at dog shows.

Breed Blueprint

Both varieties are medium sized dogs, although the Rough's coat makes him look like a big one. Not the right breed for anyone who can't abide a truly refined canine head.

In proportion to overall size, the beast's head is very light and resembles a blunt, lean wedge. The flat skull shows a modest stop and is the same length as the muzzle. Skull and muzzle are on parallel planes. At its end the muzzle is rounded, more blunt than square, and the bite is scissors. Dark eyes are proper, but one or both can be wall (whitish iris) or china (blue) on a blue-merle coated dog. The ears are set high and back. At rest, they are folded and back, at alert, ¾ friendly wild boar. They named him Deutsche Dogge. However, foreigners preferred German Mastiff, and the British renamed him Great Dane, which was good enough for Americans. He's been here since about 1880, but his numbers were limited for about three decades. A matter of public trust.

The trouble was temperament: most of the early dogs couldn't differentiate between a person and a wild boar. But by 1910 devoted breeders had turned the fighter into a loyal, gentle beast, and he was on his way to becoming the favorite pet dog of people who could afford to feed him. He is now the most popular of the very big breeds. The next decade will tell whether he can retain this rank. Many authorities (none of them German) agree that American breeding is now the best in the world. This has filled our breeders with pride—including the bum ones, who think that the praise covers their careless efforts. Thus, a first-time GD puppy buyer should proceed with caution and seek the advice of veterans at the nearest kennel club.

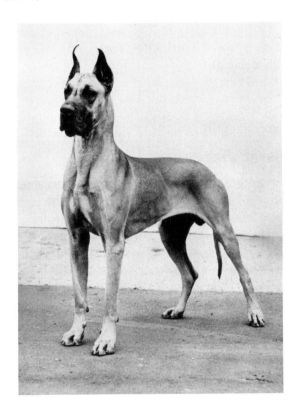

Breed Blueprint

Easy to groom but an adult needs plenty of daily exercise. A GD matures slowly until about three years of age. Often displays affection by holding one's hand between his jaws. No danger.

The long chiseled head is on the narrow side, with skull and muzzle of equal length. The stop is pronounced, the dark eyes are almond-shaped and the bite is scissors. The ears are set high and may be either natural or cropped. If natural, they drop forward close to cheek; if cropped, they are pointed and carried erect. The big nose is black. The neck is long, clean, and arched.

A GD body is short-coupled but can be a little long on a bitch. The shoulders slope, the chest is deep and broad, and the rib cage is strong. The legs carry substantial bone, and the round feet are well arched. The topline slopes from withers to tail, and balanced hindquarters, good tuck-up, and moderate angulation are proper. The tapering tail reaches the hocks and shows a little curve when it is carried up.

The GD coat is very short, dense, smooth, and glossy. It comes in four colors: fawn, blue, black, and harlequin (white with irregular black patches).

Minimum sizes are 30 inches for males, 28 inches for bitches. Breed judges prefer at least 2 inches more, both sexes. An average dog standing 32 inches will weigh about 130 pounds.

GREAT PYRENEES (53)

According to legend, this heavyweight's genealogy goes back a thousand years to the original Tibetan Mastiff, who reached Europe during the heyday of the Roman empire. He finally became the rage in Spain, where he was used as a herder and guard dog. Later, he became the pet of French nobility, and still later ('tis thought) he was the companion of Newfoundland's earliest settlers. If this is true, then the GP could be behind the Newfoundland breed. The first two beasts of the breed came to the United States (1824) from France as gifts for one J. S. Skinner. The donor was one General Lafayette. By the merest chance, Skinner did not become our first breeder, for both beasts were males.

The breed won A.K.C. recognition in 1933. Ever since, the climb to current popularity has been slow, disappointingly so for GP lovers.

In part, this can be explained by a color problem. The GP may be solid white or predominately white with markings. But since a solid white is usually considered more striking—and has proved more successful at dog shows—many breders have favored the matings of solid whites, and over several generations the true GP characteristics have begun to decline. To maintain quality, breeding back to the original rugged GP type, which was the white with markings, is a necessity. Unfortunately, some breeders won't face up to the fact. Solid white pups are easiest to sell, even though the breed standard permits the markings and dogs wearing same can be shown.

For a big breed, the GP is a fairly light eater and also can get by on minimum exercise. These days, he's pretty much a pet and show dog. For the family with room for this ambling beast, quality pups aren't difficult to find.

Breed Blueprint

The GP matures slowly, and puppy training cannot be rushed. Males tend to be more independent than females and require more con-

trol. Not for the man who doesn't believe in daily grooming.

The big, wedge shaped head runs 10 to 11 inches from occiput to nose. The skull has a rounded crown, a slight furrow, and no stop. Medium size eyes are dark brown, and the ears (set at eye level) are V-shaped with rounded tips and hang close. (In general, the head resembles a brown bear's, but with hanging ears.) Pigmentation is black and neck is short.

The short-coupled body carries sloping shoulders, a deep chest, legs of heavy bone (with a single dewclaw on each foreleg and double dewclaws on each hind leg) and close-cupped feet. The level topline runs over a flat-sided rib cage, a slightly sloping rump, and heavy hindquarters with modest angulation. The plumed tail extends beyond the hocks; in action, it is carried up and curled over the back.

The GP has a double coat—a fine, dense undercoat, and a long, heavy, harsh topcoat that's straight or slightly wavy. The proper coat colors are solid white, or mostly white with markings of badger, gray or tan.

Males stand 27 to 32 inches, weigh 100 to 125 pounds; bitches, 25 to 29 inches, and 90 to 115 pounds.

For those who haven't seen a badger, its color (on canines) is a mix of black, brown, gray and white hairs. And about those dewclaws: a show dog needs all six.

KOMONDOR (107)

No one knows how long this beast has been around, but several centuries is a pretty good bet. Hungarian herdsmen developed several breeds of sheepdogs, and this beast is the biggest of the lot and the only one designed to be more a protector of livestock than a herder. He has been in America since 1928, a full A.K.C. associate since 1938. Here he has only been used as a pet and show dog, and thirty litters a year is about average.

The Komondor, like that other, smaller Hungarian, the Puli, wears a corded coat—a coat that has never caught the American public's fancy, perhaps because it seems to promise a need for constant grooming. Overall, the topcoat looks something like a mop, with each cord (tassel) formed by a group of long, harsh, twisted hairs. Once formed, the cords are easy to brush out, and a bath does not disarrange them. Since the coat is white, a city Komondor may require a bath every week or so, depending upon how fussy his owner is. This is one of the few big beasts that adapt easily to city life, and his coat makes him comfortable in any climate. Makes a fine family pet, and American pup quality remains high.

Breed Blueprint

Very intelligent and thus fairly easy to train. Affectionate and loyal, he's one of the best of the big dogs around small fry, treating them like sheep and seldom knocking them down.

Beneath all the cords, the head looks a little short; the slightly arched skull and the muzzle are broad, with the muzzle shorter in length. The stop is moderate. The almond-shaped eyes are dark brown, and the V-shaped ears are set a little low and hang close. Pigmentation is preferably black, but a dark gray or brown nose is acceptable. The bite is preferably scissors, although a level bite is acceptable. The muscular neck is a little arched.

The body is almost short-coupled with moderately sloping shoulders and a very deep, broad chest. The legs are of strong bone, with big, tight, arched feet. For show, dewclaws—if present—must be removed. The level topline runs over a round rib cage and broad, muscular hindquarters with a slightly sloping rump, plus a little tuck-up and good angulation. The natural tail is set as a continuation of the rump, extends to the hocks, and is slightly curved toward the tip. When the dog is in action, the tail is up and at back level.

This is a double coat: the undercoat is wooly, soft, and dense; the topcoat is long, harsh, and corded, longest on the rump, loins, and tail. For show, a two-year-old dog must wear a fully corded coat. Solid white is the only proper color.

The minimum is 25½ inches for males and 23½ inches for bitches, but the average dog stands taller. At 28 inches he'll run about 100 pounds. No matter what his size, if he moves in effortless, long strides, he's at the right poundage.

KUVASZ (104)

Another of the Hungarian beasts developed as sheepdogs, the Kuvasz is a little older than the Komondor, and there's a possibility that the two breeds are related. Their histories are pretty much the same, except the Kuvasz, or at least a bigger look-alike, was used for hunting wild boar in the fifteenth century. He has been breeding true for a little over a century, and he won the A.K.C. nod in 1938, just a decade after his arrival in America.

As far as temperament and pet qualities go, the beast is similar to the Komondor. He tends to be more aloof with strangers, a virtue in these times of dognapping, and his white coat is a cinch to groom. While puppy quality has always been high in America, breed popularity has not. Maybe dog lovers feel that one big white dog (Great Pyrenees) is sufficient. There's no other apparent reason for the Kuvasz's low population. A striking dog and a fine family pet.

Breed Blueprint

A comb and brush keep the coat in shape. Nothing really wrong with this dog, and he probably wonders why he doesn't have more admirers.

His handsome head carries a broad, flat skull with a slight stop.

The medium-sized eyes are always dark and set wide apart, and medium-sized ears set high and back, hanging close. The neck is short and a little arched. A clean, squarish muzzle and scissors bite are proper.

The sturdy, compact body features sloping shoulders, a deep, broad chest, and a well-developed rib cage. The legs are of good bone, the feet compact and arched. A level topline and strong hindquarters with a little tuck-up and good angulation are characteristic. The tail carries plenty of hair and reaches below the hocks.

The medium-long coat is a little harsh to the touch. It's longest on the neck and croup, a little shorter and slightly wavy on the sides, and very short on the ears and face. The only proper coat color is pure white.

The breed standard is open-minded, merely suggesting that males stand "about 26 inches at shoulders, bitches somewhat less." At 26 inches a dog of either sex runs about 70 pounds.

MASTIFF (74)

While it is believed that this big brute's ancestors were running around in Asia and elsewhere thousands of years ago, the beast we know today had his beginnings in fifteenth-century England. He was bigger then, came in an assortment of shapes, and was used for herding, hunting, and guarding. Three centuries later the beast became popular as the heavyweight canine champion of such popular British sports as dog fights, bullbaiting, and bearbaiting. Early in the nineteenth century those sports became illegal, and breed popularity waned. But when dog shows came to the British Isles, dog fanciers rescued the breed from oblivion, and by 1880 a few breeders had a smaller version of the original Mastiff breeding true. This beast (more or less as he is today) did not fare well and was close to extinction by 1900. Credit both British and American breeders—never very many of them—with his survival.

Today, there are more Mastiffs in the United States than elsewhere in the world, but that doesn't mean that his numbers are abundant. Most are pet and/or show dogs, and some patrol large estates, the impression being that they are still excellent guard dogs.

The dog's size and looks, of course, are enough to discourage most trespassers.

The dog matures at about two years of age. If he has had plenty of human companionship, he makes a fine, docile pet. Not a good bet as a kennel dog. Since an unsound Mastiff is not a novelty, it's sound to take the advice of a veteran breeder when looking for a pup.

Breed Blueprint

The adult dog requires daily exercise and needs plently of protein in his diet. Training should be by somebody old enough to vote.

The Mastiff's big head sports a broad, slightly rounded skull that is twice the length of the muzzle and carries a moderate stop. The dark brown eyes are of medium size, and the high-set ears are V-shaped, rounded at the tips, and hang close. The broad, deep muzzle tapers a little to the nose but is decidedly blunt, and the preferred bite is scissors, but modest undershot is okay. The medium-long neck is powerful and arched.

The massive body carries slightly sloping shoulders, deep chest, and a well-rounded rib cage. The legs are of heavy bone, with big, round, arched feet. The topline is level, the hindquarters wide and powerful, with a little tuck-up. The tapering tail is set high and reaches the hocks or a bit lower.

The coat is double, with a very short, dense undercoat and short, fairly harsh topcoat. Proper coat colors are silver fawn, dark fawn brindle, and apricot. With any coat color, the muzzle, ears, and nose must be dark, preferably black.

Males stand 30 inches and up, bitches $27\frac{1}{2}$ inches and up. A 30-inch Mastiff will hit the scales at about 170 pounds. When he brushes against a dinner table, the plates bounce.

NEWFOUNDLAND (50)

See Labrador Retriever for the early days of this beast. Once upon a time the two dogs were the same, nameless breed with a big range of sizes. British dog lovers split down the middle on the matter of size. The Newf represents the choice of those who favored a big dog, and he's been breeding true since about 1860. Although developed for hauling and guard duties, he has always been better known for his pet qualities. And thanks to his ancestry, he remains an excellent swimmer.

The beast has been in America since the 1880s, but he did not attract much attention until the 1930s. Dog shows have given him a great deal of exposure, and his climb to popularity has been consistent but not spectacular. Meanwhile, the Newf has earned a deserved rep as a child's best friend—and that's quite an honor for a giant canine.

Not all breeders deserve the same reputation. Pound for pound, a sound Newf gets a high rating. The trouble is that unsound pups (weak rears, poor temperament or both) are also found in the marketplace. Over the last decade the soundest ones have been bred by the small and medium-sized kennels that have been breeding Newfs for more than a dozen years.

Breed Blueprint

Another big dog who doesn't require much exercise. Since he is not a weight watcher, his master must watch for him. A lean Newf is healthier than an obese one.

The massive head is wrinkle-free. The broad, slightly arched skull carries a prominent occiput and definite stop. The dark brown eyes are relatively small and deep set, and don't show haw. The small, rounded ears are set high and back and lie close. The deep, square muzzle is always shorter than the skull, and either scissors or level bite is proper. The long neck is strong and heavy.

The body is usually short-coupled, but bitches may be a little long. Both sexes wear sloping shoulders, a deep, broad chest, legs of heavy bone, and round, tight, arched feet with webbed toes. The topline is level over a broad back, full rib cage and very strong hind-quarters with good angulation. The croup slopes about 30 degrees, and the tail, broad at base and tapering, reaches below the hocks.

The Newf wears a double coat; the undercoat is soft and dense, and the close-lying topcoat is moderately long, straight or slightly wavy. The hair is short and fine on the head, muzzle, and ears. Preferred color is solid black, with a little bronze or white on the chest and toes okay. Also okay but less abundant are bronze and Landseer (white with black head, saddle, rump, tail).

Average size for males is 28 inches and 150 pounds, for bitches 26 inches and 120 pounds. The bigger the beast, the better his chances in the breed ring.

OLD ENGLISH SHEEPDOG (23)

An eighteenth-century British product, the famous Bobtail was de-veloped as a herder from a variety of other, unknown working breeds or nonbreeds. The shaggy beast retired as a common laborer when English dog shows came along, and ever since, he's been a popular pet and show dog in many lands. The Bobtail has changed very little in conformation from the time of his American debut (1888). Fortunately, however, his temperament has vastly improved, and he is now one of the gentle breeds.

His bobbed tail is man's idea, not nature's design. Usually, the tail is docked at the first joint when the pup is four or five days old. So Old Bobtail is really Old Docktail.

A good English Sheepdog makes a very excellent pet, but he deserves an owner who knows how to use a comb and brush and doesn't mind using them. Daily grooming is a must. A beast for the considerate dog lover. Pups come in two categories: pet shop and breeder. The pup from a breeder is always the better choice.

Breed Blueprint

This breed prefers home to roaming, peace to fighting. Easy to train but does need daily grooming and exercise. Rolls along like an amiable bear.

Under all the hair the head sports a wide, square skull and well arched forehead. The eyes are dark, the ears medium-sized, hanging close, and the nose always big and black. The muzzle is square, and the bite is level. The long neck is arched and well coated.

A Bobtail's body is short-coupled, with sloping shoulders, a deep, wide chest, rounded rib cage, legs of strong bone, and small, round, arched feet. Although hidden by the coat, the topline slopes gradually upward from the withers over the slightly arched loin. The hindquarters are round and strong, and the docked tail ranges from almost nothing to a maximum of 2 inches on an adult.

This dog wears a double coat, with the undercoat resembling a fine, waterproof pile and the abundant topcoat hard and shaggy rather than straight or curled. Proper colors are any shade of gray, grizzle, blue or blue-merled, with or without white markings. Brown and fawn are considered objectionable (by dog fanciers).

Males stand 22 inches and up, and bitches start at about 21 inches. A 23-inch beast of either sex carries about 90 pounds.

PULI (70)

The plural of Puli (Poo-lee) is Pulik (Poo-lick). Pronunciation aside, this beast is the smallest of the three Hungarian sheepdogs who are now American citizens and is the best suited to city life. In Europe he is still used to chase sheep and has been coming on strong as a police dog.

The breed has been in America since 1925 and has been a member of the A.K.C. since 1936. Although much more abundant than his cousins the Komondor and Kuvasz rolled together, the beast hasn't really caught the public fancy. But thanks to the efforts of a national breed club, more of the dogs are being seen at the shows these days, and the Puli population could be in for a dramatic increase. Of the working breeds this dog makes one of the best pets; he is very affectionate, as lively as a terrier, and usually highly suspicious of strangers.

Breed Blueprint

The Puli is high in canine intelligence and a cinch to train. A home lover, he's not a roamer and doesn't require much exercise.

Profuse, long hair hides the head. The skull is slightly domed and of moderate width, with a clearly defined stop. The big, deep set eyes are dark brown in color, and the V-shaped, high set ears hang close. The muzzle ends in a large, black nose, and the bite is either level or scissors. The clean neck is of medium length.

The body, which just misses being short-coupled, carries sloping shoulders, a deep, fairly wide chest, and a full rib cage. The legs are of strong bone, the feet round and compact. For show, dewclaws are removed. A level topline, good rib cage and muscular hindquarters with apparent tuck-up and good angulation are characteristic. When the dog is in action, the long tail curls over the back. A natural bobtail does occur, and it's okay.

The coat is double, with a dense, wooly undercoat and a long topcoat that's straight, wavy, or a little curly when groomed. Puli pups are whelped as solid whites or solid blacks. The whites remain white, and often the blacks stay the same as at birth, but they can also turn into rusty blacks or grays. All these colors are okay. Unattended, the double coat becomes corded; groomed, the coat has a shaggy appearance. Either coat is okay for show, but shaggy is more usual.

Males stand about 17 to 19 inches, and bitches go about 16 to 18 inches. For show, the maximum per sex is tops. A 17-inch dog will weigh about 35 pounds.

ROTTWEILER (66)

Although hard evidence is lacking, this sturdy beast's admirers are willing to believe that his ancestors were introduced to Central Europe by the Roman legions. Allegedly, the dogs brought up the rear, and their duty consisted of herding fresh meat-on-the-hoof for the hungry soldiers. True or false, the fact remains that a dog very similar in type but larger than today's Rottweiler (Rott-why-lurr) was famous as a boar hunter during the Middle Ages. Later this dog achieved popularity in the market town of Rottweil, Germany. There he was known as a butcher's dog and was used to drive cattle to market and guard the premises. With the coming of the rails, the need for his talents diminished and so did his numbers. By 1900 few Rotts were found in Germany.

Several dog fanciers came to the rescue and formed a breed club (1907) in Heidelberg. The purpose was to develop a working dog of great beauty. Whether the fanciers succeeded on both counts is a matter of opinion. Certainly, the Rott is an all-around worker (farm, police, army), but canine beauty is always in the eyes of the beholder.

The contemporary Rottweiler is one of the strongest breeds around and, among the strong, one of the very easiest to train. Since A.K.C. recognition in 1936, the dog has been winning acceptance as a fine family pet. Finding a quality pup doesn't require much of a search. Look for a veteran breeder (fifteen years or more).

Breed Blueprint

The Rottweiler doesn't require hard exercise during his growing period, but proper diet and early socialization are musts. Devotion and loyalty are his hallmarks. A risk is involved if the pet dog is trained as a guard dog, which is equally true of any other big breed.

The impressive head is of medium length, with a broad skull and pronounced occiput and stop. The medium-sized eyes are a dark brown, and the smallish ears are set high and wide, breaking at skull level and hanging close. Pigmentation is black. The strong muzzle is short, the bite scissors. The neck is strong, round, clean, and a little arched. The head skin is fairly tight.

His powerful body is close to short-coupled. It carries long, sloping shoulders, a deep and broad chest, and a well-sprung rib cage. The legs are of good bone, the feet round, compact, and arched, a little longer behind than up front. The topline is level, the loins strong and deep, and the hindquarters very muscular, with fair angulation and strong hocks. The high-set tail is short (docked close) and carried horizontally. Dewclaws are faults.

A proper coat is short, coarse, and flat, with a shorter undercoat on neck and thighs. The coat color is always black with markings (tan to mahogany brown) on the cheeks, muzzle, chest, and legs and over both eyes. A small spot of white on the chest or belly is okay but not desirable.

Males stand 23¾ to 27 inches, and bitches run 21¾ to 25¾ inches. A 25-inch dog will hit the scales at about 85 pounds.

Longhairs and shorthaired tans sometimes pop up in a litter. There's something wrong somewhere in that family tree, and even proper-looking pups from the litter should be avoided.

ST. BERNARD (10)

The Saint comes in two varieties: Shorthaired and Longhaired (Smooth and Rough). The breed derives its name from the Hospice du Grand St. Bernard, located high in the Swiss Alps, where the monks discovered (early in the eighteenth century) that the beasts had excellent noses and were just right for rescue work. At that time the Saint was smaller than he is today, and he always wore a smooth coat. Some authorities argue that his daddy was the old Roman Moloss, but nobody's sure.

The beast reached England in the early years of the nineteenth century. After a couple of decades the British decided that the Saint needed more size. This was acheived by crossing him with the Newfoundland. An unexpected result was a new coat type, the rough one. By 1850 the breed was on its way to popularity in England, and twenty-five years later exporting to America (both coats) had begun. Here enthusiastic fanciers formed a breed club in 1888, one of the first in this land. Still, the Saint had to wait until about 1960 before dog lovers really took him to heart. Since then Saint popularity has zoomed (the Rough more than the Smooth), and today he's fifty times more popular in America than in England.

A good Saint represents all the canine virtues one seeks in a pet dog, plus a remarkable resistance to cold. The trouble is that there are now too many undependable breeders in the act, for pups are very easy to move. Thus, many pups—more than in most of the giant breeds—carry inherited defects. Finding a bum pup is never any trouble; finding a quality pup takes a little longer. The best come from line-bred stock.

Breed Blueprint

The rough coat does require daily grooming. Under either coat a quality Saint is noted for his devotion to small fry, and he is fairly easy to train. Needs a year before he gets down to one meal per day.

The huge head features a massive skull that's wide and slightly arched, with the occiput moderately developed. The stop is very pronounced, the muzzle has more depth than length, and a proper bite can be level or scissors or even slightly undershot. Roof of mouth should be black, and overall pigmentation is also black. Brown is the right color for the medium-sized eyes and the hanging ears are set high and stand a bit off from the head at the creases. A furrow starts between eyes and runs over skull, diminishing as it reaches occiput. The skin of the forehead should carry noticeable wrinkles. The beast's neck is very strong.

The heavy body is reasonably short-coupled, with sloping shoulders, moderately deep chest, legs of strong bone, and broad, high-knuckled feet. The topline is level over a very broad back before sloping off over the rump. Hindquarters are strong and angulation is fair. The tail is broad at its base and runs both long and heavy. At rest, it's down; in action, it's up, but never absolutely erect or over the back.

A smooth coat is short, dense, and a little bushy on thighs and tail. A rough coat is of medium length, straight or a little wavy, but never curly or shaggy. Short, soft hairs are found on face and ears. Coat colors are white with any shade of red, and white with brindle patches. With either color combination, these white areas are musts: on feet, tail tip, chest, nose band, and collar (or a spot on the nape).

The minimum height for males is 27½ inches, and for bitches it's 2 inches less. At 28 inches, a Saint will go 160 to 170 pounds. While the sky is the limit for the breed, a dog standing over 34 inches is very unusual.

SAMOYED (29)

Siberia's gift to the world of dog lovers, the Samoyed (Sam-a-yed) is a member of the Spitz clan of breeds, is probably one of the oldest pure breeds still in existence and is (by far) the oldest of the sled dogs, although not the speediest. The first few Sams to reach the Western World (1890s) called England their home. They were solid whites, and their beauty won them instant fame. By 1910 the breed was getting underway in both the United States and Australia. One of the first to reach Australia (1907) was exhibited in the Sydney Zoo. An outraged Englishman saw him, purchased him, and shipped him home.

In America the breed started under the auspices of wealthy dog fanciers as the Samoyede, the name of the Siberian people. The wealthy set continued to dominate until 1947, when the final *e* was dropped. The dropping of the vowel seemed like a green light to the general public, and the Sam was on his way to vastly improved popularity. This has proved costly. While the best breeders in the world are found in America, we now have more inept breeders per capita. As a general rule of thumb for the innocent puppy buyer, the best breeders don't sell their pups to just anyone with sufficient funds. To buy a quality pup, one must have more than credit cards and prove that he's willing and able to properly care for the pup. While this may seem a bit too much, it's the best way to avoid future trouble.

Most Sams are amazingly light eaters. Interestingly, the very fine, dense undercoat sheds in patches and is a favorite nesting material for songbirds. Also, anyone who cards and spins can turn it into a fine substitute for wool.

Breed Blueprint
Thanks to a little upturn where his black lips join, the Sam often

seems to smile. Independent by nature he does require more than average patience and firmness in training.

The Sam's head features a broad, wedge shaped skull that's just a little domed. The stop is good, and the medium length muzzle tapers toward the nose, but it's never snipy. The bite is a scissors and pigmentation is black. The dark eyes are almond-shaped and set well apart, and the triangular ears are slightly rounded at tips and carried erect. The strong neck is carried up and proudly.

The body is a little long with sloping shoulders, a deep and moderately wide chest, legs of heavy bone and big, long, flattish feet. The topline runs level to arched loins and over a well sprung rib cage. The strong hindquarters have a little tuck-up and good angulation. The profusely coated tail reaches to the hocks. In action it's carried up and over the back.

An all-climate double coat. The undercoat is very fine and dense, topcoat long and harsh and standing out from the body. Males wear more ruff. Face hairs are short. Acceptable coat colors are solid white, cream and biscuit, or mostly white with biscuit.

Males stand 21 to 23½ inches and bitches 19 to 21 inches. A 21-inch Sam will go about 50 pounds.

The big disqualification for this breed is a pair of blue eyes. Once in a while, a black pup pops up in a litter, a matter of color atavism. A black Sam is a very dramatic looking beast, but not for show, and just mentioning one shocks the average breeder.

SHETLAND SHEEPDOG (13)

This lively beast takes his name from the Shetland Isles, where he was developed about a century ago. Things have always been pretty cramped on the Isles, and a small dog was needed to herd and protect the small cattle and sheep and Shetland ponies, as well as the normal-sized poultry and children. The original breeders were farmers, not dog fanciers. Thus, the Sheltie, a pint-sized Collie who may also have Border Collie in his veins. He comes in just one coat, the rough.

He was almost the Shetland Collie, but England's Kennel Club decided differently and tagged him as the Shetland Sheepdog—along with recognition—in 1909. By then, a few of the dogs had crossed the Atlantic and the first American litter had been whelped. The Sheltie has been a show dog here since 1911, but his popularity was held back by a difference of opinion among breeders as to proper size. Some wanted him under 15 inches, and others wanted him bigger, big enough to handle normal-sized sheep. The latter group crossed him back to the Collie to get the desired size.

The American Sheltie came in various sizes until 1929, when the top breeders got together to form a national breed club and agree on proper size. The decision, 13 to 16 inches at the withers, pleased everybody. Small enough for fanciers and big enough to work on normal-sized sheep.

Of all the breeds in his size range, the Sheltie makes one of the best pets. A good one is very easy to train and is an excellent choice for anyone interested in the sport of Obedience. A fine first dog for a child.

Breed Blueprint

The Sheltie makes even a bumbling trainer look like a genius. Prefers an active life, so he's not a wise choice for unimaginative or lazy owners. Loves to demonstrate his running and jumping talents.

The dog's head resembles a long, blunt wedge that tapers slightly from the ears to the black nose. The flat skull and rounded muzzle are equal in length, with a definite touch of stop. A scissors bite is proper. The almond-shaped eyes are always dark, and the small ears are set high and carried ¾ erect, with the tips breaking forward. The head sits on a strong, arched neck.

The longish body has sloping shoulders, chest to elbows, and legs of oval bone with compact, arched feet. The topline is level over well sprung ribs, and the croup carries a slope. The strong hindquarters show a little tuck-up and good angulation. The tail reaches to hocks, and it's carried up but never over the back.

A double coat. The undercoat is short, furry, and dense, and the topcoat is long, straight, and harsh and stands off from the body. Mane and frill are abundant, and the hind legs carry more feathering than up front. The hair on the face, ear tips, and feet is smooth. Plenty of tail feathering. Proper coat colors are black, blue merle, and sable (ranging from golden to mahogany), each with varying amounts of white and/or tan.

As noted, Sheltie size (both sexes) runs from 13 to 16 inches. For show, any variation under or over is a disqualification. A 15-inch Sheltie weighs about 18 pounds.

SIBERIAN HUSKY (19)

Sometimes, canine appearances are deceiving. A good Siberian Husky really doesn't look like a brute. Nonetheless, he has power to spare. The smallest and toughest of the sled-dog breeds, this beast invaded our continent through Alaska, where he was introduced in the early years of this century to add excitement to the booming sport of sled-dog racing. SH teams soon established themselves as easy winners over both the short and the long hauls. Their success did not surprise the first importers, all sporting gentlemen who had hit it rich in the gold rush and knew of the breed's amazing durability and speed. Beyond any doubt, the breed was developed in Siberia. There's still doubt about who developed him, but two nomadic tribes are credited: the Chukchi and the Tuski. The *Husky* in his name comes from one or the other or both.

The pioneer breeders in the United States were a trio of New Hampshire enthusiasts: Mrs. Nicholas Demidoff and the Milton See-

leys. They brought the breed to public attention by raising and training many of the teams used by famous explorers and by the U.S. Army
on search-and-rescue missions. Thanks to their efforts, the A.K.C.
recognized the breed in 1930, and a national breed club was formed
in 1932. Still, dog lovers held off until the 1960s before embracing the
breed. Among sled dogs, the breed is now the most popular in America.

This speaks well for his pet qualities. He has them in abundance.
A good SH makes a fine family dog. He's more agreeable than aggressive, reasonably easy to train, good with small fry, and adaptable to
any climate.

Breed Blueprint
The dog usually has a set of brown or blue eyes. However, a given
dog may sometimes have one brown and one blue. Or each eye can
carry both colors. For puppy buyers who worry about eye colors, it
should be emphasized that the breed standard approves all these combinations.

The beast's head shows a slightly rounded skull that tapers a bit toward the eyes. The skull and muzzle are the same length. The stop is distinct and the bite is scissors. The almond-shaped eyes are brown or blue, and the ears are set high and fairly close. They are of medium size and triangular in shape, with rounded tips, and are carried erect. The head sits on an arched neck of medium length.

The dog's body is reasonably compact, with sloping shoulders, a deep and strong chest, legs of good but not heavy bone, and compact, oval feet. Dewclaws, if any, are removed. The level topline extends over a well-developed, flat-sided rib cage that's broader than the loin. To the rear, hindquarters are powerful, tuck-up is slight, and angulation is good. Tail set is just below the level of the topline. The tail is well furred (fox brush) and is carried in a sickle curve over the back.

A double coat: the undercoat is soft and dense, while the topcoat is medium long, straight, and somewhat smooth-lying. All colors are okay, and even head markings are common. Nose colors harmonize with coat colors running from black (on black, gray, and tan coats) to flesh (on a solid white coat).

Males stand from 21 to 23½ inches and weigh from 45 to 60 pounds. Bitches go 20 to 22 inches and 35 to 50 pounds. For show, dogs over the maximum heights are disqualified.

STANDARD SCHNAUZER (65)

While his true ancestry is sure to remain a secret, there's some evidence in paintings that this beast goes all the way back to the fifteenth century. It is a fact that the SS was breeding true in Germany about a century ago and that he boasts one of the earliest breed standards (1880). The oldest of the three Schnauzer breeds, he's the daddy of the more popular Miniature. The odd thing about the SS is that he was designed as a cattle dog, then went on to gain fame as a ratter.

Between 1900 and 1914 several dozen of these beasts were shipped to the United States, but the breed went pretty much unnoticed until the early 1920s. By 1924 the breed had A.K.C. recognition as a terrier. Apparently, the decision was based on the Standard Schnauzer's rep as a ratter, and not much thought was given to the dog's talents on the farm and in army and police work in Germany. Eventually the A.K.C. reconsidered, and in 1945 the beast was reclassified as a working breed.

The SS is a very hardy, high-spirited dog. Although he prefers fresh air and open spaces, he adapts with ease and makes one of the best city dogs among the working breeds. His outstanding achievements in Obedience trials prove his intelligence. Breeders of quality pups are not difficult to find.

Breed Blueprint

Easy to train, but not so easy to groom. Clipping ruins coat texture, so some knowledge of stripping or plucking is required by do-it-yourselfers.

The long, rectangular head measures about half the length of back. The flat skull and strong muzzle are equal in length. The stop is slight and the bite is scissors. The medium-sized oval eyes are dark brown in color. The small, button ears are V-shaped, set high, and hang close to the head. For show, both natural and cropped ears are okay. If cropped, the ears are triangular and carried erect. The neck is clean and arched.

This is a short-coupled, heavy set dog with sloping shoulders, a deep, moderately wide chest, and a strong oval rib cage. The legs are

of heavy bone, the feet small, round, and compact. The topline is level and the hindquarters muscular, with slight tuck-up and good angulation. The docked tail (1 to 2 inches) is set high and carried erect.

This dog's soft, dense undercoat is topped by a hard topcoat of tight, harsh hairs that stand off the back. For show, the coat runs about 1½ inches and is usually trimmed close on the head, neck, chest, and belly and under the tail. The coat remains long on the muzzle to provide luxuriant eyebrows and beard. Proper coat colors are salt and pepper or solid black. The blacks can carry a little white on the chest.

Males stand from 18 to 20 inches and bitches from 17 to 19 inches. Any variation over or under is a disqualification in the breed ring. At 19 inches a dog weighs around 35 pounds.

Solid blacks are more common in Europe than America. Sometimes the black coat is soft rather than harsh and wiry, so breeders tend to shy away from it. However, a proper black is very dramatic in appearance.

WELSH CORGI, CARDIGAN (89)

Most dog lovers have difficulty differentiating the two Corgi breeds. However, for instant recognition the tail is the giveaway. If the little beast wears a long tail, he's a Cardigan; if he is tailless or wears a docked tail, he's a Pembroke. The stories behind the two breeds are somewhat similar. While they probably didn't descend from the same ancestors, both had their origins in Europe, and each, as we know him today, was really developed in the British Isles. The Cardigan was probably the first to arrive in England (eleventh century), where both Corgi breeds later gained fame as cattle dogs. While their small size made them unlikely candidates for the task, they were very tough and could herd the big animals by nipping at their heels.

The similarity between the breeds is hardly an accident. Down through the centuries they were often interbred. Indeed, for show purposes they were classified as one breed and the English Kennel Club did not grant them individual status until 1934. Since then the Pembroke has shot ahead in world popularity.

The Cardigan derives his name from Cardiganshire, where he was very popular in the past. The Welsh in his name derives from Wales, of course, and *corgi* is Welsh for "dwarf dog." Both beasts have been in America since the 1920s, but the Cardigan has always trailed in the popularity race.

There's no rational reason for the Cardie to remain in the shadows. He makes a fine pet, gets along well with children, and can get by on minimum exercise.

Breed Blueprint

The Cardie is exceptionally low-slung and surprisingly speedy. At full speed, with his tail streaming behind him, he looks like the longest beast on earth. He's also very long on affection.

His head sports a moderately wide, flat skull that runs a couple of inches longer than the 3-inch muzzle. The stop is moderate, and that shorter muzzle tapers a bit to a moderately blunt end, where the nose is always black. While scissors bite is preferred, an even one is okay. The medium to large wide-set eyes are colored dark, but blue eyes, or one dark and one blue, are acceptable for merles. The over-sized ears are set wide and back, are carried erect, and slope slightly forward.

The very long body carries sloping shoulders and a deep, broad chest. The short, strong forelegs are slightly bowed around the chest, the elbows are close, and there's a little crook below the carpus (wrist). Feet are round and compact. For show, front dewclaws, if they are present, may be removed and hind ones should be removed.

Topline is level except for a slight slope of the spine above the tail. The rib cage is well sprung, and the hindquarters are very strong, with modest tuck-up and good angulation. The long, low-set tail resembles a fox brush. In action, it streams out and up, but never curls over the back.

The coat is medium length, a little harsh, and quite weather resistant. There's a big variety of coat colors: red, sable, red brindle, black brindle, black, tricolor, blue merle. Any coat usually carries abundant white on chest, neck, feet, face, or tip of tail. A solid white coat is highly improper and so is an extremely long one.

Height (both sexes) runs around 12 inches. Average dogs weigh in at 24 to 28 pounds.

WELSH CORGI, PEMBROKE (46)

This Corgi takes his name from Pembrokeshire, just a few hills away from Cardiganshire in South Wales. For other interesting lore, see Cardigan Welsh Corgi above.

In terms of Corgi popularity the Pembroke is the easy winner. Why this is the case is anybody's guess, for the two breeds are very similar in temperament, intelligence, and talents. The only differences—and they don't amount to much—are in looks.

Breed Blueprint

While both breeds have long bodies, the Pembroke's is a little shorter and (thanks to his docked tail) looks much shorter. Compared to the Cardigan, here are the other major (minor?) differences:

Head: more tapering to muzzle; oval eyes in various shades of brown to harmonize with coat; and erect, almost pointed ears.

Body: forelegs of medium bone, with forearms turned slightly inward; feet oval, with two center toes a little longer than others; docked tail, 1 to 2 inches, never carried erect; any dewclaws, front or rear, are removed.

Coat: double, with short, dense undercoat and topcoat of medium length with flat-lying, straight hairs, usually longer on neck, chest, and shoulders. Self (base) colors of red, sable, fawn, and black and tan are proper, each with or without white markings. If present, white is okay on legs, chest, neck, muzzle, and underparts, and as a narrow blaze on head.

Size: height (both sexes) runs from 10 to 12 inches at withers, and ideal weights are 27 pounds for males and 25 pounds for bitches. The length of back (withers to tail base) is about 40 percent greater than height. For show, 30 pounds for males and 28 pounds for bitches are the maximums. And an excessively shy dog gets bounced from the breed ring.

Terrier Group

Terrier is derived from *terra,* Latin for earth. Almost all the terrier breeds were developed in the British Isles and Ireland for the original purpose of going to earth after other animals, such as the fox, badger, and assorted vermin. Sometimes, as in fox hunting, the terrier was used to complement the hound. The latter chased the fox into his lair, and then the terrier went in to finish the job. Today, most terriers are content to serve as pets. Some, of course, also serve as show dogs or compete in Obedience trials, and a very few earn their keep as ratters on farms.

It's fair to say that terriers are activists, and the smaller the breed, the greater the activity. Also, a few of the breeds require extensive coat care. Although pups of all the breeds are cute to the point of being irresistible, the average terrier does not make an ideal pet for sedate or sedentary dog lovers. Herewith, the terrier breeds recognized by the A.K.C.:

AIREDALE TERRIER (37)

The tallest and perhaps the most talented of the terrier breeds, the Airedale takes his name from a district in Yorkshire, where he was once regarded as the king of all canines. The noble beast started as a blend of several terriers. Nobody can be sure, but one of the ancestral breeds is believed to have been the long extinct Black and Tan. By 1850 this early version of today's Airedale was still on the scene, but under a variety of other names. Unfortunately, he lacked the size to tackle big animals and didn't like to get his feet wet. Both problems were solved by crossing him with the Otter Hound, and within a couple of decades the mix was known only as the Airedale. By 1880 several of the beasts were romping around in America.

One of the early greats of the breed was the English champion, Master Briar. A wealthy Philadelphian tried to buy him, failed, and was happy to settle for one of his promising sons, Clonmel Monarch. At the time (1903) Philadelphia and its environs were the hotbed of America's breed enthusiasts. Monarch fulfilled his promise, first as a great show dog and then as a mighty sire. He was also the best possible advertisement for his own breed. For the next thirty years, until the Boxer started to win away his admirers, the Airedale was one of America's most beloved breeds. The beast proved himself as a family pet, lady's guardian, farm dog, show dog, hunter of everything from rabbit to bear and mountain lion, and army and police dog.

Over the past forty years American breeders have managed to refine the beast, but he's still one of the best all-around dogs on the scene. Top breeders are not difficult to find.

Breed Blueprint

A hardy, companionable beast with an almost carefree coat. A brushing every few days and a weekly trimming of shaggy hairs suffices. A good terrier bet for small fry.

The Airedale carries a balanced head, with a long, flat skull that's equal in length to the muzzle. The stop is slight, and either level or scissors bite is okay. The nose is always black. The dark eyes are on the small side and the ears are V-shaped, set high, and fold for-

ward to the sides of head. The clean neck is of moderate length and widens toward the shoulders.

This is a smart, close-coupled dog with sloping shoulders, chest to elbows, legs of strong bone, and small, round, compact feet. Up top, the short back is level over a good rib cage, wide loins, and sturdy hindquarters with good tuck-up and fair angulation. The docked tail (about half its natural length) is set high and carried gaily, but never curled over the back.

This may not look like a double coat, but it is. The undercoat is very short and soft, and the topcoat is dense, hard and wiry, and close lying. The coat is tan on the head, ears, legs (up to elbows and thighs), chest, and belly, and sometimes shoulders. The sides and upper parts of the body are black or dark grizzle. A small white blaze on the chest is okay.

Males stand about 23 inches and bitches an inch or so less. In hard condition a 23-inch dog weighs about 50 pounds.

AMERICAN STAFFORDSHIRE TERRIER (73)

In the early years of the nineteenth century, when bullbaiting and dog fighting were popular British sports, the early version of the contemporary Bulldog was everybody's favorite. In those days, the Bulldog's head was quite similar to that now worn by this terrier. Well, there were dreamers around, and they thought they could produce a better fighting dog. To accomplish this end, they crossed him with one or more terriers and came up with a breed that eventually became known as the Staffordshire Bull Terrier. Several of these dogs reached America right after the Civil War. Here lovers of the dog fight sport decided they needed a breed with more size. What they came up with was called the Pit Bull Terrier, then the American Bull Terrier.

Nobody really thought much about the breed's potential as a pet until long after dog fights were outlawed in America. It was not until 1910 that breeders started aiming for a gentle Yankee, rather than one who was eager for battle.

To bring you up to date on dog fighting: it still flourishes in America as an underground sport. Some very nice people support it, and some of them claim it's a great spectator sport for the entire family, "very educational for children." Most dog fanciers and law-enforcement agencies tend to ignore the American subculture of dog fighting, apparently thinking it will just go away. Unlikely. Some of today's top fighters have the blood of the old Yankee Terrier in their veins.

In 1935 A.K.C. recognition meant a change of name to *Staffordshire Terrier,* but this was too close to *Staffordshire Bull Terrier.* To eliminate confusion and really set the breeds apart, the A.K.C. finally changed this beast's name to American Staffordshire Terrier in 1972.

Breeders under the A.K.C. flag have completely eliminated the original fighting instincts of the AST. The dog is now as gentle as any other terrier and completely trustworthy. For his size, he is an extremely hardy, strong, loyal beast, and he makes a fine family pet. Not likely to walk off with a stranger.

Breed Blueprint
The AST requires minimum grooming, but likes plenty of exercise and usually requires a firm hand. Quiet in the house but makes plenty of noise as a kennel dog.

His head is medium long and deep, with a broad skull, pronounced cheek muscles, and a distinct stop. The medium long muzzle is rounded on the upper side, and the jaws carry a firm, scissors bite. The dark, round eyes are set deep and wide. The high-set ears can be cropped, but natural ears are preferred. If cropped, they are very short and carried erect; if natural, they are short and carried pricked or half rose, but never fully dropped. The nose is always black, and the head sits on a clean, heavy, slightly arched neck.

This is a stocky body, with sloping shoulders, a deep and broad chest, legs wide apart and of strong, round bone, with arched, compact feet of moderate size. The topline slopes slightly from withers to rump over a strong rib cage and sturdy quarters with a little tuck-up and fair angulation. The low-set tail tapers to a point and looks a little short. It's never curled and never carried over the back.

The coat is very short, stiff to the touch, and glossy. Any color or color combination is okay, but for show solid white, or more than 80 percent white, black and tan, or liver are not favored.

Males stand 18 to 19 inches and bitches 17 to 18 inches. Figure 2 pounds per inch and then add 10 pounds.

AUSTRALIAN TERRIER (57)

Developed within the last century by economy-minded Australian dog fanciers, this little fellow represents a mix of such other small terrier breeds as the Cairn, Norwich, Scottish, Dandie Dinmont, and Yorkshire. The engaging beast has become very popular down under, where he is used on rabbit, rat, and snake and as a protector and herder of sheep. The breed found its way to England in the late 1920s and then to America in the early 1940s. Here the Aussie had to await A.K.C. recognition (1960) before winning public attention.

As terriers go, the Aussie isn't much of a noisemaker. That virtue and his size make him an excellent choice for the city apartment. Away from the pet-shop world, quality remains high and good pups are not difficult to find. A hardy, affectionate, companionable little dog who can hold his own with the small fry.

Breed Blueprint

His harsh coat is weather resistant, needs very little grooming, and sheds only slightly and gradually. Easy to train and not quarrelsome.

His long head carries skull and muzzle of equal length; the skull is flat, full between eyes, and with moderate stop. The long jaws carry either a scissors or level bite, and the nose is black. Eyes are small, dark and not prominent. The small, pricked ears are pointed or slightly rounded at the tips. The neck is long and tapering and carries a ruff.

His sturdy body is on the long side, with sloping shoulders, a deep and moderately wide chest, legs of medium bone with elbows close, and small catlike feet. Topline is level over a well sprung rib cage and strong hindquarters, with moderate angulation and hocks well let down. The docked tail ($\frac{2}{5}$ of natural) is set high and carried erect.

A double coat: undercoat short and soft, and a topcoat that's straight and harsh and about $2\frac{1}{2}$ inches in length. On the skull, a topknot of finer textured hairs is proper. Coat colors are blue-black or silver-black, each with rich tan markings on head and legs. Sandy and clear red coats are also acceptable.

A height of about 10 inches at the withers is about right, either sex. The average dog runs 12 to 14 pounds.

BEDLINGTON TERRIER (79)

This dog looks more lamblike than any other canine on earth. But he bears very little resemblance to his forefathers, who were around and breeding true by the dawn of the nineteenth century. Most were found in the shire of Bedlington (Northumberland County) where they were used on vermin, hare, and badger. They raced around on shorter legs attached to longer bodies, and their heads were more typical of terriers. And they did not wear roach backs, a physical characteristic that would have denied them their fame as combatants, when dog fights were the rage.

The new Bedlington, the dog we know today, is the result of another rage known as the dog show. It is very easy to believe—and most authorities do—that the old type was crossed with the Whippet; hence, the roach back. True or false, the contemporary Bedlington was breeding true by 1873, and by that time the dog had lost his instinct for fighting. Today he's strictly a pet and show dog.

Bedlingtons have been in America since about 1890. Here the dog's progress was stymied by early breeders who decided to bless the beast with a longer, narrower head. This refinement has worked with the Collie, but it wasn't right for the Bedlington. Fortunately, a new generation of breeders arrived on the scene, revived the head, and started the dog on the long road to A.K.C. recognition (1937). The breed's first big boost came in 1948, when Champion Night Rocket, owned by the William Rockefellers, won all the hardware at Westminster.

One of the delights of owning a Bedlington is in watching him move. At a trot his steps are short and springy, as if the ground is too hot for him. At a gallop his back seems to fold and unfold as his hindlegs reach out in front of his forelegs. In addition he's surprisingly mild, gentle, and graceful for a terrier, although as hardy as any. And he's always a conversation piece, of course. The land is full of good pups.

Breed Blueprint

If not trimmed and brushed, the coat becomes tangled and unkempt. This can be a problem, but not for anyone who is handy with scissors.

The Bedlington's head is narrow but deep and rounded, and there's no stop. The muzzle is longer than the skull, and the bite is level or scissors. The small, almond shaped eyes are deep set, with color depending on coat color. The low-set ears are triangular, with rounded tips extending to corners of the mouth. The neck is long, tapering, and clean.

His body is more compact than it looks. It features sloping shoulders, a deep chest, hind legs that are a little longer than forelegs, and those forelegs are wider apart at the chest than at the feet. The feet are a little long and compact. Any dewclaws should be removed. Up top, the roach back resembles an arch over a flat rib cage. Hindquarters are well muscled, with strong tuck-up and good angulation. The low-set tail carries a little curve, tapers to a point, and extends to the hocks. It's carried straight out, never over the back.

This is a double coat, the undercoat being very soft and fine, and the topcoat hard, a little curly, and standing out from the body. For show, about 1 inch is right. Proper coat colors are blue, sandy, liver, blue and tan, sandy and tan, and liver and tan. With bicolors, tan is found over the eyes, on the legs and chest, under the tail and inside the hindquarters. An adult wears a topknot that's a lighter shade than the coat color.

Males stand 16 to 17¼ inches, with 16 ½ inches the ideal. Bitches stand 15 to 16½ inches; 15½ inches is the ideal. Weights range from 17 to 23 pounds.

For show, eye and nose colors are important. Eyes: black (blue coat), amber (blue and tan), light hazel (sandy, sandy and tan), and dark hazel (liver, liver and tan). Nose: black (blue, blue and tan) and brown (all other coats). A breed judge has a lot to remember.

BORDER TERRIER (110)

The dog takes his name from the border country of Great Britain. There, some 150 years ago, the hill fox loved to dine on lamb and was able to outsmart and outrun both the shepherds and their big sheep-dogs. A specialist was needed: a dog big enough to give chase, and small enough to go to earth. From a mix of unknown terriers and perhaps the Dandie Dinmont, the wise men put together the early version of the BT, a beast who did the job on fox, badger, and otter. The dog became very popular in his home area, but he came in various sizes and types. Then the breed caught the eye of dog fanciers, and in 1920 they finally reached agreement on what the BT should look like and defined him with a breed standard.

The first BTs reached America in 1930. They were the least known of the many terriers, of course, and time has not favored them. There still aren't many breeders, and 60 litters a year is about average despite plenty of show exposure and adequate publicity. This sad state of affairs is likely to continue unless a few famous Americans start taking an interest.

The dog really deserves popularity. He's a convenient size for apartment and home, and his virtues include clean habits, a lack of inherited defects, adaptability, gentleness with children, and loyalty. He may look like the creation of a Disney artist, but he's a true purebred all the way.

Breed Blueprint

An average noise maker, but not quarrelsome, and comb and brush keep the harsh coat in condition. Fairly easy to train, and even pups seem eager to please.

An otter head, meaning a flat, broad skull, with wide-set eyes and ears. The muzzle is short and dark, the stop is slight, and the bite is a scissors. The eyes are dark hazel and moderate in size, and the small, V-shaped ears are set on the sides of the head and drop forward close to the cheeks. The nose is black, and the neck is clean, strong, and of medium length.

The BT is a fairly short-coupled dog, with sloping shoulders, a deep, fairly narrow chest, and legs of medium bone with small, compact feet. The topline is level over a rib cage that's carried well back, strong loins, and muscular hindquarters that show good angulation.

The natural tail is set medium high. It's on the short side, tapers, and is carried gaily, but not over the back.

The double coat has the usual short, dense undercoat and a harsh, very wiry, and close-lying topcoat. Proper coat colors are red, grizzle and tan, blue and tan, or wheaten. A touch of white is okay on the chest but not elsewhere.

Males weigh 13 to 15½ pounds, bitches 11½ to 14 pounds. The breed standard does not specify heights, but males go up to 15 inches and bitches up to 13 inches. About an inch per pound is right.

BULL TERRIER (74)

Once known as the gladiator of canines, this beast was specifically designed for the sport of dog fighting, and he goes back to crosses of the early Bulldog with other, unknown terriers in the first decade of the nineteenth century. The Bull Terrier was extremely popular as a fighter, but the need for his services diminished after 1835, the year England outlawed high society's favorite spectator sport. Illegal dog fights continued, of course, but most of the breeders who stayed with the Bull Terrier concentrated on turning him into a friendly beast. They succeeded, and along the way they also managed to come up with a new coat color, solid white, as well as to reduce ear size.

Today there are two varieties of the breed: White and Colored, the only difference being in the coat color. Since each coat is very short, this truth is apparent to the naked eye. The beast has been in America for almost a century and is now much more popular here than in his native land. He has always been more popular here than his two cousins, the American Staffordshire Terrier and the Staffordshire Bull Terrier.

A properly bred dog of this breed is not hard to find and makes an excellent family pet in the city or elsewhere, but he's not ideal for lazy people. The beast likes action, thrives on play, and doesn't mind being pushed around by children. Aside from those he knows and loves (people and dogs), he's not much of a mixer.

Breed Blueprint

Pups usually require a firm hand. An adult demands plenty of exercise, but this is offset by his ridiculously easy grooming. Just a hard brush every few days.

Viewed from the front, the dog's long head resembles a giant egg; in profile, it shows a slight curve from the black nose to the top of the skull. The forehead is flat and prominent with no sign of a stop. The small triangular eyes are set deep and high and are dark in color. Either a level or a scissors bite is okay, and the small thin ears are set close and back and carried up. The neck is long, arched, and clean.

The body carries muscular, sloping shoulders, a deep and broad chest, and feet that are round, compact, and arched. Up top, the back is short and shows a little arch over the loins. The strong rib cage is carried back, hindquarters are strong with good tuck-up and angulation, and the rather short, tapering tail is set low and carried straight out.

The coat is very short, flat, and harsh to the touch. Coat colors: *White* means a solid white, or a white dog with markings confined to his head; *Colored* means any color (brindle preferred) with white markings, but never predominately white.

The breed standard does not specify heights and weights, but the average Bull Terrier stands about 20 inches and weighs around 50 pounds. If he stands 14 inches or under, he's a Miniature Bull Terrier (see page 252) and can't weigh more than 20 pounds. In any size, a blue-eyed Bull Terrier is disqualified for show.

CAIRN TERRIER (36)

The smallest of the working terriers, the Cairn goes back several centuries to a time when nobody bothered to keep records. He was developed on the Isle of Skye and in the Highlands of Scotland and his duty was to chase and demolish every form of vermin, plus the red fox. He takes his name from the Scottish word *cairn,* meaning "heap of rocks and stones," and owes his tremendous popularity to the dog show craze. And this little beast is the daddy of the West Highland White Terrier.

America has been host to a scattering of these dogs since around 1900, although the first litter here was not whelped until 1914; today, four thousand litters a year is about average. As terriers go (active,

affectionate, and talky), a quality Cairn makes a fine family pet and a good bet for city life. Although very few have ever been used for hunting in America, a good one retains a keen nose and the old, digging instincts. Thus, if moles are present, this little dog can change a respectable lawn into a well furrowed area in no time at all. For his contribution to social status, see Norwich Terrier.

Breed Blueprint

Not for the arm-chair dog lover. Likes action and plenty of attention. One of the best of the small breeds with children.

The Cairn has a foxy head, although his coat hides the fact; proportionately, it's the shortest and broadest head among the terriers. The stop is distinct, the muzzle is short, and the bite can be either level or scissors. The medium-sized eyes are set well apart and colored either hazel or dark hazel, in harmony with coat color. The small, pointed ears are set wide (on the sides of the head) and carried erect. The nose should be black.

A proper Cairn body is on the long side, running 4 to 5 inches more in length (front of chest to back of hindquarters) than height, the ratio being about 15:10. The dog carries sloping shoulders, a deep chest, and short legs of medium bone with compact, thick feet. Forefeet are always biggest and sometimes turn out a little. Up top, the back is level over a full rib cage and strong hindquarters, with fair tuck-up and angulation. The short natural tail is set at back level and carried gaily.

A double coat, with the undercoat close and furry and the top-coat profuse, short, and harsh. Colors range from light sandy through all shades of gray and red brindle. Dark ears, muzzle, and tail tip are desired, and white is the only color fault.

For show, these are the ideal sizes: males stand 10 inches, weigh 14 pounds; bitches stand 9½ inches, weigh 13 pounds. *Ideal* means those specifications for an adult of two years who is not longer than 15 inches.

Caution for ear-conscious puppy buyers: in this breed, a pup's ears don't stand erect until he's about five months of age. If erect earlier, they may flop while he's losing his puppy teeth.

DANDIE DINMONT TERRIER (99)

Another working terrier, this small, elongated beast was fashioned in Scotland for the purpose of going to ground after vermin, fox, and badger. His ancestry remains obscure, but he was around and doing his duty by about 1760 and was known by a variety of names. None of those names stuck, however, and the present one is really the result of a literary event and one man's sense of humor. In 1814 Sir Walter Scott published his novel *Guy Mannering*. In it was one Dandie Dinmont, an oddball farmer who owned a pack of the little,

longish terriers. Although Scott never confessed to it, his intimates figured that the Dinmont character was based on his old friend James Davidson, a leading terrier breeder. Thus, Davidson started calling his favorite breed Dandie Dinmont's terrier. By the time of his death, in 1820, the public had dropped the possessive. Thanks to Scott, Davidson, and (later) Louis Phillipe, the dog went on to achieve modest popularity as a pet in England and France.

Although he's been refined a bit, the Dandie looks much the same as he did a couple of centuries ago. He's still worked abroad, mostly on fox. In America, a land he's called home since about 1890, he's mostly a pet or show dog, and he's never been one of the very popular terriers. In an average year about 260 litters are whelped. The Dandie is really a one-family dog. He has a surprisingly deep bark, and he doesn't resent living in the city. Not the best breed for kennel life.

Breed Blueprint

This terrier has a mind of his own, so training should be a little firm. The adult coat requires regular grooming (plucking). Not the quietest terrier, but one of the most devoted.

The big head carries a broad skull, a well domed forehead, and a distinct stop. The big, round eyes are set wide and low and are rich hazel in color. The pendulous ears are set back and low, hang close, and taper almost to a point. The nose and inside of the mouth are black or dark-colored. The muzzle is a couple of inches shorter than skull, and the bite is scissors. The head sits on a very muscular, strong neck.

The body is unusually long for a terrier, about twice the height at withers. The shoulders are fairly straight and set low, and the chest is deep. The forelegs are shorter than the hind legs, and the compact forefeet are a little bigger (for cushion) than the hind feet. The topline dips from the low withers and gradually arches over the loins, then slopes to the root of the tail. The hindquarters are strong, and tuck-up and angulation are good. The natural tail is short (8 to 10 inches), feathered most of the way, and tapered to a point. It's carried gaily, with a little curve.

The Dandie's 2-inch coat is a mixture of hard and soft hairs, the mix being crisp to the touch, and the head wears a soft, silky topknot. Colors are pepper or mustard, with lighter shades on the underparts of the body. A little white on the chest is okay.

Dandies (both sexes) stand 8 to 11 inches and weigh 18 to 24 pounds. On this breed, length is measured from the withers to the root of tail. Thus, dogs run from 16 to 22 inches in length—never more but sometimes 1 or 2 inches less.

FOX TERRIER (39)

Breed lovers claim that the FT can be found wherever English is spoken, and they may be voicing the truth; a surprising number of breed clubs are active in countries all over the world, and most are devoted to the interests of both varieties: Wire and Smooth. The latter is the senior variety by about a score of years, but the former is now senior in American popularity.

A British invention (circa 1780), the Smooth's ancestors remain unknown, but he was designed to keep the rat population under control and soon graduated to fox. There's still a mild debate about the Wire, and it amounts to whether or not he's the true son of the Smooth. Since the advent of dog shows, differences of opinion have

become unimportant; beneath their coats, both varieties are one and the same dog.

And both have been well known in America for more than a century and are the proud claimants to one of the earliest national breed clubs (1885). Until the 1930s, interbreeding of the two varieties was common all over the world, but that practice is now obsolete. Coat popularity depends pretty much on climate, and the Wire is king in all but the hot countries of the world.

In the United States the Wire reigns by about a nine to one ratio, a fact that has a hidden meaning for those interested in the breed as a family pet. Since there is far less demand for Smooths, most breeders of the variety produce animals of ideal temperament. Overall, Smooth quality is now superior, and the average pup of the variety is the better buy for pet purposes. This does not mean that Wires are always poor risks, but it certainly does mean that breeders of questionable Wires are easy to find and that *their* pups are always poor risks. Before falling in love with a Wire puppy, a rational buyer should check on his breeder. This is not just one man's opinion. Rather, it is the judgment of at least ten top American authorities. Let the chips fall where they may.

Breed Blueprint

A gay, active, strong dog who pleases if his owner is not a bundle of nerves. Trickier to groom the Wire, of course. The word *wise* is often used to describe the breed; that's dog talk, and it doesn't of course mean that he has the brain power of a normal child.

The head carries a flat skull and muzzle of equal length, with stop apparent but never severe. The muzzle tapers gradually to a black nose, and the bite is even or a slight scissors. The eyes are small, dark, and moderately deep-set, and the non-foxy ears are V-shaped, small, and set well back; they fold above skull level and drop forward, close to cheeks. The clean, medium long neck widens toward the shoulders.

A good FT body looks very stylish and is close to short-coupled. Up front the shoulders slope, and the chest is deep but not broad. The legs are of strong bone, with rather small, round, compact feet and toes showing a little arch. The forelegs are short and straight in pasterns and show just a touch of ankles. The back is short over a good rib cage, topline level, and the hindquarters strong for a dog of this size. Tuck-up is fair, angulation good, and hind legs carry long second thighs. The high-set tail is docked to about three-quarters its natural length.

The Smooth variety wears a short, hard, dense coat that lies flat and covers the belly. The Wire coat (also short) is hard and wiry, never wooly or silky to the touch. The predominant color (both varieties) is always white, with black or tan markings okay. For show, such markings should not be red, brindle, or liver.

An ideal male stands 15½ inches and weighs 18 pounds, and his ideal mate a little shorter and lighter. For show, small variations are allowed as long as the beast is in hard condition.

IRISH TERRIER (88)

Historians are divided on this breed's native land, but the Irish were the first to push the dog from obscurity to renown—hence, his name. All this took place a century ago, when the breed came in an assortment of shapes, sizes, and colors. Thanks to the advent of dog shows and to wise breeders, the assortment of types became one and the beast was breeding true by about 1880. Today he's pretty much the same dog as he was then, except that his ears are no longer cropped. Long ago the Kennel Club of England outlawed the cropping of ears (any breed). In America a few states have made the practice illegal (for humane reasons) but have found the law very difficult to enforce. One day, both the A.K.C. and the C.K.C. must face the issue: is fashion really more important than kindness to animals?

In recent years fewer than a hundred IT litters per year have been produced by breeders in the United States and Canada. That's the combined total, and it reflects both fine puppy quality and a mysterious lack of interest on the part of terrier lovers. Those who admire the Airedale but think he's a little too big around the house will find this breed just as talented and worthy. The IT accepts both adults and children and can be trained to perform most of the duties of the sporting and working breeds. He's handsome all the way, as long as his owner learns a little about proper grooming.

Breed Blueprint

Along with every other canine that wears a wire coat, this beast's coat turns shaggy without attention. It's always wise to get simple grooming instructions from the breeder. If you want a shaggy dog, choose a shaggy breed.

The Irish Terrier's long head carries skull and muzzle of equal length, the former flat and a little narrow. The stop is barely noticeable, but it's there. The small, V-shaped ears are set high and back, fold just above skull line, and then drop forward toward eyes, which are always small and dark. A black nose is a must. The jaws are very strong, and the bite is scissors. The lower jaw carries a touch of beard, the brow is wrinkle free, and the clean neck has medium length, with some arch and width toward the shoulders.

This is a streamlined terrier. The body is moderately long, with long, sloping shoulders, a deep but not wide chest, and a full rib cage. The longish legs are of strong, round bone, and the thickly padded feet are small and round, with arched toes and dark toenails. The topline is level, with a little arch over the loins, hindquarters are strong, with fair angulation. Low hocks to the rear and straight pasterns up front are characteristic. The high-set tail is docked to ¾ its natural length and is carried up but not over the back.

The IT's undercoat is fine and soft; the topcoat is dense and wiry and lies close to the body. It's harsh on the back, quarters and legs, less so on the sides. Coat colors are bright red, golden red, red wheaten, and wheaten. A little patch of white is okay on the chest, but not elsewhere.

A proper male stands about 18 inches and weighs close to 27 pounds, with a bitch a little shorter and not more than 25 pounds. A streamlined terrier.

KERRY BLUE TERRIER (67)

A true native of Ireland, he takes his name from County Kerry, where he was developed as an all-around utility dog. By the 1820s, he was serving as a guard, herder, and hunter. While his own ancestry remains a mystery, he just might be the daddy of the Irish and Soft-Coated Wheaten Terriers. The early dog shows (abroad) brought the Kerry to public attention and his popularity zoomed in England and several countries on the Continent. His arrival in America remains a mystery, but he was around for at least three decades before gaining sufficient support to win A.K.C. recognition in 1924.

Here, the Kerry is seldom used for anything other than pet and show duties, and overall American pup quality is the best in the world. Since he wears one of the few nonshedding coats in the dog world, the beast is beloved by housewives, especially those whose husbands know how to groom. The coat virtue is somewhat dampened

by the fact that it takes an excessive amount of grooming time to keep it in shape. That is the beast's only liability.

Every pup is whelped as a solid black. The transition to blue begins at about 6 months and is completed by 18 months. The blue color is fairly uniform, except for darker shadings on muzzle, head, ears, tail, and feet, and the "darker" can be black.

In an average year, American breeders turn out better than a thousand litters. Still, the Kerry's chances of a big jump in popularity depend pretty much on the arrival of more dog lovers who are willing to groom.

Breed Blueprint

The average Kerry holds on to youth for a long time and does not accept adulthood until he's several years old. Not difficult to train, but these frisky pups need a firmer hand than most other terriers. For patient people.

The Kerry head looks a little long. The flat skull and muzzle are of equal length, and the stop (usually hidden by the coat) is very slight. The strong, deep jaws carry either a level or scissors bite, and the black nose features big, wide nostrils. For this beast's size, both ears and eyes are rather small: the V-shaped ears crease just above the skull line and drop forward close to the cheeks with tips about level with the dark eyes. The clean, moderately long neck widens toward the shoulders.

This beast is fairly short-coupled, with long, sloping shoulders, a deep but not broad chest, legs of substantial bone, and round, compact feet with arched toes and black nails. Topline is level, the back short, loins strong, and rib cage deep and well sprung. Tuck-up is slight and angulation is good. The high-set tail does look a bit short. It's carried erect and gaily.

The blue coat is soft, wavy, and dense, and *blue* really means any shade from deep slate to light blue-gray, but never as blue as a clear sky in June. For show, breed judges don't place importance on coat color until a dog is 18 months old.

The breed's males stand 18 to 19½ inches and weigh up to 40 pounds; bitches stand 17½ to 19 inches and weigh up to 37 pounds. In the breed ring, dewclaws on hind legs are disqualifications, and so is a solid black coat.

LAKELAND TERRIER (100)

For more than a century, this British breed was known under other names. He has only been the Lakeland in England since 1924 and has owned the same name here since joining the A.K.C. in 1936. The name honors Cumberland County, a region of mountains and lakes, where the beast was developed to dig after and destroy the fox who, in turn, were destroying too many lambs. The Lakeland true family tree will never be known, but those who worry about such things believe that two or more of these terriers are behind him: Bedlington, Border, Dandie Dinmont, and Fox.

This beast has many fine qualities going for him as a pet dog, but luck doesn't seem to be on his side. Breed popularity has been declining rapidly in recent years, despite a big winning record at major American dog shows. Unfortunately for our breeders, most of

those big winners have been imports, all top dogs who had proved their worth abroad before being shipped here. It would appear that those dogs have not been used wisely at stud in America.

Despite the slip in popularity, pet quality remains pretty high. The beast is just right for the small family, since he's gay and friendly, doesn't mind small fry, is fairly easy to train, and a little trimming every few days keeps his wiry topcoat looking fine. For show, coat care is another matter, and an annual stripping is usual. The breed is often a pet-shop best seller, but that's not where to find the good ones.

Breed Blueprint

He's less noisy than many other terriers, and his bark is often surprisingly deep. Does well in the city, but requires daily outdoor exercise if he's to stay in the pink. Likes company; alone, likes Chippendale.

This dog has a rectangular head, with a flat skull and broad muzzle of equal length. The stop is modest, and the bite is either level or scissors. The V-shaped ears are small, creased at skull level, and fall forward close to the cheeks. The oval eyes are also on the small side and are normally brown or black. The nose is black, with the exception of liver with a liver coat. The clean neck looks a little long and carries some arch.

A sturdy, short-coupled little dog with sloping shoulders, a moderately narrow chest to elbows, and legs of strong bone with small, round, compact feet. Pasterns not noticeable on forelegs, and hock let down in rear. Dewclaws (if any) are removed. Up top, the withers are a little higher than the rest of the level topline. The rib cage is round and well sprung, hindquarters are strong and broad, tuck-up is moderate and angulation is good. The docked tail is set high and carried up, with the tip at about skull level.

The Lakeland wears a double coat, with the usual short and soft undercoat and a hard, wiry outer coat of medium length in a big range of appropriate colors: blue, black, liver, black and tan, blue and tan, red, red grizzle, grizzle and tan, or wheaten. Young adults often wear dark saddles, but this lightens to tan as time marches on.

Males stand 14 to 15 inches, and top weight is about 17 pounds. Bitches are 13 to 14 inches and about 15 pounds.

MANCHESTER TERRIER (76)

Another breed gift from England, this beast comes in two varieties, Standard and Toy, and the former is the father of the latter. Known as the Black and Tan Terrier until the 1920s, the Manchester is one of the oldest terrier breeds—much too old for anyone to nail down his true ancestors. His modern name is a tribute to the many breeders in and around the district of Manchester who did most to establish breed type (1875–1900). What they came up with was today's Standard variety. Once hailed as the best rat killer in the canine world, but if he's used for that purpose today, his owners aren't talking.

A peculiarity of the breed brought about the development of the Toy variety. In most breeds, a runt pup in a litter comes as no surprise, and usually he matures into an average-sized dog. But in Manchesters the runt pups often fail to achieve proper size. Once this fact was established, English dog fanciers bred runts to runts

and formed the smaller variety. The only differences from the Standard are in the size and ears. In America the varieties were recognized as separate breeds, but since 1959 they have been classed as one breed with two varieties. For the sake of convenience each variety has been relegated to a different group at dog shows.

In America the breed has had strong support for about 50 years but has never achieved the deserved popularity. Although friendly enough with his own human family, the beast tends to be aloof with others, including important, wealthy relatives who visit from time to time. And some of the dogs have minds of their own. Jim Dandy will obey Mom but not Pop or vice versa.

Breed Blueprint

The short, sleek coat makes him a cinch to groom. Happy in city or country, but prefers running room. For a family pet the Standard variety is the better choice.

The beast's head is long, narrow, and tight-skinned, with the almost flat skull carrying a median-line furrow. From the front, the muzzle tapers to the always black nose and looks a little wedge shaped. The bite is either level or a slight scissors. The small, dark, oblong eyes are set close and slant upward. The ears are set high and close. The Toy's are thin, rather narrow at the base, pointed, and carried erect. Always natural, never cropped. The Standard's are erect or button, small and thin. If cropped, they are carried erect and must have pointed tips. Most show dogs wear cropped ears, but most judges know the cropping is unnecessary.

Overall, the Manchester has a streamlined, racy look. His body is reasonably short-coupled, with sloping shoulders, a deep, narrow chest, and a strong rib cage. The legs are of fair bone, with compact, complex feet. The two middle toes are longer than the others, and the hind feet are shaped like a cat's. Front and rear, the toes are arched, the nails black. The otherwise level topline shows a little arch over the loins, and the hindquarters have modest tuck-up, good angulation, and well-let-down hocks. The natural whip tail is fairly short, set where the arch of the loin ends and tapering to a point. It is never carried higher than the back.

The beast's smooth, short, dense coat is jet black with rich mahogany tan markings over each eye, on each cheek, on the lips of the upper and lower jaws, extending under the throat, on the forelegs up to the knee, on the inner sides of the hind legs, almost up to the stifle joints, inside the ears, and under the tail (but covered by the tail). Black penciling is a must on all toes, and white is not allowed. In fact, any white marking longer than ½ inch is a disqualification. Proper or nearly proper markings are a must for a show dog.

As noted, size is the other important distinction between varieties. If a Toy weighs more than 12 pounds, he's really a Standard, and if a Standard weighs more than 22 pounds, he's a bum. An average Toy (either sex) stands about 9 inches and weighs 8 pounds. The average Standard goes 17 inches and 19 pounds.

In America, for reasons nobody understands, the Toy has become much more popular than the Standard. Perhaps good things really do come in small packages.

MINIATURE SCHNAUZER (7)

While the battle still rages over this beast's qualifications as a true terrier, he is accepted as such on our shores and is far-and-away America's most popular terrier. Pound for pound, he makes one of the very best city dogs and seems unconcerned with the mounting pressures of metropolitan life.

A native of Germany, the MS has been breeding true since the 1890s and was designed to guard livestock and decimate vermin. While his original German breeders were just as careless about keeping notes as nineteenth-century English breeders, most canine historians now agree that the MS was developed from a blend of small Standard Schnauzers and big Affenpinschers. Since he does look like a smaller version of the Standard, at least half the popular theory could be correct.

A few members of the breed reached America in the early 1900s and were used as farm dogs. Breeding started in the mid-1920s, and a decade later (after the formation of a national breed club), the general public started to become aware of the beast. Then, around 1950, the breed started to climb in popularity. Today quality pups are everywhere. But beware, for puppy factories have been in the act for a long time and other nonsense breeders are also churning out litters. For your own sake, seek a veteran breeder (see Chapter VII).

Breed Blueprint

The Miniature Schnauzer is active, hardy, and bold when necessary. Not much as a fighter or wanderer, but a fine pal for considerate children. The coat requires a hard brush, a little trimming, and plucking of dead hairs.

Except for his smaller size, the MS is pretty much a reproduction of the Standard Schnauzer.

Dogs (either sex) stand 12 to 14 inches, and 13½ inches is considered ideal for show. In hard condition, the ideal MS will go a little over 15 pounds. Good bone and coat will always make him look heavier.

NORWICH TERRIER (91)

This little dog was developed less than a century ago as a small sporting terrier. While his family tree depends on which canine authority one prefers to believe, it is known that in the early 1880s a British breeder named Charles Lawrence figured out a way to bring the new breed to public attention. He gifted several Cambridge undergraduates with pups that he might not have been able to sell, and within a couple of years, students were singing the praises of the

little fellow. The Norwich's fame spread, and he was adopted by the landed gentry as a dual-purpose dog: house pet and hunt-club favorite. In this latter capacity he was carried in a saddle bag until the hounds drove the wily fox to ground.

Almost half a century passed before the Norwich arrived in America, also as a gift. A leading British breeder, one Frank Jones, thought it was high time that the former colonists started to appreciate the little terrier. He wanted to introduce the dog through "the very best people" and figured that the recipients had to be members of hunt clubs, rather than undergraduates at Harvard. To his delight, several American hunt clubs accepted Jones's offer of gift beasts (1920, 1921), and for a few years the breed was known here as the Jones Terrier.

While the breed did not catch on here as a hound helpmate, some socially prominent members of the hunt clubs fell in love with the breed. Most of them maintained large kennels of dogs (hound or sporting breeds), and they adopted the terrier as a second breed, a handier size for the home. They also preferred the name Norwich, and the A.K.C. recognized the breed under that name (1936). Since, the Norwich and the more popular Cairn have achieved a strange social status in America, especially among breeders of sporting dogs who believe that owning either terrier (as a second breed) is the next best thing to being in the Social Register. For those who care about such imaginary social distinction, this added note: in America, a Norwich is permitted to wear either prick or drop ears, but in Britain, a Norwich with drop ears is now a Norfolk. It is not clear whether the Britishers who prefer the Norfolk Terrier are the best or the very best.

Breed Blueprint

His hard, wiry coat requires very little grooming. True terrier all the way: active, hardy, and tireless. The average American breeder continues to produce quality pups.

The Norwich head carries a wide, modestly rounded skull with good width between the high-set ears. The strong, slightly tapering muzzle is about ⅔ the length of the head. The stop is well defined and the proper bite is a scissors. The eyes are very dark and keen ("full of expression"), and the ears are either prick or drop. If pricked, they are small, pointed, and carried erect; if dropped, they are neat and small, folding at skull level and dropping with the front edges close to the cheeks and tips at about eye level, no lower. The neck is short and strong.

Although built a little low, the body is reasonably compact, with modestly sloping shoulders, a deep chest, legs of strong bone, and round, tight feet. Topline is level over a strong rib cage and heavily muscled, round hindquarters, with fair angulation. The tail is docked (medium length) and carried up.

A double coat, but the undercoat is very short and doesn't amount to much. The hard, close-lying topcoat is wiry in nature, but it does manage to seem straight, and is longer on the shoulders and neck (a mane) when the coat is in bloom. Hair on the head, ears, and muzzle is always short and smooth. For show, only very minimal trimming is permitted. Coat colors include all shades of red, wheaten, black and tan, and grizzle. White markings on chest are permitted, but not desired.

The ideal height for a dog (either sex) is 10 inches, and a 10-incher runs 11 to 12 pounds. For show, cropped ears disqualify.

SCOTTISH TERRIER (32)

Along with such other terriers as the Cairn, West Highland White, and the Dandie Dinmont, the Scottie is a product of the Highlands; specifically, the district of Aberdeen. Like the others, he is a spin-off of the old Highland Terrier, remembered (by canine historians) as a rather general breed of many sizes, shapes, and coats. The various Highland districts developed their own terrier types, beasts suited to their particular local terrains and populations of fox, badger, and rodents. Thus, in 1850 the little-known Aberdeen Terrier was developed, and in 1870 he became better known at British dog shows as the Scottish Terrier.

The first Scotties reached America in 1883, and a year later the first known litter was whelped in Indiana. By 1910 even ailurophiles could recognize a Scottie at a hundred paces, but only if he wore a black coat. For some strange reason, the little terrier's other proper coat colors have never caught the American public's fancy. This was true during the beast's golden years (1929–44), when he ranked among the top ten most popular breeds, and it holds true today. Overall, his popularity has slipped somewhat, but he's still fourth among terriers and is not likely to fade from the scene.

A good Scottie is pretty much a one-family dog and is best suited for a family of adults or dog lovers old enough to understand that a

perfect gentleman (canine variety) can also be a perfect demon. In other words, he's a gentleman with a mind of his own. Doesn't mind children but would rather outwit adults.

Breed Blueprint

A stripping comb, applied every six months, keeps the coat in shape. Not difficult. Otherwise, plucking out dead hairs with finger and thumb does the job, but it's tedious work.

The long head has medium width and carries a slightly domed skull and slight stop. The muzzle tapers a bit to a big, black, protruding nose and is about the same length as the skull. The bite is either scissors or level. The small, almond-shaped eyes are set wide apart under brows and are colored dark brown or almost black. Ears are set high. They are small, pricked, almost pointed (never cropped), and are covered with short, velvety hairs. The neck is short, thick, and muscular.

A Scottie body is moderately short, with sloping shoulders, a broad, very deep chest, short legs of heavy bone, and round, thick feet. Up front, the forelegs are either straight or a little bent, but the elbows are always close to the body and the forefeet are a little larger than hind feet. The topline is level over a strong rib cage and loin and the muscular hindquarters carry good angulation. The natural tail runs about 7 inches. It's carried up in a slight curve but never over the back.

A double coat, with a very short, dense undercoat and a hard, wiry topcoat that runs about 2 inches. Coat colors are black, sandy or wheaten, steel or iron gray, brindled or grizzled. White is not desirable, but a little is allowed on the chest.

Either sex stands about 10 inches. Males weigh 19 to 22 pounds, bitches 18 to 21 pounds. Breed judges look for balance. For show, it's best to leave a dog at home if he doesn't carry his head and tail up at all times or if he's on the timid side.

SEALYHAM TERRIER (105)

The only terrier to be named after a residence, this beast takes his name from Sealyham House, the Welsh country estate of one Captain John Edwards, a wealthy and eccentric sportsman who could not find a satisfactory breed for going to earth after fox and badger. Around 1850 the good man and some friendly farmers started to develop a new breed from available, talented mongrels. Four decades later the Sealy was breeding true. It took another twenty years before English dog lovers were aware of the little charmer. Dog shows did the trick.

The Sealy is also unique in the matter of breed recognition. The Kennel Club of England did not bless the breed until 1911, whereupon several of the beasts were exported to interested dog fanciers in the United States. Several months later, still in 1911, the A.K.C. recognized the breed. This hands-across-the-sea policy had never before happened so quickly, it hasn't happened since, and it is hardly likely to occur again.

Since that rapid recognition the Sealy has always been very popular and successful as a show dog, but he has never really caught on as a pet. While he has virtues by the dozens, he does require a firm hand, daily grooming, and more human companionship than most terriers. For the special dog lover—and not for the man who just wants to have a dog around the house in case it is invaded by fox and badger.

Breed Blueprint

A strong, wire comb that gets right down to the skin is the best tool for grooming the thick, double coat and keeping it free from grime, mats, and dead hair. For show, the coat is hand-stripped (never clipped) about twice a year.

The head is long (a little over 8 inches), broad, and strong, with a slightly domed skull, a shallow median furrow running between eyes, and a moderate stop. The dark, oval eyes are set deep and wide. The beast's ears, rounded at tips, are set high and back. They fold at skull level and fall forward, close to cheeks, with the tips extending to the outer corners of the eyes. The jaws are square and powerful and carry either level or scissors bite, and the nose is always big and black. The clean, muscular neck runs a bit over 7 inches.

Although the breed standard describes the dog as short-coupled, he's a little on the long side or of medium length. He carries sloping shoulders, a deep, broad chest, and short legs of good bone, with rather large, compact, round, arched feet. Proper forefeet are larger than hind feet, but the latter are longer. Up top, the back is level over a strong rib cage and powerful hindquarters, with good angulation and hocks well let down. The high-set tail is docked short and carried upright.

The Sealy's soft, dense undercoat is topped by a hard, wiry, fairly long topcoat that is either all white or white with lemon, with tan or badger markings on the head and ears.

An ideal dog (either sex) stands about $10\frac{1}{2}$ inches at the withers. Males go 23 to 24 pounds, bitches a pound or so less.

Body markings and ticking pop up now and again, and although canines with such coats make fine pets, their chances as show dogs aren't too good.

SKYE TERRIER (93)

Developed in about 1600 as a fox and badger deterrent, this is the oldest of the terrier breeds, and his true ancestors are not on record. He takes his name from the Isle of Skye, but the selection of the name remains a mystery, for the long, low beast was also popular throughout the Scottish mainland and on other Scottish isles. The breed's scholars assume that, around the seventeenth century, the best dogs of the breed were whelped on Skye.

For more than two centuries, the Skye failed to attract much attention away from Scotland. Then, in the early 1840s, Queen Victoria fell in love with the Skye and acquired several. This royal blessing amounted to social status, of course, and since then almost every English royal family has favored the breed as a castle pet. Thus, the Skye's popularity has remained high.

In America, the Skye has always been more popular as a show dog than as a family pet. While the beast has most of the terrier virtues, he is a one-family dog, has a low opinion of strangers, and his long coat requires constant grooming. Not a beast for a lazy man, no matter how many fox are digging in the garden.

Breed Blueprint

Many owners of pet Skyes trim that long coat back to about 2 inches. This simplifies the grooming, but the dog really doesn't look like his breed, and the owner becomes an outcast in dog fancy circles.

The head is fairly long, with a moderately wide skull that tapers into a strong, fairly full muzzle. Beneath all the hair, the stop is slight. The nose is always black and a proper bite is either level or slight scissors. Skyes eyes are medium sized, dark brown, and close set. Ears are prick or drop: if prick, they are medium-sized, set high, carried erect, and wider apart at the peaks than at the skull; if drop, they are a little larger, set lower, and close-hanging. The neck is long and arched.

The body is low and long, twice as long as it is high, with sloping shoulders, a deep chest, and short legs of good bone, with big, hare-feet. The Skye topline is level, over an oval rib cage and strong hind-quarters with good angulation. The natural tail is about 9 inches long, well-feathered, and is never carried above back level.

The short, wooly undercoat is hidden by the long (5 to 6 inches) hard, straight, flat topcoat, which hangs down on both sides from a part that runs from head to tail. Head hair is shorter and softer. The undercoat must be a solid color, but the topcoat may be of varying shades of that color. Permissible colors: black, blue, dark or light gray, silver platinum, fawn, or cream. White is acceptable only as a spot up to 2 inches in diameter on the chest.

Males stand 10 inches and bitches 9½ inches, and top weight is about 25 pounds. For show, a dog may be a little over or under in size, but not much. A flesh- or brown-colored nose disqualifies.

SOFT-COATED WHEATEN TERRIER (81)

A relative newcomer to America (1948) and one of the newest A.K.C. breeds (1973), the Wheatie is a sure bet to zoom in popularity during the next decade. Among terriers, he is unique on three counts: a soft and moderately long coat, a tendency to sound off infrequently, and a mild, rather than aggressive temperament.

The beast is a native of Ireland, where he was developed some time after 1800 for general utility work on the farm and for con-trolling the local vermin population. Although he could be Ireland's oldest pure breed, the Irish Kennel Club did not get around to rec-ognizing him until 1937, and England did not follow suit until 1943. The Wheatie's genealogy remains in the realm of guesswork, so his relationship to the Irish and Kerry Blue Terriers can only be supposed.

What really matters about the Wheatie is that there are already more breeders in America than elsewhere in the world, the great ma-jority know what they're doing, and our pup quality is very high. The breed is an excellent family choice, especially for apartment dwellers and others with neighbors who object to canine vocal exercises.

Breed Blueprint

The wavy coat gives the dog a semishaggy look, particularly on the head. Grooming is easy, and the natural look is preferred. For show, modest trimming is okay.

The head is moderately long, with the flat skull and square muzzle about equal in length. The stop is well defined. The medium sized eyes are dark hazel or brown, with prominent brows. The ears are small to medium in size. They are high set, fold at skull level, and drop straight, close to the cheeks. The nose is always big, pigmentation is black, and the bite can be level or scissors. The head sits on a strong, medium long neck.

This is a very compact dog. The body is short-coupled, with sloping shoulders, a deep chest, legs of good bone, and round, compact feet with dark nails. Topline is level over an ample rib cage and strong hindquarters with good angulation and low hocks. The docked tail (2⁄3 natural length) is set high and carried up. Dewclaws on hindlegs are removed. Up front, it's owner's choice.

The soft, wavy, medium length coat is very profuse. The proper coat color is wheaten, of course, and that means an off-white that runs close to the shades of ripe wheat, or from "shimmering silver to pale gold." At whelping time, pups carry dark red or brown coats, but the birth color lightens as the pups grow older and the adult coat color is firm by 18 months. Then, darker shadings on the ears and muzzle are okay.

Males of the breed stand 18 to 19 inches and weigh from 35 to 45 pounds. "Bitches are somewhat less," states the breed standard. Somewhat, but not much.

STAFFORDSHIRE BULL TERRIER (86)

For the lowdown on this breed's derivation, turn back to his latest edition, the American Staffordshire Terrier. It took the SBT a long time—until 1974—to gain A.K.C. recognition. Now that he has the official blessing, his popularity should increase.

Breed Blueprint

Not the handsomest terrier around, but easy to groom, reasonably quiet, and very affectionate with those he knows. Noted for his intelligence or trainability. A fine family dog.

The head features a broad, deep skull, a short muzzle, pronounced cheeks, and a distinct stop. A black nose is proper, but a pink nose is not. The eyes are dark, blending with coat color, and the bite is a mild scissors. The ears on the small side, and either rose or half pricked. Neck is strong and short and widens toward the shoulders.

This is a close-coupled dog, wide and deep up front, with legs of good bone and medium sized, well padded feet. Topline is level over well sprung ribs, rather light loins, and strong hindquarters and good angulation. The natural, medium long tail is low set, tapers to a point, and is carried low ("pump handle").

A proper coat is very smooth, short, and close to the skin. Solid white, red, fawn, black or blue are okay, as are those solids with white.

The breed stands 14 to 16 inches, depending on weight. Males tip the scales at 28 to 34 pounds, and bitches go 24 to 30 pounds.

For show, black-and-tan and liver colors disqualify. Dewclaws, if any, may be removed, and usually are from the hind legs.

WELSH TERRIER (58)

This dog was developed more than a century ago in Northern Wales, and it's easy to believe that one of his ancestors was the Airedale. He was designed as an antivermin dog, and is still used abroad for that

purpose today. Although this beast was an early arrival in the United States, it took him a couple of decades to attract public attention, and then he did it through dog shows. He has never achieved deserved recognition as a family pet, and annual American litters usually run fewer than seven hundred in number, an outrageously low figure for such a fine city and country dog. Still, the Welsh is more populous than two similar terriers, the smaller Lakeland and the bigger Irish, so that's something, even if some dog lovers continue to regard the Welsh as a miniature Airedale and thus not the real thing.

Most canine authorities agree that the best Welsh Terriers are now being bred in America. The few who disagree happen to be British. Of course.

Breed Blueprint

A lively, gay dog, he's not as noisy as the average terrier, but he's just as eager for action of any kind. The adult coat should be stripped or clipped twice a year. Latter method is easier.

The Welsh head carries a flat skull, fairly wide between the ears, with a slight stop. The small dark hazel eyes are set fairly wide, and the small V-shaped ears are set high and carried forward, close to the cheeks. The nose is always black, the jaws clean, strong, and on the deep side, and the bite level. The slightly arched neck is of moderate length.

This is a short-coupled dog, with long, sloping shoulders, a deep, moderately wide chest, and legs of fair bone with small, round, catlike feet. The topline is level over a short back, good rib cage, and strong hindquarters with modest angulation and well let down hocks. The docked tail is set high and carried up.

The Welsh coat is wiry, hard, and very close and dense. Proper coat colors are black and tan or black grizzle and tan.

A good male stands 15 inches and weighs about 20 pounds, "bitches proportionately less," according to the breed standard. For show, variance of an inch or a pound, either way, really doesn't matter. Overall quality does.

WEST HIGHLAND WHITE TERRIER (40)

Once known as the White Scottie, the Westie could be a color spin-off of the Scottie, with some Cairn and perhaps Dandie Dinmont blood thrown in for good measure. No matter his ancestry, he is another product of the Scottish Highlands and was designed, like so many of the other terriers, to work on the abundant vermin. By chance, he also turned out to be a pretty good stock dog. While there's some small evidence to indicate that the Westie (under other names) was around in Scotland as early as 1800, the dog-loving public didn't become aware of him until about 1900, when he started popping up at British dog shows. Within a decade the beast had crossed the Atlantic and breed clubs had been formed in his honor in both the United States and Canada.

Of the small terriers, the Westie makes one of the best family pets. Snap judgments about his coat have held him back from being about ten times as popular as he is. A few minutes a day with a comb and brush keeps the hard, straight, white outer coat in both clean and top condition. For show, only minimal trimming is necessary, the less the better. American pup quality is now fifty-fifty. A little breeder research is recommended.

Breed Blueprint

The Westie is easy to groom, train, and handle. A hardy, active little beast, he's a people lover and does better in the home than in a kennel. Likes plenty of human companionship but almost resents pampering.

The broad head carries a slightly domed skull that gradually tapers to the eyes and shows a distinct stop. The strong muzzle runs a little shorter than the skull, tapering gradually to a big, black nose, and the jaws show either level or scissors bite. Medium sized dark eyes are set wide and a little deep under bushy eyebrows, and the small pointed ears are set high and wide and are carried erect. The muscular neck is of medium length.

This is a strong, compact, balanced dog with sloping shoulders, a full, fairly broad chest, and the short, muscular legs carry round, arched feet. Forefeet should be a little bigger than hind feet. The topline is level over a deep rib cage, broad loins, and strong hindquarters with good angulation. The natural, high-set tail is short (about 6 inches) and carried erect, with the tip at about skull level.

The Westie wears a double coat, with short, dense undercoat and a topcoat of straight, hard hair. It's about 2 inches long on the body and runs a little shorter on the neck and shoulders. The only proper coat color—for both undercoat and topcoat—is solid white. The nose must be black, and black pigmentation is desirable on lips, eyelids, pads, nails, and skin.

The average male stands about 11 inches and the average bitch an inch less. For show, variations of less than an inch are okay. An 11-inch Westie will weigh about 18 pounds.

Toy Group

The toy breeds are generally regarded as the novelties of the dog world, in the sense that they were developed for no particular purpose other than to satisfy man's whim for something small. After all, man has dwarf trees, vegetables, cattle, and fowl—so why not canines? In modern times even skeptical dog lovers have accepted this explanation, and most contemporary canine literature either accepts it or neglects to mention the true story.

Well, the healthy truth is that the toys were developed in the centuries before plumbing and a constant supply of hot water were commonplace, and knowledge of personal hygiene was really just beginning. In those days even the best people (including royalty) had a big problem with human fleas. It came to pass that some unknown genius discovered a remarkable thing about fleas: they preferred, if given the chance, to live on dogs. Thus, the development of the lap dog, now known as the toy, a dog so tiny that it could be carried up a sleeve or in a pocket. In the days when royalty exchanged gifts as a matter of protocol, the toys were as prized as precious gems and slaves.

Since ownership is no longer privileged, the toys are much more popular today than ever before. They come in handy sizes for the city, and most get plenty of exercise running around a couple of rooms. Still, with the possible exception of the biggest toys (Shih Tzu, Pug), they are really dogs for adults and not ideal for families with small children. It's very easy to step on a Chihuahua.

AFFENPINSCHER (109)

Developed a long time ago—perhaps as long ago as the seventeenth century—this little beast's ancestors will always remain unknown al-

though the probability is that they were small working terriers who kept the German rat population under control on farms and estates. Although the Affpin cannot climb trees, swing from branches, or peel a banana, he is sometimes called Monkey Terrier or Monkey Dog, both rough translations of the Teutonic breed name. And true students of the breed claim that the dog has a monkeyish expression.

One of the little fellow's claims to fame is that he is the suspected forefather of the Brussels Griffon, also a toy but with a little more size. Over the last three decades, the Affpin's popularity has been on the increase in America, but he still trails his offspring, and seventy-five litters per annum is average.

Breed Blueprint

A spunky little dog, he's quiet most of the time, but sounds off when excited. An easy keeper, and as durable as any toy.

His head is round, his forehead well domed. Muzzle is short and pointed, with upper jaw a trifle short. Bite is either even or slightly undershot. The nose is jet black, as are the round eyes. The small, erect ears are set high, usually clipped to a point for show. Neck is short and straight.

The body is square with a fairly deep chest, front legs falling straight, and the round feet are small and compact. The topline is level, ribs are well sprung, and rear shows a slight tuck-up, with fairly straight stifle and hocks set well under the body. The tail is docked short, set high, and carried up.

Overall, the coat is hard and wiry. It's long and shaggy on the legs and around the eyes, nose, and chin, and short and dense elsewhere. Black is the ideal coat color, black with tan markings rates second best, and other dark mixtures are approved. In the fault department are white markings and light colors.

Maximums for the breed are $10\frac{1}{4}$ inches and 8 pounds. For show, the smaller the dog, the better his chances—if he's of characteristic type, that is.

BRUSSELS GRIFFON (98)

This rumored son of the Affenpinscher is, as his name implies, a product of Belgium, and chances are that he was developed as a ratter by flea-bitten dog lovers with big laps. A strong school of thought supports the theory that the Pug is another of his ancestors. If true, this would explain the two types of coat (rough and smooth) that pop up in today's litters.

For reasons unknown, the BG is not an easy breeder, and a litter's first three weeks are often touch and go. In addition, single pup litters are not unusual.

Admirers insist that the BG has super canine intelligence. Maybe. The average dog of the breed matures into either a sensitive animal or a tough cookie. For his size, he can be mighty stubborn.

Breed Blueprint

The BG is a fine pet for the patient dog lover. It's important to start training the pup at an early age, no later than his tenth week. The pup who doesn't fight the training leash is the exception.

The big, round skull features a domed forehead and a distinct stop and the large, black eyes are set wide and carry long lashes. The short, black nose carries large nostrils and looks pushed back and up. Small ears are high set, either natural or cropped—if natural, semi-

erect; if cropped, pricked. The bite is undershot, but teeth do not show when mouth is closed. Head sits on a medium length, arched neck.

This is a cobby dog, with a broad, deep chest, strong forelegs, and small, compact, arched feet. The topline is level over a well sprung rib cage and strong quarters, with good angulation and hocks well let down. The tail is docked to about ⅓ of natural, and is set and carried high.

The BG coat is either rough or smooth, and either can occur in the same litter. If rough, it is hard, dense, wiry, and long—but not quite shaggy. The wiry hair is longest around eyes, nose, cheeks, and chin. If smooth, the coat is similar to that worn by the Bulldog and Boston Terrier, and has no trace of wiry hair. Solid black is acceptable for the rough coat, but not for the smooth. Otherwise, these colors are okay on both coats: reddish brown, with a little black on whiskers and chin okay; black and reddish brown, with black mask and whiskers; and black with uniform brownish red markings.

The average BG runs 8 to 10 pounds, and 12 pounds is maximum. The biggest stand about 10 inches, but smaller dogs are preferred. The breed's disqualifications are white on coat, overshot jaw, hanging tongue, and a flesh-colored nose.

CHIHUAHUA (15)

The world's smallest canine breed is Mexico's gift to dog lovers who believe that good things really do come in small packages. The Chihuahua (pronounced Chi-wah-wah) is far and away America's favorite toy, with litters per annum climbing toward the 20,000 mark. The dog's abundance surprises the average voter, who seldom sees him away from dog shows. Most of the beasts can fit into a coat pocket or a purse, and that's the way they usually travel in public.

The modern Chihuahua was around by 1850 in the Mexican state of the same name. In one small shape or another his ancestors were around for several prior centuries in Central America, and there's nothing wrong in believing that those tiny canines were worshipped by the Aztecs in the same ways that the cat was revered by the ancient Egyptians. The first A.K.C. registered Chihuahua (1904) was the appropriately named Midget.

Two coats, smooth and long, are proper, and the former is far more popular in this land. Wearing either coat, he usually gets along with relatives but not with other breeds. Another oddity is skeletal: sometimes the skull carries a molera (space where the bones have not joined). Hence, if Sweetheart's skull shows molera, he can be accused of having a natural hole in his head. He never knows and does not care.

Breed Blueprint

Surprisingly hardy and intelligent—and often long-lived (15 to 20 years)—this is an ideal apartment dog. The biggest problem is keeping him at proper weight. Tendency is to overfeed.

The head is domed, with lean cheeks and jaws, a distinct stop, and a short, slightly pointed nose. The ears look big and are carried erect on the alert, and at 45 degrees in repose. The big, full eyes are set wide apart, with dark and ruby colors preferred, but light eyes okay on blondes. The bite is level. The head sits on a slightly arched neck.

The body has a little more length than height, still more so in bitches, and carries sloping shoulders, a good but not overdone chest, straight forelegs, and small, tight feet with nails moderately long.

Topline is level over rounded ribs, muscular hindquarters, and a slight tuck-up. Tail is moderately long and is carried sickle-fashion, up or out or in a loop over the back with tip just touching.

Smooth coat is soft, close, and glossy. The long coat is also soft, flat or curly, with some undercoat, and fringe on the ears, feathering on feet and forelegs, pants on hind legs, ruff on neck, and plumed tail. For smooth or long coat, any color is okay: solid or combination, and solid color coats are more popular in America.

The breed weighs from 1 to 6 pounds, with 2 to 4 pounds about average. A 4-pounder will stand about 6 inches, a 6-pounder about 8 inches. A docked tail, cropped ears, and a thin, bare coat are disqualifications for show.

ENGLISH TOY SPANIEL (115)

A favorite of Britain's upper classes since the sixteenth century, the breed has remained pretty much the same down through the years, except for the refining of coat colors in modern times. Mary Stuart knew this toy in France and may have brought several home to Scotland. It's probable that the ETS reached France from Spain or Italy some time before that, and there are dreamers who believe that the breed reached those countries from China or Japan. The theories are numerous, including one holding that undersized Cocker Spaniels were mixed with an unknown oriental toy to produce this dog. The true origin amounts to reader's choice.

While the ETS has had a dedicated following in America for more than a hundred years and was shown in numbers at our dog shows prior to 1900, the breed has never achieved much popularity on this side of the Atlantic; fifty litters a year would set a new American record. One of the breed's drawbacks here might be the fact that the ETS has four varieties, each identical in conformation but different in coat color. To compound the confusion: for show purposes the four become two varieties. Or look at it this way: each show variety consists of two color varieties. Finally, one of the original four varieties is called the King Charles, and it's easy to confuse his name with that of the Cavalier King Charles Spaniel, who is a little bigger and not recognized (although he is listed) by the A.K.C. Another ETS variety is the Prince Charles. Enough said . . .

Breed Blueprint

No matter what coat he wears, the ETS is one of the best family dogs among the toys, but he is usually wary of strangers. A good toy choice for the family with small children who are not tail and ear pullers.

The ETS carries a domed head, and on a very good one the half-circle extends almost to the upturned, short, wide black nose. The big dark eyes are set well apart, and the stop between them is pronounced, often deep and hollow. The long, low-set ears hang close and extend well below the short muzzle. The bite is level.

Thanks to the long coat, the cobby body looks bulkier than it really is. The coat and feathering also hide a wide chest, a rounded rib cage, stout legs on compact feet, a short broad back, and fair tuck-up and angulation. The docked tail runs 1½ inches, has about 4 inches of silky feathering, and is never carried above back level.

The coat on all varieties is long, silky, soft, and wavy but never curly. A profuse mane extends down the front of the chest. And there's always plenty of feathering on the ears, feet, and on the back of the legs. As for those coat colors, grouped by variety:

King Charles and Ruby. King Charles: black with tan markings over the eyes and on the muzzle, chest, and legs. Ruby: solid chestnut red. Note: on either coat, any white is a disqualification.

Blenheim and Prince Charles. Blenheim: white with red chestnut markings evenly distributed in large patches; also, red ears and cheeks and white blaze. Prince Charles: white with large black patches, black and tan spots over the eyes and on the muzzle, chest, and legs; also, tan lining on ears and vent.

The EST tips the scales at 9 to 12 pounds. A 12-pounder will stand about 10 inches at the shoulders.

ITALIAN GREYHOUND (77)

Canine authorities agree that this little pooch was around at least two thousand years ago and that he was the result of intentional dwarfing by breeders of the ancient gazehounds. From the beginning the IG has been regarded as a pet, and for hundreds of years he was a big favorite of European aristocracy. The ladies loved him.

By the seventeenth century the little beast was established in Britain, but he did not become popular there until Victoria's reign and failed to win favor in America until about 1870. Although a bit more refined these days, the IG is pretty much the same now as he was then. The dog's star started fading in both countries around 1900, and a couple of decades later his numbers were practically nonexistent in England. This sad state of affairs was corrected by importing breeding stock from the United States in 1920—the first time this had ever happened. Until then America had been importing this and most other breeds from England.

Over the past several decades American breeders have been producing the top dogs of the breed, and our pup quality is very high. The IG is not well known outside the dog fancy, and his chances of any real popularity remain slim. Still, he outnumbers the bigger Greyhound by about three to one. That's something anyway.

Breed Blueprint

Despite his delicate looks, the IG is hardier than most of the toys and usually has a surprisingly deep bark. His shedding is next to nil. A high-stepping, elegant little fellow and always a conversation piece.

The head features a long, almost flat skull with a slight stop. Medium-sized dark eyes and small ears that are held back and folded at right angles to the head are also characteristic. The muzzle is long, fine, and tapered, and the bite is scissors. The slender neck is long and arched.

The IG body is short-coupled, with long, sloping shoulders and a deep, narrow chest. The straight legs are of fine bone, and the hare-feet carry arched toes. The withers are high and the topline curves over drooping hindquarters with good tuck-up and angulation. The slender tail is set and carried low, tapers to a curved tip, and extends to the hocks.

The IG's glossy, soft coat is fine and very short. Any color and markings are acceptable, with one exception: the tan markings normally found on other black and tan breeds (e.g.: Bloodhound, Coonhound, Manchester Terrier).

Ideally, dogs (either sex) stand 13 to 15 inches. Figure 10 pounds, give or take a few ounces.

JAPANESE SPANIEL (85)

Another toy who made canine history, the JS (also known as the Japanese Chin) was the first foreign breed to reach America before it got to England and Europe. For this, thanks go to Commodore Perry, who discovered the breed while opening Japan (1853) to the wonders of the West. When Perry sailed for home, several of the little dogs (all gifts) were passengers. Two survived the long journey. Although they were never bred, the two dogs served to popularize the breed, and hundreds were imported before and after the Civil War. In Japan the breed was pretty much the property of royalty and had been for a few centuries. In the United States, however, the only qualification for ownership was money, and for a long time a $1,000 pup was a bargain. Thus, most of the breeders were wealthy people. Abroad, members of the Rothschild family owned the biggest kennels.

A national breed club was organized by leading American breeders and fanciers in 1883. The JS seemed destined for great popularity, but another toy was coming along and catching the public fancy.

The newcomer, also from the Far East, was the Pekingese. By 1900, because of the Peke, the JS had peaked. These days, a 100-litter year would be big news.

Breed Blueprint

For a little dog, this one has a big mind of his own; he loves or dislikes for life. His coat needs a little grooming several times a week. Look for a friendly, lively pup.

The head should appear big on the body, with the skull broad and rounded over the front. The eyes are big, dark, and set wide. The V-shaped ears are small, set wide and high, and carried slightly forward. The nose is the same as the coat markings, the muzzle is short, and the bite, although not specified, is usually level or a slight scissors. The neck is fairly short and thick.

The body is short-coupled, with a wide chest. The slender legs are well feathered and carry small, fairly long feet. The topline is level over a little tuck-up and fair angulation. The tail is carried up and over the back, twisting to either the right or left from the base and flowing over the back to the opposite side. It should carry profuse hair.

The long, straight coat is dense and silky, with the appearance of a ruff on the neck and plenty of feathering on the thighs and tail. It's parti-colored: either black and white or red and white. *Red* actually includes all shades of sable, brindle, lemon, and orange. Whether black or red, patches should be distributed evenly over the body, cheeks, and ears.

The standard does not specify sizes, beyond "the smaller they are the better, provided type and quality are not sacrificed." For show, classes are sometimes divided by weight: under or over 7 pounds. A 7-pounder will stand about 8 inches if he's in good condition.

For show, a black and white must wear a black nose.

MALTESE (42)

This native of Malta is known to be about three thousand years old, but how the breed evolved remains a mystery. It is known that the first members of the breed came to England in 1841, thence to the United States in 1875, and then on to Canada. This little bundle of white fluff achieved popularity in Canada before the First World

War, a couple of decades before catching on here. The breed became extinct on Malta, but imports corrected the situation.

Abroad, people who worry about such matters often subscribe to the theory that the Maltese is a member of the terrier family, while the worriers on this side of the Atlantic favor the spaniel clan. Although lively, the dog does not carry the instincts of either family. Thanks to great success at the shows over the past two decades, the Maltese is now more popular and populous here than anywhere else in the world.

Breed Blueprint

A fine breed choice for the family that must have a toy, even though small fry are already present. The breed is affectionate, does get along with children, and is among the hardiest of the toys. Not a good choice for the owner who hates grooming.

His medium length head looks in proportion, with a slightly rounded skull, a moderate stop, and a muzzle that tapers but is not snipy. The bite is either even or scissors, and the nose is always black. Maltese eyes are dark and round. The drop ears are set low and hang close, and are so heavily feathered that they look much larger than they are. The neck is just long enough to permit high head carriage.

The body is very compact, with sloping shoulders, deep chest, straight and fine-boned forelegs and small, round feet with black toe pads. The topline is level over well-sprung ribs, strong loins, a slight tuck-up, and moderate angulation. The tail, resembling a long-haired plume, is carried gracefully over the back, its tip lying to one side of the quarters.

Although it looks like a double, this is really a single coat. It hangs long, flat, and silky over the sides of the body and almost to the ground. While it's legal for the long head hairs to hang, they are usually tied up in a topknot—by the owner, not nature. Ideal coat color is pure white. Light tan or lemon on the ears is permissible but not desirable.

Proper size depends on weight, and 4- to 6-pounders are preferred. Just under 7 pounds is the maximum. The biggest dogs go up to 12 inches, but 8 to 10 inches is about average.

MANCHESTER TERRIER, TOY

For details please go back to the Manchester Terrier, the Standard variety of this breed. Except for ears and size, this Toy is the very same dog.

MINIATURE PINSCHER (59)

It's common practice to assume that this breed was bred down from the much bigger Doberman Pinscher. Except for size, the two breeds do resemble each other in looks, but the popular assumption is erroneous. Aside from looks, the only thing the two breeds have in common is their native land, Germany.

The Minpin was developed about three centuries ago, 200 years before the Dobie. The belief is that he was bred down from black and tan terriers of the time, and his instincts seem to confirm this: here and there a few prove to be natural ratters and some are used to hunt hare. Still a useful little dog, then, if given the chance. And he has the distinction of being the first toy breed to be accepted by the masses: peasants owned and loved him just as much as members of the aristocracy.

This spirited little dog with a hackney gait arrived in America shortly after the First World War, but he remained pretty much unknown until 1929, the year the national breed club was born and he was recognized by the A.K.C. Since, his American popularity has been on the slow-and-steady side.

Breed Blueprint

An active little beast, he thrives on exercise, is very self-possessed, and thinks that he's a big dog. Grooming is a cinch. The best toy for an action-loving owner, but too high spirited for a nervous person.

The Minpin's head is wedge shaped, with the flat skull sloping toward the reasonably strong, tapering muzzle. The nose is black (but self-colored on chocolates), the bite is even. The dark oval eyes are set wide, and the ears are set high and upstanding (if cropped, pointed and erect). The clean neck is slightly arched and flows into the shoulders.

A compact body (although bitches can be a little long), with sloping shoulders, chest to elbows, and forelegs of strong bone with well-arched, catlike feet. Topline is either level or sloped slightly to rear over a well-sprung rib cage, muscular hindquarters, and moderate angulation. Tail is docked short (1-inch maximum), set high, and carried erect.

The smooth coat is hard, short, straight, and lustrous. As for proper coat colors: solid red or stag red; black with sharply defined tan markings on cheeks, lips, lower jaw, throat, twin spots above eyes, on chest and lower half of forelegs, inside of hind legs and vent region, and lower portion of hocks and feet; and solid brown or chocolate with rust or yellow markings. Thumb marks (black spots) or a white area more than $\frac{1}{2}$ inch long on feet or forechest are disqualifications.

Proper Minpins stand 11 to $11\frac{1}{2}$ inches at the withers. For show, a dog under 10 or over $12\frac{1}{2}$ inches is disqualified. At 11 inches, figure 8 to 9 pounds.

PAPILLON (83)

A dwarf spaniel with a solid-colored coat and drop ears once ran across the landscape of Italy, France, and Spain. If the breed had a name, nobody remembers, for the running took place some three hundred years ago.

Except for his color, ears, and name, the dog hasn't changed much since then.

The coat now carries two or three colors. Although drop ears are still okay, most of the little fellows now wear obliquely erect ears,

resembling the spread wings of a butterfly. Hence the name Papillon, which is the French word for that fluttering insect.

Some sources place the arrival of the breed in this country in 1915, and others are sure it was 1923. All agree that the A.K.C. gave its blessing in 1935.

Breed Blueprint

A toy for all seasons. The coat provides proper insulation in cold or warm climates. A dainty little dog, although some are amazingly ferocious on dangerous mice.

The small head carries a slightly rounded skull with a distinct stop. The thin, tapering muzzle ends at a small, round, black nose, and the bite is a scissors. Ears are set wide and back, drop or erect, always large with rounded tips, and the dark eyes are of medium size, never pop or bulging. Neck has medium length.

The body is a little on the long side, with sloping shoulders, chest of medium depth, and fine-boned forelegs with thin, elongated feet. The topline is level over a good rib cage, strong hindquarters, clear tuck-up, and strong angulation. The long tail is set high and is carried up and arched over the body, with plume hanging to either side.

The coat is long, silky, straight, and abundant, with feathering, and the hair is short on skull and muzzle. A proper coat carries white with patches of another color, or it can be a tricolor (white, black, and tan). A white blaze is very desirable. Solid colors are disqualifications, and so is any liver.

The breed should stand 8 to 11 inches, and a dog over 12 inches is disqualified for show. To figure weight, take height and add 1. Thus, a 9-incher will go about 10 pounds.

PEKINGESE (12)

The Peke's ancient history is anyone's guess. In 1860, when the British sacked Peking, the loot the troops took home to England included several of these toy dogs, each weighing less than six pounds. One of the canine captives was presented to Queen Victoria. Her stamp of approval was enough to make any breed popular in the British Isles. Victoria, by the way, named her pooch Looty. An honest woman.

Since about 1910 this has been the most popular toy breed in the Western World. In America it has been the most popular toy most of the time, sometimes outranked by the Chihuahua. This may also

be the most spoiled breed in the Western World—or anywhere, for that matter. Owners claim that the Peke has a special arrogance, and that they often feel inferior in his presence. It's as if the little dog knows that his Oriental ancestors only associated with the emperor and his entourage. Once a palace pooch, always a palace pooch.

Breed Blueprint

The heavy front, bow legs, and light rear give the Peke his rolling gait. A weekly grooming keeps the double coat in shape, but this is not a breed for lazy owners. Independent by nature, the Peke requires a firm hand and early training. Quality pups aren't hard to find.

The big, broad head carries a skull that's flat between the ears and wide between the eyes with a deep stop. The dark eyes are big and round, the heart-shaped, drop ears carry long feathers, and the black nose is broad and flat. The wrinkled muzzle is very short and broad, the bite even; neither teeth nor tongue show.

A Peke's compact body is heavy up front, with a broad chest. Hind legs are a little lighter in bone than forelegs. The short forelegs (forearms bowed) carry flat, turned out feet. The topline is level over well sprung ribs, and good tuck-up. The high-set tail is carried up and over the back to one side or the other; it's covered with long, profuse, straight feathers.

The undercoat is very thick, and the flat topcoat is long, straight, coarse, and soft to the touch, with plenty of feathering and a profuse mane. All colors are okay. For show, black masks, "spectacles" around the eyes, and lines to the ears are a plus.

At 8 inches a dog will weigh about 12 pounds. Over 14 pounds is a disqualification, as is a flesh-colored nose.

POMERANIAN (22)

This toy is a fine example of how rapidly breed size can be reduced if wise breeders really put their minds to the task. Down through a few centuries the original Pom was well known as a herding dog in Central Europe. He stood about 18 inches and weighed around 30 pounds, and the best of the breed were found in and about Pomerania (a province in northeastern Germany). Along about 1860, a few were exported to England, already the home of a sufficient number of herding breeds. A few breeders admired the dog's pet qualities, and they set about reducing his size. A couple of decades later American breeders joined the action, and by 1900 we had a pocket edition of the old Pomeranian. The contemporary Pom was under 10 pounds and stood about 9 inches, and he was coming along strong at the dog shows.

The refinement continued. Today's Pom is lighter in bone and pounds, a little shorter, sports smaller ears, and wears a denser double coat. He ranks third in popularity among America's toy breeds, and one of these days he may even overtake the Peke and Chihuahua.

Breed Blueprint

Very intelligent, easy to train, and a people lover. However, he's a natural yapper and craves action. Not for lovers of peace and quiet.

Overall, the head is foxlike: wedge-shaped, with a flat skull, distinct stop, and fine but not snipy muzzle. Dark, almond shaped eyes, small ears set high and carried erect, a black nose (or self-colored on a brown or blue coat), and scissors bite are proper. The neck is quite short.

This is a short-coupled dog, with sloping shoulders, a deep but not wide chest, and straight forelegs with small, compact feet. The topline is level over a rounded rib cage and strong hindquarters with

slight angulation. The high-set tail is carried up and flat over the back and boasts profuse hair.

The Pom wears a double coat, with the undercoat short, soft, and dense and the topcoat long, coarse, and harsh. Feathering in the usual places. Any solid color is okay, and so is any solid color with shadings of same or with sable and black shadings. Also approved: black and tan and parti-color.

Poms weigh 3 to 7 pounds, with 4 to 5 pounds ideal for show. A 5-pounder will stand about 6 to 7 inches. Rear dewclaws are removed, front ones are optional.

POODLE, TOY

The smallest of the three varieties of Poodle. For the lowdown on this one, as well as the other two, please refer to Poodle.

PUG (35)

In days of yore Dutch traders of the old East India Company brought this breed home from the Orient, land of short-muzzled dogs. For almost a century, he was called the Dutch Mastiff, but by 1840 he was in England and had a new name, the one that identifies him today. Before the word *Pug* became obsolete, it was a term of endearment.

In no time at all this sweetie pie became extremely popular in England. His color was fawn until about 1885, when black members of the breed were imported from China. Ever since, either fawn or black has been proper, and over the past several decades the black coat has been more popular. This toy is now much more abundant in America than England. This is Pug Country to the tune of about ten thousand litters a year.

Breed Blueprint
Pups from show stock are the ones to seek. This toy's constant snorts and grunts annoy some people, but admirers find the sounds puggy, or endearing. Requires minimal care and gets along reasonably well with children.

The head is large and round, with large, deep facial wrinkles. The dark eyes are big and prominent, and his small ears are thin and soft and can be either rose or button. The square muzzle is very short, the bite either level or slightly undershot.

A Pug's body is short and cobby, with a wide chest and very strong legs of moderate length, with medium sized feet that carry black nails. The topline is level over a full rib cage and a sturdy rump. The tail is curled as tightly as possible over the hip; a double curl is regarded as perfection.

The short, smooth coat is very fine and soft. Silver fawn, apricot fawn, and solid black are the approved colors. Fawns should have black markings and trace. Although white on the chest and feet is not uncommon, it's never appreciated.

Pugs weigh 14 to 18 pounds. Heights aren't specified, but 10 to 11 inches is average.

SHIH TZU (30)

The breed has been a member in good standing of the A.K.C. since 1969, but its name remains the most mispronounced in the dog world. Simply say "Sheet zoo" and slur the two words together. Practice makes perfect. In Chinese, the name means "lion." Yes, another of the Orient's fabled lion dogs, and this breed is regarded as one of the finest artistic developments of the Ming dynasty, a royal-family favorite. Supposedly, this little toy looked like a lion in miniature. The ancient Chinese had wild imaginations but no wilder, perhaps, than those of current breed lovers who insist that the Lhasa Apso is the daddy of the Shih Tzu. If that is the case, the dog dates back to the Tibet of A.D. 600.

By the dawn of this century, the Shih Tzu was believed to be among the canine breeds that had not survived the changing scene in China. This belief was shattered in 1930, when a British lady living in China discovered several of the dogs and shipped them home to England. Later an English officer serving in China found a few more, and they were also exported. Thus, the first breeding in the West was in England. From there, breeding stock was sent to various European countries and Australia and finally to America (1948). The breed has really caught on and is here to stay. In Canada the breed is regarded as non-sporting.

Breed Blueprint

Needs more companionship than most toys, plus a fair amount of daily exercise. Daily grooming prevents a matted, messy coat.

The head is broad and round, wide between the eyes, and with a definite stop. The big eyes are dark and round, the large, long ears drop from a medium set, and pigmentation is black. The square, short muzzle runs no more than an inch, and the bite is either level or slightly undershot.

The body is a bit long, with a broad, deep chest. The short legs are of strong bone, and the big, firm feet carry hair between the pads. The topline is level over sturdy hindquarters, the high-set, heavily plumed tail is carried up and well over the back.

This is a double coat, with a wooly undercoat and a long, dense topcoat that's sometimes wavy but never curly. The topknot is usually tied up. All colors are okay.

The breed stands 9 to 10½ inches and weighs from 12 to 15 pounds. For show, judges permit some variance, but anything over 18 or under 9 pounds is off limits.

SILKY TERRIER (45)

A comparatively recent breed, the Silky is the result of a judicious cross of the Australian and Yorkshire Terriers. First named the Sydney Terrier after the Australian city of its origin, the breed gained fame abroad as the Australian Silky Terrier. Presumably the dog was designed purely for pet purposes. For economy the A.K.C. dropped *Australian* from his name during registration ceremonies in 1959.

By then the little dog had been in this country for more than a decade. Credit for his discovery and importation goes to Americans who served down under during World War II. The Silky's true terrier spirit won their hearts and pocketbooks. The climb to great popularity has been steady, and it continues.

Breed Blueprint

The wedge-shaped, longish head carries a flat skull that's a little longer than the muzzle and a shallow stop. The little eyes are dark and the high-set, V-shaped ears are small and pricked. The nose is black, the bite scissors.

Overall build is light. The low-set body is long, with a 6:5 ratio of length to height. Sloping shoulders, a deep chest reaching the elbows, straight legs of fine bone, and small, catlike feet are characteristic, as are a level topline, strong hindquarters, low hocks, and moderate angulation. The high-set tail is docked and carried erect.

The adult coat runs up to 6 inches and is flat and silky. The proper color combination is blue with tan markings on the muzzle and cheeks, at the base of the ears, below the pasterns and hocks, around the vent, and over each eye (a spot). The topknot should be silver or fawn.

Dogs stand 9 to 10 inches and weigh 8 to 10 pounds. Under 8 inches is not desired.

YORKSHIRE TERRIER (18)

This daddy of the Silky is only about seventy-five years older and a bit smaller than the son. The breed is probably a spin-off of the Skye but was developed around Lancashire and Yorkshire rather than in Scotland. He was once a big favorite of the working classes. Then came the dog shows. Good-bye, factory slaves. Hello, pre-jet set. By 1875 the Yorky was a favorite of Britain's upper classes and by 1880 he had been adopted by a few wealthy Americans as a status symbol.

Prior to 1900 the Yorky came in various sizes and weights. Some tipped the scales at 3 pounds and others at 16. Selective breeding brought the breed to its current size. In the process the coat also improved to its now fine and silky texture. In England, he's very high in popularity among all breeds, and the top toy. In America, he's popular enough and still climbing.

Breed Blueprint

Among the toys, the Yorky is one of the most delicate. An indoor beast, his coat requires plenty of care, but it's almost a nonshedder. Pups are black and tan for about three months.

The head looks small and the skull is flat. The muzzle is of medium length, the bite is either scissor or level, and the nose is black. Medium-sized eyes should be dark, and correct ears are small, V-shaped, set high, and carried erect.

The body is very compact. Forelegs are straight with elbows close, and the small, round feet have black toes. That topline is level over a short back, angulation is moderate, and the docked tail is carried a bit above back level. Hind dewclaws, if any, are removed.

The long coat is the glory of the breed. It is very fine and silky, must be perfectly straight, and is usually trimmed at floor length to permit freedom of movement. The fall is long and is usually tied up with one or two bows. Hair on the muzzle is also long, while the ear tips and feet are generally trimmed short.

Proper coat colors are blue or tan. If blue: a dark steel blue, not mingled with fawn, bronzy, or black hairs. If tan: all tan hairs, darker at the roots, then shading to a lighter tan at the tips. No intermingled sooty or black hairs are approved.

Yorkies should not exceed 7 pounds. A big dog will stand 9 or 10 inches. Wise breeders shy away from bitches under 5 pounds.

Non-Sporting Group

The non-sporting group was designed to accommodate those beasts who did not fit conveniently into one of the other groups. Time changes all things, including the original talents of some breeds. Although developed as a sporting dog, the Poodle no longer retrieves fowl from water, the Dalmatian has ceased to be a working dog, and nobody knows what "apsoing" meant, hence the presence here of the Lhasa Apso. As all people who are kind to animals know, the Bulldog is no longer adept at bullbaiting, and the Chow Chow hasn't been used for hunting in hundreds of years.

These days, the purpose served by all the breeds in this group is companionship. They are the friends of man, and nothing more is really expected of them—beyond winning huzzahs at dog shows.

Two recently recognized breeds classified as non-sporting are the Bichon Frise and the Tibetan Terrier. The former is really a toy, but placing him here instead of in the toy group eliminates possible confusion with his look-alike, the Maltese. As for the Tibetan, he is not in the terrier group because he is not and has never been a true terrier, nor does he really belong in any of the other groups.

Although the smallest of the groups, non-sporting has more diversity than the others, and it includes America's most popular breed —the Poodle.

BICHON FRISE (63)

This little white toy (bee-shon free-zay) dates back to about the twelfth century, and according to ancient rumors, he was developed somewhere in the Mediterranean area from one or more water spaniels who long ago ceased swimming. The beast has had his ups and downs in several countries, notably Spain, Italy, and France. A popular lap dog of royalty in one century and the favorite of commoners in the next. A late arrival (1959) in the United States, the Bichon won favor in a hurry and made the A.K.C. roster in 1973.

Only three other countries (France, Italy, and Belgium) recognize the breed, but the little dog's popularity has overflowed into Canada and the C.K.C. won't be able to neglect him for many more years.

Breed Blueprint

The Bichon is one of the hardiest of the little breeds. Eager to please, easy to train. The adult coat requires daily attention with comb and brush. Top-quality pups still the rule.

His head is in proportion to his size, with the skull broad and a little round, the stop slight. The big round eyes are either black or dark brown. The medium length ears are dropped and are covered with long, flowing hair. The round nose and pigmentation are black, the muzzle is of medium length and is neither heavy nor snipey; and the bite is scissors. The neck is rather long.

The body is a little long, with sloping shoulders, deep chest, and good rib cage. The straight forelegs carry round, tight, catlike feet. The topline inclines gradually from the withers to a slight rise over the large, muscular loin, and the hindquarters are well angulated. The tail is carried in a curve and lies on the back.

The Bichon wears a double coat, with the undercoat short and dense, the topcoat profuse, silky, and loosely curled. Coat color is white or white with cream, apricot, or gray on the ears and/or the body. For show, the coat is usually cut to 2 inches and brushed to give the powder-puff appearance. The hair is scissored to show the eyes and give the head and body a rounded appearance. Pups are clipped short.

Bichons stand 8 to 12 inches. Figure maximum weight at about 10 pounds. Black hair on coat and a corkscrew tail are both serious sins.

BOSTON TERRIER (27)

The Bostonian barks in Chapter II.

BULLDOG (41)

The pride and joy of England, this easily identified beast was around and bullbaiting as long ago as the thirteenth century. In those days— and for the next 500 years—he was a bigger, longer dog and looked more like a coarse Bull Terrier than he does today. Nothing is known about B's ancestry, but his descendants are a matter of record; B's blood flows today through the veins of the Bull Terrier, Boston Terrier, French Bulldog, and Bullmastiff.

The Bulldog of olden times was bred for viciousness, and the need for him faded when bullbaiting became illegal in 1835. Fortunately, a few dog lovers hated to see him disappear and set themselves to the task of developing a Bulldog who was good-natured and could qualify as a trusted friend of man. They achieved their goals, and in so doing, changed breed conformation; the result was reduced size, a more compact body, a shorter muzzle, and a heavier front. Today's type was pretty much set by 1875. Within a few years several good Bulldogs had been imported here and were winning trophies at the Yankee shows. A national breed club—one of America's earliest—was formed in 1890. For some years now, our breeders have been producing the world's best, and the Bulldog has been one of the big stars of the show circuit.

Breed Blueprint
This famous snorter can't be forced into doing anything, but persistent training will pay off. Long on memory, and can turn on the speed when necessary. You don't have to be a Yalie to own and enjoy.

The circumference of the Bulldog's large skull (measured in front of the ears) is at least as great as his height at the withers. From the front, the head appears very high, broad, and square; from the side, it looks high and short. The dark eyes are set low and wide and in line with a definite stop. The high set ears are small and thin and placed wide apart; they are never cropped, and rose are preferred. The big black nose is turned upward, the muzzle is very short and broad, and the massive jaws are undershot. The neck is short, thick, and arched.

The body looks broad, low, and short-legged. The heavy, wide shoulders slant outward, and the chest is very broad and deep. The forelegs are short, stout, and straight, with a bowed outline, and the compact feet are high knuckled. The hind legs are longer than the forelegs, and the hind feet are pointed well outward. The odd topline shows a little dip behind the shoulders, a rise over the loins (which are higher than shoulders), and a sudden arch to the tail. The short, strong back is broader at the shoulders than at the loins. The tail, either straight or screw, is always short and carried below the base.

The smooth coat is short, straight, and flat. In order of preference, coat colors are red brindle, all other brindles, solid white, solid red (fawn or fallow), and piebald. Solid black is undesirable.

The breed standard calls for males of 50 pounds and bitches of 40 pounds, but 5 pounds more (both sexes) is usual. A 55-pounder will stand a little over 16 inches. For show, a flesh-colored nose disqualifies.

CHOW CHOW (44)

Most authorities agree that this dog was around in China 2,000 years ago. He was a beast for all classes of people: a pet for royalty, a hunting dog for workers, and a tasty dish for anyone who was hungry. Despite that last fact, the breed name is not pidgin Chinese for "edible food." Rather, it is pidgin English for "knicknacks," or "a mixed bag of things" and dates back a couple of centuries. The masters of East India Company ships trading with the Orient listed various items in their cargo under the general classification of chow-chow. Toward the end of the eighteenth century the first members of the breed to reach England were imported on those ships.

England's dog fanciers didn't take the breed very seriously until

about a hundred years ago, when importing dogs became the rage. Americans followed suit, and the breed was firmly established here by 1900. Today the breed is very well known, although not as popular as it was in the 1920s, when the CC was the darling of society, a favorite of Park Avenue strollers and Newport bathers.

Breed Blueprint

The CC is usually independent, aloof, and wary of strangers. A great family pet, he responds to gentle handling but can't be pushed into anything against his will. About five minutes a day with brush and comb will keep his coat in shape.

The massive head sports a broad, flat skull with a moderate stop and a fairly short, square muzzle. A scissors bite is proper. The big nose is black, as is the tongue, and the almond-shaped eyes are dark and deep set. The small, wide-set ears are slightly rounded at tips and are carried up and tilted forward. The neck is strong and full.

A CC comes in a square, cobby body with slightly sloping shoulders, a broad and deep chest, and forelegs of heavy bone with round, catlike feet. His topline is level over a straight, strong back, well-sprung ribs, and broad, powerful loins. The high-set tail is carried over and close to the back along the spine.

This is a double coat: the undercoat is soft and wooly, and the coarse topcoat is straight, dense, and off-standing. Any solid coat color is okay, with lighter shadings on ruff, tail, and breechings.

The unique thing about this breed standard is that it neither specifies nor even suggests size. But the good CCs stand 18 to 22 inches and weigh from 40 to 60 pounds.

For show, there are these disqualifications: nose other than black, except for blue dogs, who may have solid blue or gray noses; tongue red, pink, or spotted with red or pink; and drop ear (or ears).

DALMATIAN (33)

The breed's name derives from Dalmatia, a province of olden Austria, but whether the horse's best friend originated there remains doubtful. But it is known that this spotted beast has been around for more than four hundred years on the Continent and almost as long in the British Isles. In the beginning, the Dal was an all-purpose hunting dog, then a farm dog and guardian of livestock, and finally the companion and protector of horses engaged in hauling carriages, coaches, and fire equipment. He has been in America for about one hundred fifty years and has been firmly established as a reasonably popular pet since 1890, when people realized that the Dal could be happy away from horses.

Many owners regard him as the perfect, courteous watchdog, since he'll bark an alarm but refrain from biting. As canines go, the Dal is a clean dog, almost catlike in his cleansing habits. A great breed for children.

Breed Blueprint

The Dal can take any climate and requires minimum care. One of the best family breeds. The trick is to find the right breeder. A poorly bred pup often develops into a nervous wreck. And who doesn't know that every pup is solid white at birth?

Overall, the head structure is rather like the pointer's, with a flat, fairly broad skull that's free of wrinkles and ends in a moderate stop. The round, medium-sized eyes are set well apart, and color depends on coat markings: if black, the eyes should be dark (black, blue, or brown); if liver, eyes are a lighter tone (gold, light brown, or blue). The high-set natural ears are wide at the base, taper to a rounded point, hang close, and are (preferably) spotted. The nose and

pigmentation are black on the black and white, brown on liver and white. The neck is long and arched.

The Dal's body is designed for speed and endurance, with sloping shoulders and a deep, moderately wide chest. The straight, strong forelegs are of heavy bone, with compact, arched feet. The topline is almost level, with a little arch over the loin, the back is powerful, ribs are well sprung but never barreled, and both tuck-up and angulation are moderate. The medium-set, tapering tail should reach the hocks. It is carried in a slight upward curve but never curls.

A proper breed coat is short, hard, dense, and fine. Color and markings are very important. There are two coat types, but both have pure white as a ground color. The spots, whether black or liver, should be clearly defined (not intermingled), running from the size of a dime to that of a half-dollar, with the smaller spots on the face, ears, head, legs, and tail. For show, a patch (sizable mass of color) is a disqualifier, as is a third color or any markings other than black or liver.

The breed stands 19 to 23 inches, and over 24 inches is a show disqualification. For approximate poundage, double the number of inches and add 5. Thus, a 21-incher will weigh about 47 pounds.

FRENCH BULLDOG (101)

The Bulldog Revolution (1850–1900) involved dog fanciers in three countries: England, France, and the United States. In the beginning, as British breeders were striving to perfect the contemporary version of the Bulldog, a few nonconformists bred away at producing a toy edition of the same breed. In the long run, both groups succeeded, and that is why the Kennel Club of England recognizes both the Bulldog and the Miniature Bulldog, although the A.K.C. does not recognize the latter. Well, the French Bulldog, who is also descended from the Bulldog, was originally developed in France, mostly from Miniature Bulldog stock.

Although the two small B breeds are about the same size, the FB looks less like the big B. Could that be the reason why the FB won the hearts of American dog lovers? Who knows? It is known, however, that American breeders are more responsible than the French for standardizing and popularizing the FB. Why, the first breed club was American (1890), and so were the first great dogs of the breed. Since 1900 the top FBs have been bred in America, and the best in other countries have come from imported American stock. The breed was designed for pet purposes and was very popular prior to the First World War. Frenchie deserves to be much more popular than he is today. Why he isn't remains one of the mysteries of the dog game.

Breed Blueprint

An easygoing little dog who tries to please and usually does. His hall-mark is a pair of bat ears, an achievement of American breeders. Not easy to find pups of this breed, but it's worth the effort.

The large head carries a flat skull, a rounded forehead, and a distinct stop. The short, broad muzzle is laid back, with the lower jaw undershot and the short nose colored black (or lighter on light colored dogs). The round dark eyes are set wide and low (far from the ears). A proper neck is thick and arched, and carries loose skin at the throat.

A Frenchie's body is short and round, with a broad, deep chest. The short, straight legs are set wide apart with compact, firm forefeet and slightly longer hind feet. Up top, there's a roach back, broad at the shoulders and tapering over the loins, and those loins should be a little higher than the shoulders. A good tuck-up, hocks well let down, and a low-set, short, tapering tail that's carried down in repose.

The coat is short, fine, and dense. Acceptable colors: brindle, fawn, white, brindle and white, and any other color that does not disqualify, as below.

Frenchies come in two classes: under and over 22 pounds. Over 28 pounds is too much. At 22 pounds, an average dog would stand 12 inches.

For show, these coat colors disqualify: solid black (without trace of brindle), black and white, black and tan, mouse or liver.

KEESHOND (43)

The Keeshond (pronounced Caze-hawnd) is one of the very few breeds named after a man—actually, his nickname, Kees. The man was Cornelis de Gyselaer, a leader of the Patriots Party in Holland about two hundred years ago. Kees owned a pet dog, and the party selected this dog as its mascot. That will not make much sense unless one recalls that the opposition, better known as the House of Orange, already had a Pug as a mascot. In the end, the Orangists won, but ever since, the Keeshond has been accepted as the national dog of Holland in most countries except Holland. The breed may be the daddy of the Pomeranian, and the reverse could also be true. There's no doubt that the beast is a member of the Spitz family and that he was developed for pet purposes.

In both Holland and Germany, the Kees achieved his greatest popularity as a barge dog, and a small barge without one aboard was regarded as lacking class. The dog also gained favor on farms as a companion and luxury item, but he never did catch on with the upper classes. As other breeds were introduced into Holland, the Kees lost ground, and by 1900 his numbers were declining at an alarming rate. When a breed revival occurred in the 1920s, it was in England, not in Holland. A decade later American fanciers introduced the breed here. The friendly beast did not make much of an impression until he started winning at the shows after the Second World War. He has enjoyed his greatest popularity in recent years. Today's best pups are from American and British stock.

Breed Blueprint

The Keeshond is highly regarded as a one-family dog, and some make modest watchdogs. The coat looks more troublesome than it really is. Grooming with a stiff brush once a week usually keeps it in shape.

The head is wedge shaped, or foxlike, with a distinct stop. The dark brown, obliquely set eyes never protrude, and the small, triangular ears are set high and carried erect. The nose, pigmentation, and muzzle are black, and scissors bite is proper. Correct expression is important, and this depends pretty much on the "spectacles," which are formed by delicate pencil lines and markings. The neck is long and arched.

This is a short-coupled body, with a deep chest and well rounded rib cage. The straight forelegs are of good bone, and the compact, catlike feet carry black nails. The topline slopes slightly downward from the withers to the rump, and tuck-up is moderate, angulation slight. The high-set, feathered tail is carried tightly curled over and close to the back.

The thick, downy undercoat is hidden by a long, straight, harsh topcoat. Hair on the legs is smooth and short, except for feathering up front and trousers in the rear; on the head and ears it's short and soft. Coat color is always a mix of gray and black, with black tips providing shading. Legs and feet are cream colored.

For show, ideal heights are 18 inches for males, 17 inches for bitches. Average weights run 30 to 35 pounds.

LHASA APSO (20)

One of several Tibetan breeds, this little dog was a resident of that land of mystery for several centuries before the Western World heard of him. He takes his name from the sacred city of Lhasa, where he is still known as Abso Seng Kye, which translates as "bark lion sentinel

dog." Apparently, Tibetans were highly suspicious of one another and of foreigners, and they kept a big watchdog (Tibetan Mastiff) chained outside their doors. And since they were heavy sleepers, they also kept a little watchdog indoors (Lhasa Apso), to provide double security. The little one is credited with having a very keen sense of hearing.

The first known members of the breed arrived in America in 1933. Known as Lhasa Terriers, they were gifts to friends from the Dalai Lama. The breed won overnight popularity, and dog fanciers couldn't wait for pups. The breed even overcame a change of name (1935) to Lhasa Apso. The A.K.C. decided that the beast was not a terrier but an apso. So what's an apso? Might be *rapso,* the Tibetan word meaning "goatlike." The Tibetan goat is also small and wears a shaggy, rather unkempt coat.

Breed Blueprint

He's friendly enough with the family but often wary of visitors. Active, bright, and fairly easy to train. His double coat requires attention several times a week. Really a toy breed, but even pups resent that thought.

Beneath all the furnishings, the narrow skull is almost flat, falling away behind the eyes, which are always dark brown and of medium size. The ears are set at eye level and back, hang close, and reach the lower jaw. The nose is black, the muzzle straight and blunt but never square. Bite is either even or a little undershot.

The body is a little on the long side, with a medium sized chest and a good rib cage. The straight forelegs carry round, catlike feet. The topline is level over strong loins and well developed hindquarters with fair angulation. The screw tail is carried up and over the back, and an end kink is okay.

The coat is long, straight, dense, and hard. Approved colors are golden sand, honey, dark grizzle, slate, smoke, parti-color, black, white, and brown. For show, there are other considerations, such as dark tips on the ears and beard, head furnishings with good fall over the eyes, good whiskers and beard, and heavily feathered ears, legs, feet, and tail.

These dogs stand 10 to 11 inches. A big one might weigh as much as 14 pounds.

POODLE (1)

The Poodle reigns as the world's most popular breed. In America, of course, this is the number-one breed by an almost ridiculous margin. In A.K.C. registrations he is two to one over the runner-up, the German Shepherd Dog. And when the total count for all recognized breeds is considered, one finds that the Poodle represents about 20 percent of all the purebred dogs in America.

One reason for his great numerical superiority, of course, is that he comes in three sizes, or varieties: Standard, Miniature, and Toy. They are counted as one breed by dog fanciers, for they are all governed by the same standard of perfection. What confuses the innocent dog lover is the fact that the A.K.C., for show purposes, lists each size as a separate breed, with the Toy in the toy group, not the nonsporting.

The Standard is the daddy of the other two; both were bred down from him. Since 1950 the Miniature has outnumbered the other two, and the Toy is now in the second spot. Considered as a separate breed, the Standard would probably occupy the thirtieth place on the popularity poll.

This big variety is believed to be more than four hundred years old, a native of either Germany or France and probably the son of the Portuguese Water Dog (see page 270). In Germany the Standard Poodle was used as a sporting dog (retriever), and in France he gained early fame as a truffle hunter and later as the darling pet of society. He is no longer so big or so husky as he was in those days, but otherwise, if he has been properly bred, he's pretty close to what he used to be.

Of the three Poodle varieties, only the Standard is used for hunting—and not often. Otherwise, the breed, whatever the size, has become a star pet and show dog, as well as an outstanding performer in Obedience trials. If he's not headed for a show career, the Continental clip is more trouble than it's worth. In a plain old kennel clip, he makes a handsome beast. (See below for details on coat styles.)

Breed Blueprint

The Poodle is noted for a high degree of intelligence, but the big problem is finding the right breeder. A good pup is sure to please, but a bum pup will be more trouble than a hoot owl on pot, and twice as nervous. Coat is a nonshedder.

The head features a moderately rounded skull with a slight stop. The very dark and oval eyes are set far apart, and the ears hang close from their set at or slightly below eye level. The muzzle is long, straight, and fine, the chin is definite enough to preclude snipiness, and the bite is scissors.

The body is squarish, close to short-coupled, with sloping shoulders and a deep, moderately wide chest. Straight, parallel forelegs, and small, oval, arched feet are typical. The topline is level over a short back, broad loins, and good angulation. The docked tail is high set, straight, and carried up.

A Poodle coat is harsh and very dense. All solid colors are okay, and varying shades of the same color are permitted for show. A particolored coat (two or three colors) at the skin is a disqualification.

Coat style is an important part of Poodle life. For the dog who serves only as a pet, a kennel clip is usual. The coat is clipped to about an inch on the body and is much shorter on the legs and face. Shaping for a little body outline is a matter of owner's choice. On the other hand, there are formal clips for the dog who pursues a show career. The three approved clips (any other coat style is a disqualification):

Puppy. Only pups (under one year) may wear this clip. The coat is left naturally long, except on the face, throat, feet, and base of the tail, which are shaved. Then there's a pompon on the end of the tail. For neatness a very slight shaping of the coat is okay. Now, a pup doesn't have to wear this coat. He can also be shown in one of the other two coats, and most senior pups are presented in one or the other.

English Saddle. Dogs one year and older must be shown in either this clip or the Continental (see below). The face, throat, feet, fore-legs, and base of the tail are shaved, leaving puffs on the forelegs and a pompon on the end of the tail. The hindquarters are left with a short blanket of hair, except for a curved, shaved area on each flank and two shaved bands on each hind leg. Elsewhere, the body wears full coat, and it may be shaped to ensure overall balance.

Continental. The only other choice for dogs one year and older. The face, throat, feet, and base of the tail are shaved, and so are the hindquarters, with pompons optional on the hips. The legs are also shaved, leaving puffs on the forelegs and bracelets on the hind legs. A pompon is left on the end of tail, and the rest of the body is left in full coat, with shaping okay.

The breed standard is specific about heights, but not weights. Here are the proper heights, per variety, and also reasonable weights:

Standard. Over 15 inches. Most are bigger. For 20 inches, figure 45 pounds.

Miniature. Over 10 inches and not more than 15 inches. At 15 inches, figure 20 pounds.

Toy. Up to 10 inches. Figure about a pound per inch.

For show, a dog is disqualified if he (she) is not within heights specified for variety.

SCHIPPERKE (56)

The breed name (pronounced skeep-er-ker, the last *r* almost silent) is Belgian, and that's very nice, for this little black beast is a native of Flanders. It's probable that he's been a friend of man for more than four hundred years, and it's suspected that he's a descendant

of an extinct herding dog that was also black but much bigger. Once a popular canal-boat and barge dog in Belgium, Holland, and Germany, he has always been popular with the working classes in those countries. The breed was in America by 1890, won A.K.C. recognition in 1904, then suffered through years of ups and downs while breeders and judges changed their minds about proper type. The formation of a national breed club brought about single-mindedness among fanciers, and the breed climbed slowly to its current modest popularity.

The beast is unusual in several respects. Sometimes he's born without a tail. Minus a tail or wearing a short docked one, he does not (in silhouette) really resemble any other canine breed. And if trained as a watchdog, he is very thrifty with his barks, sounding off only when necessary.

Breed Blueprint

He's one of the best dogs in this size range around children. Often used on vermin and infrequently on rabbits and other small game. Long-lived, very active, attention-loving, and easy to groom.

The head is foxlike, with a fairly wide skull narrowing at the eyes and looking slightly rounded in profile. The stop is medium.

The dark brown eyes are small and oval, the small, high-set ears are triangular and carried erect (drop or semierect ears are a disqualification) and the small nose is black. The muzzle tapers, and the bite is even (tight scissors but not badly overshot or undershot is permitted). The head sits on a short, full, slightly arched neck.

The body is short and cobby, with sloping shoulders, a broad, deep chest, and forelegs of medium bone, with small, round feet. The neck ruff makes the broad shoulders look high, but the topline is actually level or sloping slightly toward the rump. The back is short and strong, ribs are well sprung, and the hindquarters are a little lighter than the forequarters. A rounded rump and docked tail (no more than 1 inch long) complete the picture.

This beast's coat is abundant and slightly harsh to the touch. It's short on the ears, fronts of legs, and hocks; fairly short on the body; and longer on neck (starting behind ears), forming a ruff and cape. For finishing touches: a jabot between the forelegs and a culotte of long hairs on the thighs, the points turning inward. Ah, yes, all the above are supported by a hidden, very dense, short undercoat. The only proper coat color is solid black; any other color disqualifies a dog for show.

Dogs up to 18 pounds are permitted by the breed standard. Most dogs stand 12 to 14 inches and look very sturdy up front.

TIBETAN TERRIER (90)

This breed is not a true terrier, but he was on hand in Tibet so long ago that researchers have been unable to establish his actual age and ancestry. It is known that the TT was developed as a companion and that for several centuries his strongest admirers were the holy men of Tibet. The monks were his breeders, and pups were given away (never sold) as good-luck charms to worthy individuals. The shaggy beasts dwelled exclusively in Tibet until about 1920, when several popped up in India. A few reached England in 1932, and it took another twenty-four years for the breed to invade America. A year later (1957) the first American litter was whelped in Virginia, and the A.K.C. recognized the breed in 1973.

Some dog lovers can't tell a TT adult from an Old English Sheepdog pup. The latter carries a bobtail or no tail. And then there's

that other Tibetan, the Lhasa Apso. He's longish, whereas the TT has a boxlike build. When you get down to cases, a TT really looks only like a TT.

This breed is coming along rapidly in the popularity sweepstakes, and thus far the quality of pups has been high. Usually, newly recognized breeds attract a coterie of eager beaver know-nothing breeders, but that hasn't happened yet to the TT.

Breed Blueprint

Easy to train, reasonably quiet, and not much of a roamer. The undercoat usually sheds annually, the topcoat every three years. The dog requires weekly grooming and extra combing when he's shedding.

The medium long TT head carries a flat skull the same length as the substantial muzzle, with a definite stop. The wide-set eyes are big and round, dark hazel in color, and the V-shaped pendant ears are of medium size, a bit rounded at the tips, and hang close. The nose is always black, and a level bite is preferred.

This is a boxlike body, compact and powerful, with sloping shoulders, a deep chest reaching the elbows, straight forelegs, and big, round feet. The topline is level over sturdy hindquarters and hocks well let down. The feathered, high set tail is carried up and curled over the back, sometimes with a kink at the tip.

A double coat: the undercoat is dense and soft, while the top-coat is profuse, long, straight, and rather fine. The head carries a long fall over the eyes, plus a beard on the lower jaw. Overall, heavy furnishings, including feet. Proper coat colors are white, cream, gray, smoke, black, and golden; any of those as solids or parti-colors or tricolors.

Dogs stand from 14 to 16 inches and weigh from 15 to 30 pounds.

IV

The A.K.C. Miscellaneous Breeds

The A.K.C. rarely drops a recognized breed from its roster, but sometimes it adds a breed. The choice of the newly recognized breed is never willy-nilly, and the honor is only bestowed after it becomes apparent to all thinking dog lovers that a breed has a very good chance for permanency in America. Prior to recognition the breed must serve time as a candidate. Individual dogs of the breed are listed, rather than registered, by the A.K.C.

There are always a half dozen or more candidate breeds, and each is a member of the miscellaneous group. The first step to recognition, then, is to become listed as miscellaneous, and a breed earns that distinction through application; the breed's owners and admirers ask the A.K.C. for the rating and agree to certain A.K.C. conditions. One condition is that the fanciers maintain a very complete stud book—a record of the breeding particulars of all matings in the breed.

These days, to be considered for full A.K.C. recognition, a miscellaneous breed needs about fifteen hundred properly listed dogs, fairly evenly distributed throughout the country. That number of dogs usually assures a future for the breed in the United States.

At all-breed dog shows the miscellaneous breeds are shown in a special class. However, dogs of the breeds cannot win championship points. Thus, the candidate breeds never boast of champions.

Happily, however, dogs of the candidate breeds may be entered in Obedience trials and tracking tests and are eligible for the degrees.

Since precise population figures of the miscellaneous breeds are not released, a popularity ranking for them is not included herein. The year noted in parenthesis following the breed name indicates the date of original acceptance in the miscellaneous group.

AUSTRALIAN CATTLE DOG (1941)

Originally the candidate was called Australian Sheepdog; then the name was switched to Australian Heeler (1952) and finally to the current listing (1965). In his native land, this beast is famous for his work on the open range, where his specialty is rounding up and driving cattle by nipping at their hind legs. Thus, the designation of *heeler*. If another name change is in the works, Australian Cattle Nipper might be appropriate.

The tough, wise beast was developed down under and was breeding true by 1850. His ancestors include a mix of the big Black Bobtail (a long extinct herding dog), the Smooth Collie, the Dalmatian, and the Dingo (wild dog). The Australian Kelpie is often mentioned as another ancestor, but it's more likely that the reverse is true.

Since only a minority of dog lovers own cattle, the majority have remained unaware of this dog. His chances for popularity and recognition by the A.K.C. appear to be slim. Too bad, for he has a high degree of canine intelligence and can adapt to almost any environ-

ment. In looks he somewhat resembles a German Shepherd, although he's smaller in size.

Breed Blueprint

The Australian Cattle Dog is as kindly and lovable as a good Collie and has a trouble-free coat. But he requires plenty of exercise. His long stride really covers ground, but he can stop and turn on a dime.

The ACD head is V-shaped, with a broad, slightly domed skull and a moderate stop. The eyes are dark and oval, the high-set ears are pricked and inclined outward, and the nose is black. The tapering muzzle is of medium length, the bite scissors. And he wears a very strong neck of medium length.

The body is a little long, with 10:9 ratio of length to height. Sloping shoulders, a deep chest, straight forelegs, and round, arched feet. The topline is level over a good rib cage, broad loins, and hindquarters with moderate angulation. The tail has brush, reaches the hocks, and is carried down when the dog is at rest and never above its set when in action.

A soft, dense undercoat is topped by an outercoat of slightly harsh hairs that are fairly short except on the legs, which carry feathering. Colors are mottled blue, with or without black markings; blue head with black and tan body, plus the usual tan markings; or red speckled with darker red markings on the head.

The average dog stands 18 inches and weighs 33 pounds. Up to 20 inches is okay for a male, but that's the limit. Weight should be watched. If this beast doesn't get sufficient action, he piles on the pounds.

AUSTRALIAN KELPIE (1941)

What the previous dog is to cattle, this beast is to sheep, and he's also very famous for his work. He is known as a keeper, since he keeps a flock in order by pushing the sheep with his head and shoulders rather than by nipping. The Kelpie was breeding true by 1870. In his family tree are the Border Collie, the Dingo, and perhaps the Cattle Dog.

In America the beast's story and status are pretty much the same as the Cattle Dog's, but the Kelpie's numbers are even fewer. The two breeds are quite similar in looks, size, intelligence, and endurance. The Kelpie is just a little lighter in build.

Breed Blueprint

The keeper is not interested in cows, but he's willing to substitute small children for sheep. Easy to train, remarkable for obeying hand signals at great distances. Another exercise lover.

On the foxlike head, the skull is slightly domed and quite broad. The stop is distinct, the muzzle tapers, and the bite is a scissors. The nose color conforms to coat color, and the same goes for the dark or lighter almond-shaped eyes. The ears are set wide and carried erect and outward. The arched neck has fair length.

The Kelpie's body is a little long, 10:9, with sloping shoulders, chest fairly deep, forelegs of fine bone, and round, deep, arched feet. The topline is level over a full but not too rounded rib cage, muscular loins, and broad hindquarters with a little tuck-up and good angulation. The tail reaches to the hocks and hangs in a slight curve (at rest) and up but not above base level (in action).

The harsh coat is short, straight, and dense, and comes in a choice of colors: black, black and tan, red, red and tan, fawn, chocolate, and smoke blue.

Males stand 18 to 20 inches, and bitches 17 to 19 inches. Weights run from 25 to 30 pounds.

BEARDED COLLIE (1974)

Some four hundred years ago, when Scotsmen were trading sheep for Polish grain, the Poles ran a little short on their commodity and tossed in a few of their sheepdogs for good measure. Mixing those dogs with other, unknown ones produced the Bearded Collie, a sheep-herding specialist designed for work in rugged country. This bearded pooch could be related to the Old English Sheepdog but not to the other collies.

Although the BC became a great favorite of Scotland's working herdsmen, he did not win favor as a pet of the upper classes, and his numbers started dwindling in the British Isles as this century began. It's quite possible that the dog was saved from extinction by a Mrs. G. O. Willison, a British woman who accidentally came into possession of a bitch, launched a successful search for a male, and became a breeder. In 1923 Mrs. Willison was the world's only breeder of the BC, but these days there are scores of them on both sides of the Atlantic.

The breed is almost sure of A.K.C. recognition in the next few years and is already recognized by the C.K.C. A people lover, the shaggy beast is a fine choice for dog lovers who haven't been able to make up their minds about an Old English. The two breeds have a great deal in common.

Breed Blueprint

The BC looks bigger than he is and makes an impressive if harmless watchdog. Okay with children, needs exercise and daily grooming with a brush. Most oldsters are as playful as pups.

The head consists of a broad, flat skull, with a moderate stop and a fairly long foreface. His nose is usually black, but brown is okay on a brown or fawn coat, and the bite is even. The medium-sized ears are set wide and high and droop after a slight rise at the base. The wide-set eyes are big and bright and of a color tone to match the coat. The neck is strong and arched.

The BC body is long and lean, with sloping shoulders, a deep chest and forelegs of good bone with oval, arched feet. The topline is level over a deep and long rib cage, strong loins, and hindquarters with good angulation. The moderately long, natural tail is low set and carried low (at rest) and up but not over the back (in action).

A double coat: the undercoat is soft and furry, and the topcoat is harsh, strong, and flat. The hair is sparse on the bridge of the nose, longer on the sides, and forms a long beard. Longish hair covers the ears and tail. Proper colors (with or without white Collie markings) are slate gray, reddish fawn, black, all shades of gray, brown, and sandy.

Males stand 21 to 22 inches and bitches 20 to 21 inches. On a 21-incher, 60 pounds is about right.

BORDER COLLIE (1934)

This is one of the world's best herding breeds, and recognized as such in America since Civil War days. Time has not impaired the beast's instincts, and with very little training he becomes an outstanding herder of sheep, cattle, swine, and poultry. On the American farm, ranch, and range, he remains our very best working dog and is probably the reason why Australia's Cattle Dog and Kelpie haven't achieved real popularity on these shores.

While his family tree is uncertain, this beast may be a spin-off of the Bearded Collie and other, early sheepdogs. In his native land (Britain) he has undergone a few name changes: Shepherds Collie,

English Collie, Working Collie, and finally the current appellation. Although not related to the popular Rough Collie, the Border continues to wear the old-fashioned head once worn by the Rough, or before the long, narrow muzzle became the rage.

If the Border were to become an A.K.C. recognized breed tomorrow, the beast would be rated as popular as the Boxer. But the chances of that recognition are slim, and most dog fanciers fail to understand the reason. It's quite simple. The beast's admirers would rather not have him fall into the wrong hands: people more interested in showing than working him. As a candidate breed, the Border can compete in Obedience trials, and he does—often in brilliant fashion. That particular A.K.C. sport is okay, since it proves the dog's intelligence. Elsewhere, the Border shows his stuff in sheepdog trials, and has (in America) since 1890. Breeders have maintained high quality. Although it is not an impossible feat, one must search very hard to find a bum pup.

Breed Blueprint

The Border remains undiscovered as a popular family pet but makes one of the very best. Great with small fry and his high trainability makes him a joy to own. One dog can handle several hundred sheep or two children.

His head features a fairly broad skull and a slightly blunt muzzle with a moderate stop. The bite is level, and the nose is black. His large, dark eyes are set wide and his ears are wide at the base, taper to a rounded point, and are carried semiprick.

This dog's body is a little on the long side, with sloping shoulders, a deep chest, and strong forelegs that are just a bit shorter than the hind legs. The feet are oval and well arched. The topline is mostly level, with a slight rise over the loin, and the hindquarters are strong, with a good tuck-up and angulation. At full stride, the shorter forelegs pass between the wide-set and reaching hind legs. The low-set, natural tail is bushy and is carried low with a slight upward swirl.

A double coat, with the undercoat soft and furry and the topcoat dense, harsh, wavy or slightly curly, and of varying lengths. Proper coat colors: black, gray or blue merle with white points (neck, breast, face, feet, tail tip), or (less often) black, white, and tan.

Males stand 18 inches and bitches 17 inches, and the beasts run from 30 to 45 pounds. Those are American specifications. Dogs imported from England and Australia are often bigger and heavier.

CAVALIER KING CHARLES SPANIEL (1962)

This is the original English Toy Spaniel (see page 202) of the sixteenth and seventeenth centuries, and the beast would be nonexistent today if it were not for the persistence of one Roswell Eldridge, an American dog fancier with a mission. Thanks to old paintings, he was familiar with the original beast's looks and preferred that version to the modern, refined toy with the exaggerated head, shorter muzzle, and smaller size. And it came to pass that about fifty years ago, Eldridge decided to rescue the original from oblivion by selective breeding. A few other breeders joined him, and within two decades they had the old version of the Toy breeding true again. This revived breed is already recognized in England and Canada, and it's a sure bet for future recognition by the A.K.C.

Breed Blueprint

The CKCS in the only toy spaniel who really looks like a member of the spaniel family. Gentle, affectionate, active, and quiet for a toy.

His head looks flat on top because of the high-set ears. The stop is slight and the nose is black. The tapering muzzle runs at least 1½ inches and is never snipey, and the bite is scissors or level. The big, dark brown eyes are round and set wide, and the long, feathered ears hang close. Neck is long, arched, and clean.

The body is short-coupled, with sloping shoulders, moderately deep chest, straight forelegs, and compact feet. The topline is level over a good rib cage and muscular hindquarters with fair angulation. The lively tail is carried level with the back and can be natural or docked. If docked, two-thirds of the natural length is the minimum; it must not be too short.

The coat is long, silky, soft, and free from curl, although it can be slightly wavy. Feathering on ears, legs, feet, and tail is desirable. A quartet of proper colors: ruby, black and tan, Blenheim (rich red markings on a white ground), and tricolor (black markings on white ground with tan markings over eyes, on cheeks, inside ears, inside legs, and on underside of tail).

This little pooch stands 12 to 13 inches and weighs 13 to 18 pounds. The average dog is in the pink at 15 pounds.

IBIZAN HOUND (1968)

The breed name comes from Ibiza, one of the Balearic Islands in the Mediterranean, where the beasts have thrived since early in the sixth century. Prior to that time—perhaps for thousands of years—this hound or a similar-looking one was a popular hunting dog in Egypt. Carvings on ancient tombs verify the claim.

As a hunter, this beast has many talents: coursing, trailing, pointing, and retrieving. He has also been used as a herder and watchdog, but in modern times his chief function has been as a pet. A newcomer to America, he has only been here since 1956 and is still a stranger to most dog lovers. Although he comes in three coats—wire, long, and short—only the last is approved on this side of the Atlantic. Unless many more dog fanciers succumb to his charms, the Ibizan doesn't stand much chance of early breed recognition.

Breed Blueprint

This hound has great speed and unusual high- and broad-jumping talents. Not unhappy in the city but needs plenty of running to stay

healthy. Hates to be left alone and will accept another canine as company.

The Ibizan's narrow head carries a long, flat skull with a prominent occiput and barely defined stop. The small, oblique eyes range in color from clear amber to caramel, and the prominent prick ears are set high and wide, but centered at eye level. With those small eyes and big ears, the dog always looks alert. The muzzle is elongated and slender, so that the flesh-colored nose extends beyond the lower jaw, and the bite is scissors. The neck is long, slender, strong, and arched.

The body is reasonably short-coupled, with sloping shoulders and a deep, long chest (breastbone prominent). The straight forelegs are of fine bone with long-toed harefeet. The topline is level to a little arch over the loins and a slightly sloping rump. Hindquarters are relatively vertical, and angulation is good. The long tail is set low and carried in sickle, ring, or otter fashion, according to mood.

The coat is smooth and short: shortest on the head and ears, longest at the backs of the thighs and under the tail. Solid white, lion, and red are the preferred colors, but they are in the minority, so white-and-red and white-and-lion are okay.

Males stand 23½ to 27½ inches and bitches 22½ to 26 inches. At 26 inches, a dog will weigh about 50 pounds.

MINIATURE BULL TERRIER (1963)

This is the pocket edition of the Bull Terrier, and is his offspring, of

course. The little beast is a British product and goes back over a century, although most of the serious breeding has been since 1900. He has been a recognized breed in England since 1943 but has not achieved significant popularity there. Why the little dog hasn't caught on in the United States, where toy lovers abound, remains a mystery.

The MBT is an excellent choice for the apartment dweller who would like to own three Bull Terriers but thinks they're a little big for his two small rooms. Six of this pocket edition won't crowd him. For the lowdown on breed specifications, check the Bull Terrier. Except for size, the standards are identical.

Maximums for this little beast are 14 inches and 20 pounds. No minimums.

SPINONE ITALIANO (1934)

On these shores the beast is also known as the Italian Pointer. However, nobody is quite sure whether pointers or setters are behind him or if his big head and ears mean that a hound or two got into the act. Here's what we do know about this beast: he was developed in northern Italy and was breeding true about a hundred years ago; he is Italy's most popular hunting dog and is highly regarded by leading sportsmen in most other European countries; he performs the traditional duties of the pointing breeds, excels in swamps and deep woods, and can easily perform as a retriever if properly trained. Indeed, just in case anyone wants to start a new ancestral rumor, the Spinone's double coat sheds water like a Labrador's.

The only trouble with this breed in America is that pups are very difficult to find. Although the beasts have been here off and on since 1921, we have never had more than five breeders at any one time, and there were only two active breeders in 1974. Fortunately, there's always a fine supply of pups on the Continent.

Breed Blueprint

The Spinone doesn't have speed, but he will go all day in the field and is an extremely efficient worker. Designed for country living and makes an excellent family pet. Even temperament.

His head is big and long, with the moderately wide and slightly domed skull equal in length to the square muzzle. The stop is shallow, the nose is brown or flesh-colored, and the strong jaws carry an even

bite. The large ears are set high and wide and hang close to the cheeks, and the light brown or yellow eyes are framed by bushy eyebrows.

The squarish body has long, sloping shoulders, a deep chest, straight and strong forelegs, and round, compact, arched feet. The topline runs level over a strong back to a slight arch over the loins. The sturdy hindquarters have good angulation. The docked tail (6 to 8 inches long) is thick at the base and is carried horizontally or a little up.

The Spinone wears a weather-proof double coat. The undercoat is smooth and dense, and the topcoat is rather short (about 2 inches) and is rough, hard, and slightly wiry. Proper colors are solid white and white with yellow or light brown patches. If marked, the yellow or brown sometimes also shows as ticking.

This beast stands 20 to 26 inches, and that's a little under the European standard. At 26 inches, a dog will weigh about 60 to 65 pounds.

V

The C.K.C. Recognized Breeds

As of 1975 the Canadian Kennel Club recognized 136 breeds or varieties of purebred canines. Almost all the A.K.C. recognized breeds are included in that head count, and so are a few of the A.K.C. miscellaneous breeds. The C.K.C. does not list any candidate breeds.

In addition to the A.K.C. breeds, the C.K.C. recognizes several others. Whether they will ever make the grade with the A.K.C. depends on the whim of dog fanciers and perhaps the mood of St. Francis of Assisi. Meanwhile, the lowdown on the breeds will be found in this chapter.

Dog fanciers and canine authorities on both sides of the border are usually confused about the breeds recognized in one country and not the other. It is easy to forgive them. Until these very pages canine literature has failed to clarify the burning issue. Despite this oversight, the breeds, their admirers, and both countries have survived.

Canada's very own recognized breeds are presented herein by the group. Unless otherwise noted, the C.K.C. also recognizes all A.K.C. breeds in a given group.

Sporting Group

POINTER, GERMAN LONG-HAIRED

The popular belief that this is the German Shorthair in a long coat is far off the mark. A blend of the old-fashioned Gordon Setter and French Spaniel, the GLP dates back to about 1860 and was an extremely popular hunting dog in Germany in the early 1900s. Since that time his numbers have declined, and he hasn't staged a real comeback anywhere in the world. There can't be more than seventy-five adults in all of Canada. The breed's future there can't be predicted.

The dog has retained strong hunting instincts. He's remarkably easy to field train, and a senior pup often performs like a three-year-old veteran of another breed on upland birds.

Breed Blueprint

The GLP has plenty of endurance, but looks a little light, compared with other German Pointers. His full coat takes about eighteen

months to develop and can be counted on to shed excessively in summer. A great family dog, okay with children.

The long head consists of equal-length skull (slightly domed) and muzzle (tapering but not snipey, and a slight arch over bridge of nose). The slight stop is more of a slope, the nose is dark brown, and the bite is either level or slight scissors. The high-set ears are broad at the base, rounded at the tip, and hang close. They are of medium size and so are the round brown eyes. Neck is strong and clean.

His body is a little long and looks streamlined, with sloping shoulders, a chest deeper than elbows, and straight and tight forelegs with compact, almost round feet. The topline is level over muscular loins and a slightly sloping croup. Tuck-up and angulation are strong. The high-set tail is carried straight out or with a slight upward curve.

For show, coat is of great importance. Overall, it should be smooth, slightly wavy, and water-repellent. It runs 1 to 2 inches in length, is firm to the touch, and is never curly. It's short on the back and sides, longer on the neck, chest, and belly, and wavy and overhanging on the ears. Good feathering is found on the tail and backs of legs. Solid brown is the preferred color, but brown with a light spot on the chest is okay, and so is white with brown patches and small spots.

For either sex, 22 inches is the minimum height. The average dog stands about 25 inches and weighs about 55 pounds. This dog should be strong and muscular, but if he looks massive up front, he is really a bum. For show, the following colors disqualify a dog: black, red, solid white, and white with only small markings.

PUDELPOINTER

In the Germany of a century ago, there were more breed-conscious sportsmen per square mile than anywhere else in the world. These gentlemen weren't satisfied with the canines on hand, and they probably set a record for developing new sporting breeds. Among these new breeds was the PP, designed as a general hunting dog for any cover (field, woods, swamps, and water) and for use on any game (winged or four-footed). To achieve the PP, they crossbred the wooly Barbet Pointer with several forgotten French shorthairs and finally the English Pointer. Most authorities assume that the Standard Poodle was involved, but don't bet on it. In the good old days the German words *pudel hund* meant "water dog."

This beast remains a better-than-average, all-around hunting dog, although he's now having a pretty rough time proving it. In Canada —and everywhere else, for that matter—it would be fair to classify him as a rare breed. Sad, but true. Needs friends.

Breed Blueprint

The PP's biggest drawback is his aggressive personality. Dislikes inactivity, and will wear out both himself and owner if not restrained as a pup. Not for Abercrombie & Fitch type sportsmen.

The head is long and broad, with a balanced forehead and muzzle. That muzzle is also broad, the stop is distinct, and the bite is even or scissors. High-set, close-hanging ears are medium length and more pointed than rounded at the tips. The big, round eyes are dark amber in color, and the head sits on a medium long, strong, arched neck.

A good PP body is a bit long (10-to-9 ratio), with tight, sloping shoulders, and chest to elbows. The forelegs are straight and strong, the feet are round and compact. The topline is level over a short back, strong loins, a sloping croup, and excellent angulation. Hocks are fairly high, and the rather slim tail is docked to a length of 6 to 8 inches. It is covered with hard, dense hair but lacks feathering.

The PP wears a double coat. The undercoat is fine and wooly, while the topcoat is dense, hard, and of medium length. It fits close (flat) and beard and eyebrows are well developed. Approved colors run from dark liver to "autumn leaves," but if the individual dog carries concentrated Pointer blood, a black coat is okay. With approved colors, a little white on chest and paws is permitted.

The breed standard does not specify size. However, 24 inches and 55 to 60 pounds is about average. In other lands, minimums are 22 inches for males and 21 inches for bitches. Obviously, breeders look for dogs with good size and substance.

RETRIEVER, NOVA SCOTIA DUCK TOLLING

Now at the rare-breed level, but not as rare as the Pudelpointer. Most of the breeding, and thus most of the dogs, are found in the Maritime Provinces. For breed lowdown, see Chapter II.

TAHLTAN BEAR DOG

Another rare breed. So rare that none of the beasts have been registered in the last two decades, and nine out of ten canine authorities agree that the dog is on the verge of extinction. It is logical to assume that the C.K.C. will drop the TBD from its roster of recognized breeds, but just when remains a question. The only existing representatives of the breed are in the rugged reaches of British Columbia, and anyone interested in meeting one should hire a guide.

Of all the recognized breeds, least is known about this one. The beast may or may not be a true native of Canada, for absolutely nothing is known about his family tree. Many moons ago, at least fifty years' worth, he was still employed as a hunter by the Tahltan Indians, who favored bear and lynx steaks. To preserve his strength, the little dog was carried in a hide sack, then released when game was sighted. It was his job to circle and harry the bear or big cat, holding it at bay, and provide distraction while the hunter crept up within killing range. Usually, the TBDs worked in pairs.

The beast is an oddball. His tail is unique (see below), and he barks and yodels like a coyote. A bitch comes into season only once a year, and a litter is always small, never more than four pups.

Breed Blueprint

The TBD is a tough cookie but active, engaging, and affectionate with those he knows. Gets along well with other domestic pets. Owner has a sure subject for endless dinner conversations.

The head has a reasonably flat skull that's equal in length to the tapering, sharp muzzle. The bite can be either even or slight scissors, the nose is always black, and the stop is distinct. The dark, round eyes seem to be just right in size, but the bat ears look much too big. Those ears are set high and wide, are very broad at the base and taper almost to a point, and they are carried erect with orifices to the front. The big ears and brow give the dog a startled expression. The head sits on a strong, medium-length neck.

A TBD body is a little longish, with sloping shoulders, a deep and broad chest, straight forelegs of good bone, and small, compact, arched feet. Topline is level over a round rib cage, strong loins and quarters, and good angulation. The short, natural tail is high set and is carried level or a little up. It is a bushy tail and pretty much the same thickness from set to tip; no other canine breed wears such an appendage.

The coat is short on the face, head, and ears and runs longer (up to 1 inch) on the body. It's dense, rather coarse, and a little harsh to the touch. Proper coat colors are black or a blue gray, either as solids or with irregular white markings. Tail should be bushy.

The beast stands 12 to 16 inches and weighs a corresponding number of pounds, plus a pound or two more.

Hound Group

DREVER

A twentieth-century breed, the Drever is a native of Sweden and the offspring of Germany's Dachsbracke, whose own ancestry remains in limbo. Abroad the Drever is also called the Schwediche Dachsbracke, and everybody knows that he looks like a streamlined Basset Hound.

The Swedish word *drev* means "hunt." On a hunt the beast is used as a trailing hound. Not a speedster, but he owns an excellent nose and a voice that transforms the chase into a musical event. One of Sweden's most popular dogs, although the breed wasn't recognized

by the Swedish Kennel Club until 1949. Drevers have been in Canada since about 1960, but the beasts do not have the comic qualities of Bassets and chances for popularity remain doubtful.

Breed Blueprint

The Drever is used on big game abroad but on nothing bigger than hare and fox this side of the Atlantic. As a family pet, he rates on a par with the Beagle. Pups take their time learning and should not be pushed.

A large, long head, with the skull broadest between ears and narrowing progressively toward the well developed muzzle. The black nose sports wide nostrils, and the bridge of the nose is straight or a little arched. The upper lip overlaps the lower jaw, and the bite is scissors. The stop is slight, and the eyes dark brown with thin lids. The ears are of medium length (for a hound), a little rounded at the tips, and hang close with the forward edges against the head. The neck is long and strong, with fairly loose skin.

The body is rectangular, definitely longer than high (10:8 ratio), with sloping shoulders, a very deep chest, strong forelegs and firm, well padded feet with straight toes. The topline slopes a little to a slight arch over the rump, and tuck-up is fair, angulation good. The long tail is set as an extension of the croup. It's thick at the base and is carried either down or slightly raised but never over the back.

A Drever coat is short, close, and thick, and shortest on head, ears, and upper side of tail. All colors are okay, but there should be some visible white on the front (including neck), tip of the tail, and paws.

Males stand 12½ to 15¾ inches and bitches 12 to 15 inches. For a 14-incher, figure 28 to 30 pounds.

FINNISH SPITZ

The most recent (1974) breed added to the C.K.C. roster, the FS is regarded as the national dog of Finland, where he has been the most popular beast for several decades. An eighteenth-century spin-off of the Laika (Spitz) family, the dog was once bigger, longer, and lower to the ground. Devoted modern breeders boiled him down to his present size and type. In the process this hunting dog lost his yen for tracking game of all kinds and became a specialist on upland birds. As such, he ranges far and wide and freezes on point in the manner of a proper pointer or setter. Then just to make sure that the hunter can locate him, he emits a series of sharp barks.

As a pet and show dog, the FS has been gaining popularity in Sweden and England. He is certainly catching on in Canada, and his American admirers are growing in number. In the long run, a sure A.K.C. bet. His American future as a hunting dog is open to question; we like our bird dogs to be quiet when they're on the job.

Suomenpystykora is the breed name in Finnish, and a rough translation is "cock-eared dog." Not to be confused with *Suomenajokoira* or "drop-eared dog."

Breed Blueprint

The FS is great with the family, and prefers home to roaming. To avoid his tendency for shyness, he needs plenty of early exposure to outsiders and different social situations. He's cautious by nature but learns in a hurry.

The clean, medium-sized head carries a slightly domed skull, a distinct stop, and a narrow and tapering muzzle. The nose is black, and the bite (unspecified) is usually scissors. The pricked ears are set high and wide and are pointed, and the dark eyes are medium sized. Because of coat, the muscular neck looks short.

The square, short-coupled body carries fairly straight shoulders, a deep chest, and strong forelegs, with rounded feet. The topline is level

over a deep rib cage and a strong rear with a fair tuck-up and medium angulation. The tail curls from the base in a curve up and over the back Norwegian Elkhound style. This is a must, and a tail carried slackly is a major fault.

A proper FS wears a double coat. The undercoat is short and dense, and the topcoat is short and close on the head and on all but the backs of the legs, where it's a little longer. On the body the hair is fairly long and either erect or half-erect. On the shoulders it is stiff and coarse (especially on males), and on the tail long and thick. Coat color is clear brownish red or yellowish brown on the back, with lighter shades elsewhere. White is permissible on the feet and as a narrow stripe on the chest. Sparse, black-tipped hairs on the back are also okay. The undercoat is a much lighter shade of topcoat color.

Males stand $17\frac{1}{2}$ to $19\frac{1}{2}$ inches, bitches $15\frac{1}{2}$ to $17\frac{1}{2}$ inches. Figure about 2 pounds per inch.

Working Group

BELGIAN MALINOIS and BELGIAN TERVUREN are not recognized as separate breeds. Rather, each is accepted as a coat variety of the BELGIAN SHEEPDOG, who is recognized. For differences in coats, check the three breeds in Chapter III.

BEARDED COLLIE

Listed as a miscellaneous breed by the A.K.C. See Chapter IV.

ESKIMO

One of the oldest of the sled dogs, this beast probably originated in Siberia and then found his way to the Arctic region—and to fame as the indispensable helper of the Eskimo. After several centuries as a sled puller and pack carrier, hunter and herder, he gained new and wider fame as the favorite sled dog of early Arctic explorers.

The A.K.C. once recognized the Eskimo but dropped the breed after annual registrations declined to zero. A similar decline in numbers is now apparent in Canada, and withdrawal of C.K.C. recognition would appear to be only a matter of time. While the average beast of the breed is almost sure to be a hard worker, he does not make much of a pet. Eskimo temperament cannot usually be trusted from here to across the street, and the dog is unhappy when confined indoors.

Breed Blueprint

The Eskimo is not for the average dog lover or a family with children. Really a draft animal and designed for a cold climate; doesn't do well in temperate zones.

The head is wedge shaped, with a flat, broad skull and fair stop. The slanted eyes are small and deep-set, and the triangular ears are short, firm, carried erect, and turned forward. They are well covered with hair, inside and out. The big nose and other pigmentation are black or brown. The medium-long muzzle is strong, the jaws powerful, and the bite scissors. The neck is short, heavy, and very muscular.

The Eskimo's rugged body is a bit on the long side, with sloping shoulders, a deep, broad chest, and a well sprung rib cage. The straight, strong forelegs carry big, longish, thick-padded feet that are well protected by hair. A level topline, muscular hindquarters, and moderate angulation are characteristic. The large, bushy tail is carried up or curled over the back.

This is a double coat. The undercoat is very dense and wooly, up to 2 inches in length. The topcoat runs 3 to 6 inches. It's coarse and looks shaggy. All canine colors are okay, as solids or in combination. Mostly they're black, white, black and white, wolf or blue gray, and all shades of tan and buff.

Males stand from 22 to 25 inches and weigh from 65 to 85 pounds. Bitches are 20 to 23 inches, 50 to 70 pounds. Much bigger and heavier dogs of both sexes are not uncommon.

Good luck.

Terrier Group

SOFT-COATED WHEATEN TERRIER is not recognized. See Chapter III for the breed lowdown on this A.K.C. beast.

Toy Group

SHIH TZU is recognized by C.K.C. but not as a toy. North of the border this breed is found in the non-sporting group (see below).

CAVALIER KING CHARLES SPANIEL

Listed as a miscellaneous breed by the A.K.C. See Chapter IV.

MEXICAN HAIRLESS

The A.K.C. used to recognize this breed but has not since 1960. Canada stands alone in the world, and this does not seem to be enough to save the breed from eventual extinction. Of the hairless breeds, only the Chinese Crested Dog would appear to have a chance for much popularity.

Well, the MH has been a resident of Mexico for the past hundred years (minimum) or maybe two thousand years (maximum) and may have originated in Africa, China, Turkey, or—who knows?—in old Mexico.

The dogs are mostly, although not entirely hairless, of course; hair does not appear on the body proper. Many authorities claim that the dog's body temperature is a constant 104 degrees, but this has

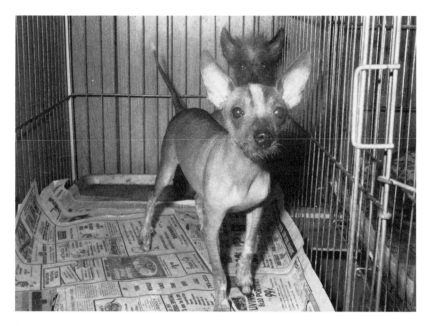

been disproved too many times; temperature really is normal (101.2 degrees). The skin does feel warm or hot to the touch, depending on one's touch.

Breed Blueprint
The MH is for the dog lover who prefers a novelty. Does not require grooming, of course, but wears a dry hide if skin cream is not applied every week or so—and more frequently in hot or dry weather. A little on the nervous side and very wary of outsiders.

The slender head carries a narrow skull with very little stop, lean cheeks, and a long pointed muzzle with scissors bite. The eyes are of medium size, do not bulge, and are hazel, yellow, or dark in color. Large, delicate bat ears (up to 4 inches in length) are set laterally and are carried obliquely erect on the alert. Neck is long, slender, and slightly arched and is carried high.

The body is reasonably short-coupled, with a deep but narrow chest and long, slender forelegs with harefeet (and black or pale nails depending on skin hue). The topline is level over a well rounded rib cage and a slightly rounded rump. There's good tuck-up and angulation. The low-set tail is long and smooth and tapers to a point, and is carried up but not over back level.

An MH is coatless, of course. His skin is smooth and soft, devoid of hair and wrinkles, and is warm or hot to the touch. Any skin color is okay, solid or mottled; bronze, gray, and pink are common. The skull is topped by a tuft of coarse hair, a bit forward of center and sometimes shadowing the brow. In addition to the tuft, a little fuzz on the lower half of the tail is okay.

Dogs stand 12 to 20 inches and weigh up to 35 pounds. Most of the beasts run to the maximum size. For show, fuzz or hair anywhere else amounts to a disqualification, and the same goes for cropped ears or a docked tail.

In canines, there seems to be a genetic link between absence of coat and dentition. Often an MH lacks premolars or a couple of incisors. Missing teeth are not rated as disqualifiers.

Non-Sporting Group

BICHON FRISE is not recognized by C.K.C. See Chapter III for this A.K.C. breed.

SHIH TZU

Considered a toy by A.K.C. See Chapter III.

VI

The Rare Breeds

Canine authorities are seldom unanimous about anything, but a majority do agree that the modern world is inhabited by more than four hundred pure breeds of dogs. A few of these experts insist that there must be at least seven hundred breeds. Since some authorities do not travel and those who do cannot cover all areas of the globe, and since rivalry does exist in high places (most seers do not communicate with their peers), it is impossible for dog lovers to arrive at a firm grand total.

Still, the minimum figure of four hundred breeds should satisfy just about everybody. These beasts represent all sizes, coats, colors, and purposes, complete coverage of man's needs in canines. Some are well known in many countries, others in a few, and still others only at home. And a great many have never set four feet in America. Not yet, that is.

Almost every year, at least one or two new breeds arrive on this side of the Atlantic. "New" to dog lovers here, that is; the breed is usually a very old one in its land of origin. There are about forty such breeds in America. Some will become a permanent part of the scene, while others will fail to attract admirers and fade away. In the beginning there are always a few dog lovers with high hopes for a new breed, but neither they nor America's canine authorities can predict the breed's staying power. While we have more canine authorities per capita than any other land, they are cautious about predicting anything beyond the fact that each will find a publisher for his or her autobiography.

When introduced here, a new breed is classified as a rare breed. Again, the breed may be abundant elsewhere in the world—and that's almost always the case. But making the grade in America is something else again. The odds are stacked against success. We already have a sufficient number of recognized breeds to satisfy the demands of the most discriminating dog lover, no matter what his personal hang-ups, his bank account, social status, vocation, and dwelling. Indeed, there are so very many recognized breeds that some have fallen on sad times and their numbers (per breed) are fewer than those belonging to the new and rare breeds.

It can be argued—and it often is in the highest echelons of the dog fancy—that America already has too many recognized (or listed) breeds and can survive without any rare ones. While this is more or less true, truth isn't everything; it is certainly not a deterrent to citizens who continue to import, herald, and support the rare breeds. Each of these enthusiasts is sure that his rare breed is the best of the lot and that finding at least a little support won't be too much of a problem. The woods are always full of people anxious to own something different and to get in on the ground floor. However, finding a small army of supporters and convincing some of them to become breeders *is* a problem.

The rare breeds identified on these pages may or may not be the best of the current lot, a decision that depends upon one's personal taste in canines. Each of these breeds meets certain criteria: residence here long enough to assure permanency, a growing population, and most important, puppy availability. And each breed, according to unidentified sources, will eventually become a recognized breed.

In no particular order, these are the selected rare breeds:

PORTUGUESE WATER DOG

This beast was in existence a long time ago, so long ago that there's little point in speculating about his ancestry. On the other hand, some authorities claim that the PWD is the daddy of the Irish Water Spaniel, and an army of researchers hold that he's the original forebear of the Poodle. One fact is known: all through the PWD's personal history, he has been the fisherman's best friend. Until modern times he served as a crew member aboard the ships of the big fishing fleets, and his duties included carrying messages (ship-to-ship and ship-to-shore), fetching fish that escaped the nets, diving for and retrieving tackle, and performing sea rescues. Among canines this dog is one of the best swimmers—and the very best deep diver. And he has also proved himself on land as a herder, guard, and hunter.

Once an extremely popular dog at all fishing ports in Europe, his numbers declined as the fleet's need for him disappeared. By 1960 there were only fifty or so in all the world and most were in Portugal. The first American litter was whelped in 1965 and the second in 1971. In 1975 the world population was about one hundred adults, and eighty of them were in the United States. Some serious breeders are in the act. They are quite aware of the very unusual situation: if the breed is to be saved from extinction, the salvation will take place in America. A national breed club has been formed, and the breed's future here looks promising.

The PWD makes an excellent family dog. He's short-coupled, medium-sized, and wears either a wavy or curly coat that runs to solid blacks and browns, with touches of white okay. It's a shaggy coat and a nonshedder. Feet are webbed. A big dog stands 22 inches

and weighs about 55 pounds. An average beast of the breed will go 20 inches and about 45 pounds. Both his close-hanging ears and his medium length tail are natural. On alert, the latter is carried up and over the back.

GREATER SWISS MOUNTAIN DOG

This is one of a quartet of Swiss breeds who (according to legend, not records) evolved from dogs left behind by the Roman legions some two thousand years ago. Of the four, the only one recognized by the A.K.C. is the Bernese Mountain Dog, who is similar to the Greater Swiss but a little smaller and covered by a longer coat. The GSMD is the largest of the Swiss breeds and was once the farmer's favorite for herding, hauling, carrying, and guarding.

The breed has been recognized by the Swiss Kennel Club since 1910, but the first beasts of the breed did not arrive in America until 1968, and the first litter was not whelped until 1970. Since that time there have been other imports and more litters, and a national breed club has been formed. As of 1975 there were about sixty adults in the country, but that figure should build in a hurry. The club has been

vigorously promoting the breed and picking up new members and owners.

Another fine family dog for those who believe good things come only in large packages. Easy-going and easy to train. This dog's powerful body is a little on the long side. He wears a double coat: a very short, dense undercoat and a topcoat that runs a little over an inch and is straight and smooth. A proper coat is mostly black or bronze, with rust red markings and a white blaze and a white patch on chest. White is also okay on the feet, tail tip, back of the neck, and as a ring around the neck. The drop ears are natural, as is the heavy tail that's usually carried down. Males stand 26 to 28 inches and weigh up to 150 pounds; bitches are somewhat less.

CANAAN DOG

An amazing example of natural selective breeding, for man had no hand in the development of this beast. His wild ancestors roamed all over North Africa, eastern Mediterranean lands, and the Orient. While roaming, they selected their own feral mates, and finally, in this century, the beasts were breeding true. The wild pure breed was nameless

until 1934, when a program was established for training guard dogs, and beasts of this abundant wild breed were successfully caught and domesticated.

The Canaan Dog has been in America since 1965. A breed club was founded that same year, and there are now more breeders here than in Israel, where the army continues to use the dog for guard and messenger work. The beast has also proved himself as a herder and seeing-eye dog. If and when listed by the A.K.C., he is sure to show his stuff in Obedience, and a big jump in popularity is almost sure to follow.

This is a medium-sized, fairly short-coupled dog, and his frame is on the light side. His fine undercoat is hidden by a topcoat of straight, harsh hairs running up to 2 inches, plus feathering. Just about any color scheme is okay, but sandy to reddish brown and black are common and big patches of white are the rule. Prick ears are typical, and the long, bushy tail curls over the back when he is on alert; both ears and tail are natural. About 22 inches and 55 pounds are average for males, and bitches go a little smaller.

PHARAOH HOUND

A member in good standing of the Greyhound family, the PH dates back to the Egypt of more than three thousand years ago and is a cousin of such A.K.C. accredited beasts as the Saluki and Basenji and that miscellaneous fellow, the Ibizan. A speedster, the Pharaoh Hound was once used to chase down gazelle. In the absence of gazelles he can be used on hare. Some of his ilk think they are terriers and will go to ground.

Despite his speed, the PH did not reach England until the early 1920s and didn't cause much excitement there until the late 1960s. The breed is now recognized by the Kennel Club. The first American arrivals (via England) were dated 1969. A national breed club was launched in 1970, and the dog has been picking up new friends every year. America now has a plentitude of adult PHs and a good distribution of serious breeders. A pretty sure bet for an A.K.C. listing in the near future.

A beast with a very curious nature and a real need for exercise. In build the PH is quite similar to the Ibizan Hound, although his prick ears seem much larger. When the dog is alert, the natural whip-like tail is carried up and curved but not over the back. The coat is

fine, short, and smooth, so grooming is never a problem. Rich tan is the preferred color, and white is okay on the tail tip, toes, chest, and (as a center line) face. The average dog stands 26 inches and weighs about 50 pounds.

TIBETAN SPANIEL

The smallest of the Tibetan breeds, this pooch is really a toy and does not display any of the spaniel-family talents. He was developed many centuries ago, apparently as a companion dog for the lonely religious men in the lamaseries, although imaginative canine historians believe he also served as a watchdog. Just about everybody agrees that the

beast must have been used as a gift dog. The Tibetans didn't have much else to give to important outsiders, so they gave dogs.

This breed is better known in England than in America. Here, the TS got off to a strange start (1967) when an innocent dog lover bought one from an importer of many breeds. The new owner thought he had bought an oddball Pekingese and was amazed when an authority told him what the little beast really was. A mate was imported from England, and the first American litter was whelped on Easter morn of 1969. The breed club was organized in 1971. The TS population continues to grow but not by leaps and bounds.

The little dog is aloof with strangers but hardly dangerous. A TS body is a little long, the face is short, the drop ears are natural, and so is the plumed tail that's carried in a curl over the back. The dog wears a longish double coat, with the topcoat soft, silky, and flat, except on the flowing cape. TS colors range from white, cream, and fawn to red, black, and tan, and tricolor. Maximum height is 11 inches, and weight is seldom over 12 pounds.

CHINESE CRESTED DOG

This is the toy of the hairless breeds. The little beasts were breeding true in China by about 1850, and any history prior to that date amounts to gossip. The breed has been extinct in China for about half a century but has held on elsewhere. Off and on the CCD has been a resident in America since 1900. These days there are no more than two hundred adults in all the world, and the only enthusiasm for the

breed is found in England and America. The breed is now making progress is both countries, but American fanciers just can't seem to get together in a cooperative effort to popularize the little hairless wonder. He is not currently recognized by any national kennel club, although the A.K.C. carried the beasts in its miscellaneous group until 1965.

Powder puffs, or pups with coats, do pop up in litters. While this may be comfortable for them, they find life a little dull, since they are not used for breeding. On normal adults skin tones are usually dark in summer, light in winter. Almost but not quite a nonshedder, for a proper beast does wear a head crest of flowing hair, as well as hair on the feet and end of the tail. Not really a hothouse dog, but he doesn't like subzero temperatures any more than a human nudist does.

A pet for adults only, the CCD is affectionate, clean, and odorless. His head sports a long brow, distinct stop, sharp muzzle, and prick ears. His longish body looks streamlined, and the slender tail is carried up and level with the back. Skin colors are blue gray, gold, and pink, either as solids or with irregular patches of white. If white is present, it usually shows spots of the ground color. Dogs stand anywhere from 8 to 15 inches, but 10 to 11 inches and the same number of pounds are preferred.

AUSTRALIAN SHEPHERD

The family tree is pretty much the same as those of the Australian Cattle Dog and Australian Kelpie, the big difference being that the breed arrived here earlier (1850s) and the refinements since then have taken place here. Of these three herding breeds, this is the only one not recognized in Australia—or here or anywhere else, for that matter. The breed club dates back to 1957, and it is far and away the most active of our rare-breed clubs. It's also the most ambitious, staging its own specialty shows and Obedience trials, all in accordance with the rules and regulations of the A.K.C. but not under its auspices. The breed club awards its own championships and Obedience degrees, a unique undertaking for the supporters of any breed. While the activities have helped promote the Australian Shepherd in both the United States and Canada, they could be the reason why the breed has not won a listing with the A.K.C.

The beast is built along the lines of his cousins, with prick ears and natural tail, and endurance to spare. His different appearance can be credited to coat. His straight, harsh topcoat runs over 1 inch in length and is colored blue merle, black, red merle, or red, all with or without tan markings. The merles seem to predominate. Whatever their color, the dogs stand 18 to 23 inches, and (for work) the smaller sizes are preferred. At 20 inches, a dog will pack about 30 pounds.

In addition to the many pure breeds who are a part of the American canine scene, there are countless combination breeds, the ones generally classified as mixed or mongrel. This land is filled to overflowing with them, and the best computer could not possibly tally the total number of these breeds running around on a given date; new and usually unexpected combinations occur every hour of every day.

Every twenty-four hours about thirty thousand mongrel pups are whelped. Most of them are the results of unplanned (by man) matings and they arrive as unwanteds. Some will be sold for a few dollars, some will become gifts, and others will be destroyed. Of those that survive to adulthood, about half will become homeless and spend their days as solo strays looking for the next meal and shelter or as members of a feral pack that lives off the land (wild animals, mostly deer) and the farmer's young livestock and poultry.

The overwhelming majority of homeless dogs are mongrels. They are found everywhere—in the city, suburbs, and country—and the very best research puts their current population in the United States at about 15 million. These vagabonds also breed, of course. Their surviving pups do not make good pets, nor do they help diminish America's problem of surplus canines. We have many more dogs than dog lovers.

Mongrels will always be with us. Even in these days of many pure breeds and the easy availability of their pups, there is always at least a minor demand for mixed-breed pups. Some intelligent people still argue that a mongrel pup must be more intelligent and healthier than a purebred. The theory is interesting, but the facts of inheritance prove that it is nonsense. And then there are dog lovers who just can't afford the price of a purebred but have their hearts set on dog ownership. Such an individual, if he can provide a proper environment for a pet, is the answer to any humane society's prayers.

Among other objectives, the humane societies are dedicated to finding good homes for the unwanted pups and dogs under their care. They place only 10 percent of their charges and must destroy (in time) the rest to make room for the steady stream of new unwanteds. This humane destruction is costly in terms of lives, to say nothing of dollars. In the average big city more than one hundred thousand canines must be put down each year. A humane society pup is always a safer bet than the gift pup offered by the surprised owner down the street. The society does not release a pup unless it is in the best of health and has preventive shots against future diseases.

All the canine breeds in the world are either pure or mixed, with a single exception:

JACK RUSSELL TERRIER

This breed is quite popular in England and is enjoying a small boom in America. It is not recognized by any of the world's kennel clubs—and chances are, it never will be. While the JRT is a definite terrier type, the type has many variations.

The breed goes back less than a century, and the responsible

breeder was one John (Jack) Russell, a British parson, sportsman, and one of the founders of the English Kennel Club. He was not really trying to develop a new breed; his intent was to breed dogs that would go to ground in a hurry. Over a period of about two decades he mated the best working terriers he could find, never mind their breeds. This was specialized breeding of a new kind: for talent rather than looks.

Apparently, Russell didn't give a hang about conformation. Nevertheless, he ended up with beasts that looked more or less like each other, and he had a hard time keeping up with the demand for pups. After his death friends and admirers gave his name to the accidental breed. The JRT never did catch on as a society favorite and was never promoted as a show dog, but the beast gained favor as a reliable vermin-killer and as a pet. And some of the breeders who carried on with the beast concentrated on certain refinements, each to his own taste. There never has been and there may never be a breed standard accepted by all admirers.

The JRT continues to prosper under an unknown number of breed standards, but the differences are not very great and are mostly confined to the ears, tail, and coat. Early versions of the Fox Terrier are supposed to be among this beast's many terrier ancestors. Today, he's about the same size as the modern FT but a little longer and with a few more pounds. Overall, the body has more heft. The muzzle is shorter, the head is broader, and the ears are prick or semiprick. The tail is usually docked to about 3 inches, but natural tails are also worn. In coat, color, and markings most of the beasts are quite like a proper Smooth Fox Terrier. Wire-haired strains exist but are in the minority.

It's a wonder that the JRT is still with us. Dog breeders are usually very opinionated people, and the fact that this beast has survived so many different opinions and still manages to resemble himself must be rated as at least a small miracle.

VII

The Truth about Breeders

At this point in history, America's domestic canine population is out of control. Short of a great catastrophe, such as the sudden ending of the world, there doesn't appear to be any way of correcting the surplus of dogs: an imbalance of 15 million (as of 1975), or that many more dogs than owners. There are many explanations for this strange state of affairs and one of the most rational comes in two parts: first, our leaders have failed to recognize the inherent danger in the growing belief that loving or owning dogs is just as patriotic as respecting apple pie, motherhood, and the flag; second, when it comes to dogs, many patriotic people are irresponsible.

These patriots include a majority of the producers or breeders of even *more* dogs. The current American production (whelping) rate is about two thousand pups per hour—every hour, every day. Tens of thousands of breeders keep the production lines rolling; most of the product is purebred, and nowadays the supply exceeds the demand. The excess does not disturb the breeders. Each one thinks that the other fellow should get out of the game. The commercial breeder feels that the hobby breeder is hurting business, the hobby breeder is convinced that the quality of purebreds will decline if the commercial and impulse breeder are not outlawed, and the impulse breeder thinks the other two should jump into the nearest lake and let him attend to his own affairs.

From any sensible dog lover's viewpoint, the commercial breeders are the biggest sinners in dogdom. Their establishments are known as puppy farms or factories and all are dedicated to supplying the pups for pet stores and other retail outlets. The *modus operandi* of the average puppy farmer is reasonably simple: he simply breeds a bitch each time she comes into season, making sure that the stud dog is of the same breed but not paying much attention to anything else. It is very important for the pups to look like their breed, since all will be sold with A.K.C. papers. Quality is unimportant. Quantity, on the other hand, is the name of the game. Pups are weaned far too early for their health and shipped in flimsy crates to distant markets. Obviously, a litter weighs less and thus is cheaper to ship at four weeks than at seven or eight.

A puppy farmer deals in several of the most popular breeds, the ones he's reasonably certain of placing. The number of pups he produces depends on his own ambition and on whether the operation is his only vocation or a sideline. Either way, he's interested in harvesting dollars, and he couldn't care less about temperament, soundness, sizes, and other specifications of a given breed's standard.

While puppy farms are found just about everywhere in America, the midwestern states are the true hotbeds of these commercial ventures. Kansas got the jump on the other states and still holds the lead. On a clear night the stars twinkle over sorghum, soybean, and sunflower fields, plus several thousand puppy farms. There and in nearby states the breeding of purebred canines is big business—so big, indeed, that some of the flourishing puppy farmers find it expedient to subcontract part-timers. And like any big business, this massive puppy production has created its own specialists. There's the broker, who operates as the middleman between the breeders and the mail-order houses, pet-store chains, and research laboratories. And then there's the stud queen (or king), a rather strange but still appropriate designation for the owner who offers the stud service of a dog at a low, low fee. Usually, she (he) owns a stud dog or so in several breeds and keeps them all as busy as bees. It's cheaper for a puppy farmer to pay the low fees than to own and feed his own team of studs.

Sometimes one of the sires is a champion of record. When he is, he's sure of being mated very frequently for as long as he can stand. A champion, of course, is often an excellent representative of his breed. But as we shall see (Chapter XI), he can also be a bum. That's show biz. This is rarely understood by the innocent puppy buyer. If the pup's pedigree reveals that the sire is a champion, the buyer is eager to believe that said sire is one of the world's great dogs. The puppy farmer may not know much, but he is aware of the sales magic inherent in the title of champion. Generally, it's the poor champion or bum who services the puppy-farm bitches, but the breeder can demand more dollars per head for the pups.

What the commercial breeder does repeatedly in a big way the impulse breeder does just once or twice in a small way. Every year a vast army of these nitwits breed their bitches for reasons that are no more valid than slim whims. Almost always the owner of the bitch knows absolutely nothing about the breeding of canines but is willing to put his trust in luck and nature. The bitch's quality and physical condition, required care, exercise, and nutrition are thoughts that never cross the breeder's mind. And chances are that he would be astonished to learn that breeding some bitches is a very big threat to their lives and that others shouldn't be bred because of something known as the laws of inheritance.

By and large, the impulse breeder is content with the knowledge that a purebred bitch who successfully mates with a purebred dog of the same breed will eventually whelp a litter of purebred pups. The reason or whim that guides his decision to breed is usually described (by him) as a because, and it seldom represents in-depth thinking. The breeder usually believes that his reason is original, but that's seldom the case. The commonest becauses:

"She has just as much right to sex as you do." This means that every bitch deserves the full life, and it's best (and healthiest) to fill it with puppies. This theory has never been proved. Indeed, the spayed bitch has no idea that she's missed anything.

"It amounts to a practical sex education for the children." Well, maybe, but most kids come away thinking that sex means getting glued together for a time and their parents were too dumb to explain why.

"I wanted to breed. Why not?" No comment.

"I wanted to keep one of Sweety's pups." And what about the other pups? Did the breeder feel an obligation to see that they were placed in proper homes? Nope. Too much trouble.

There are many more impulse breeders than commercial breeders. The former breed for the hell of it, the latter breed for profit, but both help to populate the land with inferior pups of dubious quality and high risk. The chief difference between them is not in their puppy results, but in their motivation. It relates to human quality. To be perfectly clear: the average puppy farmer is a creep, while the average impulse breeder is more likely to be an individual of social quality, such as a college or bank president, the mother of seven worthy children, or a successful professional in a crowded field. To become an impulse breeder, it is not necessary to have a college education, nor does it help. Still, most of the people in this category are well educated and regarded as good citizens and may even occupy very high office. Aside from their attitudes toward dogs, reasonably responsible people.

The category also has a subdivision known as accidental. Breeders in this category are identified by such confessions as "I told Poopsie not to leave the yard while she was in heat" and "I didn't even know she was in season, but the vet says she'll have pups in a couple of weeks." Since many of the accidental breeders are experienced parents and even more experienced grandparents, one wonders how they have lived so long in complete ignorance of a bitch's appetite for sex while in heat and the signs of the season for that appetite. There doesn't seem to be any solution to this problem, and it's a safe bet that unplanned breeding will continue to contribute several million mongrel pups per annum to the American scene. Not all those pups will survive long enough to find homes, but enough will to gladden the hearts of the dog-food companies.

The commercial and impulse breeders produce better than half the annual crop of purebred pups. Under pressure or in strict confidence, a deeply religious canine authority will admit that all those pups must be of questionable quality.

And so we come to the hobby breeders, who most closely resemble purists in the dog game. In recent times, they have been producing better than 2 million purebred pups a year, including most of the good ones. The purists are a cut above the commercial and impulse breeders, for all have honorable intentions, above-average knowledge about their favorite breed, and the belief that a planned breeding program will bring satisfactory results. They regard the breeding of canines as a science or a fine art or both, respect their own opinions and those of others who agree with them, and often get so involved that their vocations go to pot. For the hobbyist, breeding is time-consuming and mind-boggling.

Most don't mind making a few dollars, are very happy to break even, and not too distressed if they stay in the red forever. The hobby keeps them happy and healthy and often earns them at least a local reputation as a canine authority. Who could ask for anything more? Well, a minority do. They want to put money in the bank, and the only way to do this is to increase the volume of litters, cut costs, and sell pups to all comers. While all the effort doesn't increase the bankroll by much, this type of hobby breeding is flirting with loss of status and coming closer to the level of the puppy farmer. Indeed, some of the money dreamers sell their surplus pups to distant retail outlets. When "Pups from private breeders" appears in an outlet's advertisement, it usually means pups that a too ambitious hobby breeder was unable to sell to private parties. They are never that breeder's best pups.

In the dog game there's no such human animal as a professional breeder. Whether they like it or not, all of the hobby breeders are amateurs, although there's no law around to prevent any one of them from declaring themselves professionals. At the same time, dogdom's governing bodies do not approve, designate, or license any breeder as a professional. Perhaps the closest approximation of a pro would be the hobby breeder who has been active in purebreds for a minimum of twenty years, averaging from one to three litters a year. It does take about ten years to realize that one does not know everything or even very much about breeding. There's so much to learn if one is really dedicated to producing good pups with any consistency, and there's nothing like experience—about ten more years of it should do the trick. Thus, if the veteran hobby breeder is not an idiot, other purists won't sue when she calls herself a professional.

She? Yes, she, most of the time. In declining order of numbers hobby breeders are: women, wife-and-husband teams, and men. Some children of both sexes are also breeders, but they are the only ones who take the designation seriously. Officially, according to the A.K.C. and the C.K.C., the breeder of a litter of purebred pups is the owner of their dam. Thus, a baby who still doesn't know the difference between horses and dogs can be a breeder. In such cases, his parents are usually too cute for further comment here.

Hobby breeders come in both sexes and all ages, and their grand total on any day of the week is about two hundred thousand, give or take a few thousand. While that total is fairly constant, the breeders are not; turnover is continuous. The average purist stays with the hobby for about five years, just long enough for a few litters of pups and the realization that the interest is too time-consuming or costly or unrewarding in terms of success. Some of them, of course, simply decide that breeding purebreds just isn't their cup of tea.

Most of the hobbyists own fewer than four adult purebreds of the same breed, and often all are females. Thus, the purist's kennel is usually one in name only, for all of the dogs are house pets and a kennel structure does not exist. Pups are whelped in a corner of a room, and the degree of worship for the beloved bitch often dictates whether that corner is in the kitchen or living room. When the pups outgrow the corner, a spare bedroom is often converted to a temporary raising pen.

That's the small and simple end of the breeding spectrum. At the other, elaborate end are the kennels of the very wealthy purists, each housing up to 150 dogs (not counting pups) in several breeds. Half a century ago America was rather cluttered with such kennels, for social prestige was attached to owning good dogs by the numbers. To a considerable degree the wealthy did own the dog game. The crash on Wall Street, the depression, and several wars changed that picture, and today there are fewer than 300 large kennels. A couple of them are so big that they amount to kennels within kennels. In each case, the wealthy owner has imported entire kennels (dogs and people) from England and added them to his existing spread.

As in the good old days, none of the big kennels make a profit. Unlike the old days, owning a biggie is no longer a sign of social distinction. But it's more economical than raising and racing horses, and the satisfaction is enormous. To their credit, the purists at this costly level leave the deep thinking, planning, and doing to the hired hands, who often know their canines. This leaves the owners free to take the bows, as the occasion demands. Those occasions are infrequent. A few million dollars can buy many things, but not instant knowledge about the proper breeding of canines. Still, that money makes it possible for a hobbyist to hang on to his best pups or those assumed to be the best and to give away or sell the others.

Whether they are aware of the fact or not, all breeders—commercial, impulse, and hobby—practice one of three particular forms of breeding with each mating: outbreeding, inbreeding, or linebreeding. Commercial and impulse breeders usually practice the first type, and most are not even aware of the fact and wouldn't give a damn if they were. The aware purists do know about the three methods. Unfortunately, most of them also go with outbreeding, proving that they are only dimly aware. For those who care, a closer look at the three methods:

Outbreeding, or outcrossing. The mating of unrelated dogs of the same breed. This is by far the most popular type, practiced by about 85 percent of the hobbyists. It is very easy for them to believe that a good-looking bitch and a handsome stud must produce beautiful offspring. It doesn't take much more effort to convince themselves that wonderful pups will result if only one of the dogs is good-looking, for he or she will overcome the other's faults. And when both mates fail to resemble the breed standard, their pups are sure to be okay because everybody knows that two negatives make a positive.

Those beliefs are erroneous, of course. The nicest thing one can say about outbreeding is that it's fine for gamblers and others who think that potluck is better than nothing. What this type amounts to is a mix of strains (bloodlines), with little or absolutely nothing known about the dominant and recessive genes of either canine. To put it bluntly, outbreeding generally ignores the known and proven science of genetics, and conformation aside, it's not the prudent way to produce pups who are sound in body and steady in temperament.

There is another and slightly brighter side to outbreeding. While the chances are slim in an average mating, the genes can blend in just the right proportions, and a pup or two (never all) in a litter will mature into proper beasts of the breed. Those cases are infrequent, probably only occurring when the mating has been secretly blessed Above.

And then there are beasts with special magic. More about them up ahead. Here it is only necessary to know that one of them, when mated, takes a great deal of the gamble out of outbreeding. The trouble is that there aren't many of them, and most hobby breeders who have heard of them don't know where to find one.

Inbreeding. The opposite of outbreeding, this amounts to mating *closely* related beasts, or those *within* the immediate canine family. A bitch is bred to her father, brother, or son; a male is bred to his mother, sister, or daughter. About 1 percent of the hobby breeders are inbreeders, and most are either newcomers or veterans in dogs. The latter produce the best physical results.

Once again, it's the story of dominant and recessive genes. After observing a strain of dogs through several generations, the veteran breeder has been able to determine the beasts who carry and throw certain desirable qualities, the results of dominant genes. In a typical case, a litter sister and brother will obviously be carriers. When mated, the doubling of genes means that the quality of the pups can be predetermined. In any pure breed, this is the best way of producing a litter of perfect-looking pups. Always provided, of course, that the breeder knows his job. If he does, he can go right on producing generation after generation of beautiful pups, all sure to mature into close carbon copies of the perfect dog described in the breed standard. As far as conformation goes, inbreeding can be almost foolproof.

The big trouble is temperament. All the world knows that canine temperament is inherited, although what a pup starts with can be influenced by environment. Still, a shy pup cannot be completely cured, and shyness comes along with inbreeding—as early as the first generation, and certainly by the third. Sooner or later, shy pups are the sure products of inbreeding. And that's why we don't have many inbreeders. There are always purists around who think they can lick the personality problem, but none have ever succeeded.

Linebreeding. The mating of related dogs in the same family strain but never as close as the same litter or next generation. Thus, a dog and his granddaughter are a match, and so are a bitch and her grandson. As with inbreeding, dogs are mated with the idea of stamping dominant qualities. Preserving proper temperament is seldom a problem.

Linebreeding is what our breed authorities are really talking about when they discuss the science of genetics. This breeding method, or science, is the best one known, and doubters are free to consult the tomes of proof related to the miracles achieved with horses and cattle. It is the preferred method of veteran breeders, most of whom are found in the sporting and working breeds, where both conformation and temperament remain all-important. Granted that the breeder is not in a hurry, this method produces the best puppy results.

The problem is that strict linebreeding cannot continue forever. The deepest thinkers don't know the reason, but somewhere this side of infinity the repeated breeding back of a given bloodline to the same bloodline will produce a litter whose members display a common fault. It's as if some of the zest has gone out of the strain despite nature's best intentions. Perhaps a long dormant recessive gene popped into action while all those wonderful dominant genes weren't looking.

Almost always the fault that shames the strain is physical—a scissors bite, when a level one is proper, perhaps—and it can be corrected. A talented linebreeder rejects the entire litter for future breeding, waits a couple of seasons, and then mates the same brood bitch to a different stud. This time, the stud is of an unrelated strain, and the trick is to find one whose dominant genes will correct the fault. If he's wise and lucky, the breeder will find the right stud dog in an animal that has earned a reputation as a prepotent sire, a dog with a proven record for stamping his best features on all his offspring, no matter what the faults of their dam. In this case, one of the mighty sire's tested and proven gifts would be a perfect bite.

This amounts to outbreeding, but it is a necessary shot in the arm for a planned breeding program. The pups represent some of the future breeding stock that will help rejuvenate the linebred strain. Since this introduction of new blood happens so infrequently and the stud must be the right one, perhaps it would be best to call it selective outbreeding. Done the right way, it does not constitute a gamble.

The prepotent sire is a beast with special magic. He does not warrant the designation unless this is his sixth time out as a father, with five litters out of different dams, and all the pups superior to their dams. His female counterpart is a brood bitch known as founder or old pie. She has a solid rep for delivering pups of merit, and it doesn't matter much who her mate is, as long as he's not an outright bum. Quite often she appears overdone, and a breed judge might fault her for having too masculine a head or being too long in body and too wide in loin or too deep up front. Not a breed beauty, but built for motherhood, and she does not throw her slight faults if that's what they are. She'll be a bigamist, with at least three litters of quality pups to her credit. By the time she has qualified, the bitch is often too old to be bred again, and that's why active founders are rarer than prepotents.

Founders are not abundant in any of the pure breeds. Since conformation is all-important, the inbreeder does not hold on to them. The average outbreeder wouldn't buy one because he hasn't heard of them or because what he's heard hasn't made sense. The linebreeder who owns one wouldn't sell her. She's a joy—and his insurance for the future.

The saddest news about linebreeding is the number of practitioners: at most, only 15 percent of the purists are linebreeders. Although it is the best of the breeding methods for canines, it seems to be fading away. In any breed the price tag for linebred pups is usually the same as for outbred and inbred. And if the linebreeder is an honest man, he's the only breeder with a fair chance of predicting what a given pup will look like at maturity and what he'll be like if the home environment is reasonably normal. To do this, the linebreeder doesn't need a crystal ball. He knows his strain's genes.

America is not in any danger of becoming overcrowded by linebreeders and linebred canines. Outbreeding, whether planned (by commercial, impulse, and hobby breeders) or accidental (irresponsible owners) or in the raw (stray and feral dogs), is what has caused the current canine surplus. This imbalance of too many dogs and not enough owners is sure to continue and perhaps worsen unless the breeding of canines is brought under control.

There is not much hope on the horizon. To their credit, the dog game's seers did predict the coming of an era of canine over-abundance. On the other hand, the credit must be limited, for they did not enforce any preventive measures.

One obvious control would be cutting down the number of breeders. The idea is so obvious that it has gained support in several states, and groups are now at work devising ways and means. The licensing of breeders, per annum or per litter or both, is being planned. In the United States that would require new legislation at the state level (in every state) and then enforcement. Those dreams have little chance of coming true. All dog lovers assume that their right to breed dogs at will is guaranteed by the Constitution. And the concerned groups will always be outnumbered by groups that make a profit from dogs.

The breeders who are in the act for real profit are the commercial ones. The impulse set isn't concerned. Most of the hobby breeders hope to make money—and many claim that they do—but the big turnover in the ranks every few years indicates otherwise.

A consumer-education program to enlighten ambitious dog lovers about the money to be made in breeding dogs might be more effective than legislation. The truth is that very few hobby breeders make money. Those who claim a profit are either amateur puppy farmers or deluded souls who keep incomplete records on overhead, such as the hourly rate for their own time.

VIII

The Art of Buying
the Right Pup

If there's such a human animal as an average puppy buyer, he's an adult who gives at least a little thought to choice of breed and not much else. A Beagle is a Beagle, and he'll pay top price without complaint if the pup is an A.K.C. or a C.K.C. registered Beagle.

It's that kind of simple thinking and instant buying that makes it possible for hundreds of thousands of breeders to turn out and unload millions of purebred pups every year. Since an overwhelming majority of those breeders do not know what the hell they're doing, only a minority of the pups can possibly represent breed quality. The more popular the breed, the greater the numbers of careless and idiot breeders—and the greater the odds against finding a quality pup. Since he usually costs no more than a bum pup, the search for him is worth the effort.

A quality pup is, of course, a little beast who will mature into a reasonable facsimile of his breed standard in terms of conformation and temperament. If he is to be just a pet and companion, then minor breed faults are unimportant. Those same faults become very important if he is to be used for breeding or show or both. In other words, he doesn't have quality enough for either.

There's an art to finding canine quality, and it begins with this vow: "I shall not buy from a pet store, mail-order house, or a breeder who was recommended by my neighbor, minister (priest, rabbi), doctor, banker, butcher, or postman." Adhering to that vow will increase one's chances of success.

The first big step toward that goal consists of locating potential sources of pups and visiting them. Breeders, of course, with line-breeders at the top of the list. The tip-off to the breeding method will be found in the pup's pedigree.

DECODING THE PEDIGREE

Whether he's purebred or mongrel, every pup has a pedigree. It's his family tree and—in the case of a legitimate purebred—a piece of paper carrying the written record of his ancestry. If the record is to make much sense, it should go back a minimum of three generations and list the names of the pup's great-grandparents on both sides of the family.

If the breeder does not immediately wave the pedigree before the potential customer's eyes, he will usually make it available upon request. In the case of many breeders the request may have to be repeated. The first paper offered is often the pup's A.K.C. or C.K.C. individual or litter registration. It does list the names of his sire and dam, but that's a limited pedigree, just a start. For practical purposes, a pedigree really should include *their* sires and dams and *their* sires and dams; not counting the pup, it should carry the identities of fourteen other dogs. Try that one on your nearest pet-store clerk.

The most important names on the pup's pedigree are those of his sire and dam. Each of them is a warehouse of inherited genes—dominant and recessive, good and bad, strong and weak—and the pup is a blend of their gifts. The influence of a grandparent has already been diluted and that of a great-grandparent more so. Going back another generation: any one of the sixteen great-great grandparents contributes very little of the pup's make-up, less than $\frac{1}{2}$ percent. The frequently voiced boast, "This pup's great-great grandsire was the greatest dog of the breed England ever saw!" does not alter that blunt fact of life.

In the dog game, sincere breeders use a kennel or strain prefix to identify their dogs. Thus, English Setter breeders Mary and John Botch might use Mojo as a prefix, as in the case of their mighty stud dog, Mojo Hot Shot. In practice, the erstwhile prefix often wanders. Bum Shot of Mojo, for example. Or perhaps Pride of Mojo's Best Shot. In any position (fore, middle, or aft) the prefix usually reveals the breeding method. Most of the time a purebred pup's sire and dam will not carry matching prefixes. Thus, Mojo Hot Shot × Echo Valley's Sweet Sue. That's outbreeding.

Mojo Hot Shot × Mojo Crazy Mary (or Crazy Mary of Mojo) indicates inbreeding or linebreeding, and probably the latter. On a pedigree from a veteran linebreeder, the same prefix will predominate in the three generations behind the pup. In inbreeding, all the prefixes will probably be the same. When in doubt, there's no law against asking. An inbreeder will usually announce his *modus operandi*. His *modus vivendi* is not our business. Live and let live.

The only tricky thing about the prefix system relates to change. A linebred pup's pedigree will sometimes show two or three different prefixes in the preceding generations. Upon questioning, one discovers that all represent the same blood strain. This breeder (X) started with dogs of a strain bred by another breeder (Y) and originally developed by a third (Z). X is Bunko, Y is L-Grekko, and Z is Inflayshun, but each prefix represents the same strain in this case.

A breeder's choice of prefix is based on whim, and it can relate to almost anything, including the breed, land of origin, owner's surname or nickname, place of residence, and a talent for coining cute words. For a short course in current prefixes known to fame in the American dog game, consider Westfield (Bulldogs), Chinook (American Malamutes), Pugholms (guess!), Ho Dynasty (Pekingese), Kinvarra (Irish Setters), Marberlane (Kerry Blues), Vin Melca (Norwegian Elkhounds), Fezziwig (Old English), Therectory (Bloodhounds), On Time (English Cockers), Westphal (Cockers, Dachshunds), High Farms (Golden Retrievers), Eastern Waters (Chesapeakes), Foxden (Fox Terriers), Dottidale (Dalmatians), Quibbletown (Great Pyrenees), Palyn (Rough Collies), Mon Plaisir (Bernese Mountain Dogs), Shaggar (Tibetan Terriers), and Danelagh (Great Danes).

LOOKING, GUESSING, AND HOPING

Unless one has been born under a lucky star, the time spent searching for a quality pup varies with the breed. The more popular the breed, the more populous the foolish breeders and the greater the abundance of bum pups. The wise dog lover spends extra time rather than extra money when buying.

No matter how expert he is, a stranger cannot possibly look at a litter of pups and select the sure bets for the future. Nor can any honest breeder guarantee what a given pup will turn out to be. The closest assurance would come from a veteran linebreeder whose virtues include keen observation and long memory. It is possible for him to recall other litters of pups carrying the same blood, to compare the present litter with them, and to reach such a decision as "This pup is a carbon copy of the great Jumbo Mumbo at the same age of nine weeks. If this pup develops along the same lines, he'll be a winner."

Note that the statement does not include a positive assertion. This does not mean that all breeders play it safe. Many are so high on their own genius that they can point to a five- or six-week-old litter and proclaim, "Every pup will make a good pet, but these three are show quality and will win their championships with ease, so I'm asking a little more for them. How can I be so sure? Here, take a look at this pedigree. The sire is a champion, and there are four more behind him." The speaker has to be an outbreeder with a limited knowledge of genetics. Give him ten more years. If he lasts that long, maybe he'll learn.

To be almost sure of what the pup will be as an adult, eight months is a safe time for judgment. That's for all breeds except the toys. They mature in a hurry, and a linebreeder knows what he has at five months. If what he sees is top quality, he might not sell.

As long as a senior pup has had plenty of human companionship, there's no real reason for not buying him. The very thought sends chills up the spines of breeders, for they hate to hold on to pups for more than ten weeks. It is also contrary to traditional beliefs about bringing pups home at very early ages, the earlier the better. Somehow, that's supposed to help the pup, his new family, and the world. No. What it does is keep puppy prices down, so the subject will not be pursued herein.

Back to the pup and his quality: his pedigree is a tip-off. If he's linebred, the risk is smallest. And his breeder's quality usually shines through all the talk.

If satisfied, the buyer should next look in the direction of the pup's living relatives. At any breeder's kennel the dam will be present. It takes some bitches longer than others to recover from whelping and weaning, so she might not be in top shape. Still, any glaring faults—physical deviations from the breed standard—will be evident. And her temperament will be as usual. In any breed she should not be shy or threatening. Herding breeds are often (and instinctively) aloof, but that's not shyness; it's being "sensibly suspicious," as the Puli breed standard put it.

Four times out of five the sire won't be on the premises. But he's just as important to the pup's future as the dam, and that's sufficient reason for making arrangements to pay him a visit. If he doesn't look right or tries to climb a pole, then all his pups are big risks.

But if he's a prepotent sire, or the dam is a founder, you have little to worry about. Old pies have never been abundant, but more were around prior to the 1920s, when even leading breeders thought nothing of mating a bitch in her first or second season, and once a year thereafter. Today, however, once every two years is considered quite enough, and three litters in a lifetime are the limit. The brood bitch has a long life ahead of her, but she's at the end of the line as a first-rate reproductive machine and additional pups won't be good bets. Unless he has a hole in his head, a breeder does not mate her after she's seven or before she's two.

Not before she's two? How come? We're coming to that.

THE SINS OF THE FATHERS

The worst personality trait a pup can inherit is shyness. It usually comes direct from the dam or sire or both, but it can also skip a generation. Either way, the pup is in for a hard time and so is his master. The little beast will always be shy to some degree and will never be much steadier than he is on his first birthday. Up to that date, the aware owner can keep the shyness within acceptable bounds by exercising special care, protection, and patience.

If not checked, inherited shyness will turn any pup into a doggone pest and nuisance: a fear biter, instant piddler, destroyer of cherished things, or obstinate canine. Since this personality quirk normally shows up by the eighth week of a pup's career, any innocent dog lover—even one who doesn't believe in the laws of inheritance—should be able to spot the shy pup or pups in a given litter. While those are the pups to avoid, they often become best sellers. A child's heart goes out to a shy pup, a case of instant love develops, and the family takes home trouble. One of the best reasons around for not taking small fry along on the search for the dream pup.

Shyness can also be developed by environment. The preventive is plenty of human companionship during the pup's growing months. Since most are raised as house pets, company is part of the daily routine and a beast does not become skittish. When one does, it's because of mistreatment or continued noise and excitement in quantities that would also send a human baby crawling up the wall. The big danger is when the pup is raised outdoors and must amuse himself while confined by a chain or kennel fencing. The lack of sufficient company often turns the pup into what's known as a kennel-shy case —and nine times out of ten, a very noisy one.

Intelligent handling will correct induced shyness, as long as the pup spends most of his wakeful hours with a person or two. Enough. Here we are concerned with inherited sins and how to avoid them.

The incurable structural defect is hip dysplasia (HD). Any pup of any breed can carry this affliction, although it's more common in the heavy breeds (over forty pounds). Usually inherited, it is seldom apparent before four or five months—and only then when the case is very severe. HD amounts to a malfunction of the hip socket and the femur head. The socket is too shallow or otherwise abnormal, and the femur has not developed properly; the result is a misfit, and the effect on the canine depends on the degree of HD. In a severe case a dog may be lame, drag his hindquarters, or have trouble getting up from a sitting or lying position. Sometimes the pain causes him to whimper and whine. A very slight degree of HD is not apparent to the naked eye and must be discovered by X-ray.

If the HD is mild in a pup of six months, it may not worsen. On the other hand, it could—and even cripple the dog. One sure thing is that HD, if present, will not go away. Not entirely. And if it is not there at six months, it might be at a year or two years.

If at two years both the sire and dam are tested and found to be the wearers of clean, or normal, hips, the chances of their bringing HD pups into the world are considerably reduced (and marginal in some breeds).

Until recent years breeders who cared about producing sound pups had their breeding stock X-rayed by their friendly veterinarian and depended on his verdict. Canines who came up with HD were then eliminated from breeding programs. While this was a big step in the right direction—and the practicing breeders deserved all the applause—it didn't prove to be much of a deterrent for HD. Less than one percent of the breeders bothered with X-rays. Those who did had to assume that the vet knew how to position the dog for the radiograph. If he did, the radiograph would show the degree (if any) of HD. Provided, of course, that the vet knew how to interpret what he saw.

While the local vet might know more about reading hip plates for HD than any other person in town, that doesn't always mean that he knows as much as a vet in the next town—or as much as a specialist. Thus, local interpretations were sometimes misinterpretations or guesswork. Despite the best intentions, HD dogs continued to be bred.

Today the HD game that breeders play with or without their friendly vets has new rules. America's dogdom, previously blessed by the A.K.C. and C.K.C., has again been blessed, this time in the form of the Orthopedic Foundation for Animals (OFA), with headquarters in Columbia, Missouri. For a small fee a team of OFA specialists in HD will study a radiograph submitted by a vet at the request of the canine's owner. At the time the plate is made, the dog must be older than twenty-four months, and one day older is okay. In due time the OFA renders an official opinion. If all is well in the hip department, the OFA issues a Dysplasia Control Registry certificate stating that "no evidence of hip dysplasia was recognized."

OFA findings of excellent, good, or fair means that, as far as hip-joint conformation goes, a canine is okay for breeding. A borderline, mild, moderate, or severe rating means that the dog should not be used for the production of pups. By mating only OFA certified (approved) dogs, a breeder is doing his best to produce sound pups. That's true, whatever the breeding method.

Any intelligent person who has been in the dog game for more than a week has heard about HD, and all American breeders capable of reading in any language are aware of the OFA. Unfortunately, most breeders—eight out of ten—make no effort to determine the soundness of their dogs. While the number of OFA certified dogs grows every year, it still isn't easy to find pups whose sires and dams are officially clean. Finding such a litter is cause for jubilation. However, the champagne celebration should be delayed until both dam and sire have actually been observed. OFA certification is not a guarantee against shyness or a terrible temper or other faults. But at this time it is the nearest thing to a guarantee that a pup will not become an HD case. While heredity is certainly the major cause, absolute control may never be achieved, since it would mean total commitment by all breeders, and everybody knows it's silly even to dream about that.

Still—for a wild few moments—consider the unlikely time when HD dogs are no longer bred. Except for oddball cases, would HD disappear after several generations of clean hips? No. Down through the decades, wise dog lovers have warned puppy buyers about not over-feeding those pups. The warnings haven't been very effective, and most people continue to sing "a fat and healthy puppy" as if the words belonged in the national anthem. Obesity helps a canine as much as it helps a mortal—not at all. In the case of a pup, his growing bones are soft and not designed to support any unnecessary pounds. Viewed as a machine, a dog's driving power comes from his hind-quarters, and overweight often damages a pup's hip sockets or femur heads. The result is HD. This time as a gift from a foolish and some-times fat owner and not from the pup's sire or dam.

Whatever his breed and age, the canine should be kept in lean condition. Lean, rather than thin. The ribs are easy to touch. They do not protrude, nor are they buried, but can be found just under the skin. In the case of beasts that do not wear smooth coats, it's a matter of finding and judging by feel.

A PUP IN THE PINK

If he's lean and full of bounce and has the look of the devil in his eyes, the pup is probably healthy. And yet a pup boasting of those three virtues might not be in the pink of condition. Sometimes closer inspection pays off. A sick pup or one who will be sick tomorrow is not the one to purchase and take home today. He represents trouble and expense. A pup is a risk if he shows any of the following:

(1) Runny or mucus-discharging nose or eyes or both.
(2) Discolored or yellowish teeth. (Only pearly white teeth in a setting of firm, pink gums are proper.)
(3) Dirty ears. (They should be clean inside, pink and smooth.)
(4) Patchy or scaly coat; one or both would indicate a skin disease, perhaps mange or wet or dry eczema. A dirty, smelly coat indicates a breeder who doesn't care and shouldn't be trusted.
(5) Coughing, sniffling, or wheezing.

The breeder to trust is the one who is not trying to unload pups that are shy or fat or that show any of the above five symptoms. And trust him even more if he offers these proofs that he's a person who cares about the welfare of baby canines.

(1) Simple affidavit signed by veterinarian as testimony that pup has been wormed. Date should be affixed. A litter is usually wormed right after weaning, in the fifth or sixth week.

(2) Another affidavit, signed on a later date, testifying to the fact that the pup has received a *temporary* shot to protect him from the three dread diseases of distemper, hepatitis, and leptospirosis. Since the pup inherits about six weeks of immunity from his healthy dam, the shot is usually given in the sixth week. It continues his immunity for several more weeks, until he is due for his first permanent shot, at ten to twelve weeks (local veterinarian's choice). Since a sensible breeder will not release a pup under eight weeks of age, he will have the affidavits on hand and happily turn them over to the new owner. More proof that he really cares.

SEX: THINGS THAT EVEN CHILDREN SHOULD KNOW

Like their owners, canines are social animals, believe in family life, and come in two sexes. On the puppy market, bitches are often priced a little lower than males. The girls have always been harder to move than the boys, a fact that has become a strange American tradition. Seven out of every ten dog owners prefer male puppies. They are so bullheaded on the subject that even those who are willing to pay a high price for a male pup would absolutely refuse to accept his litter sister as a gift.

The great tradition has been built on two bitchy words, *messy* and *troublesome*. The only thing messy about a bitch in heat is her discharge. In season the female is guilty of dripping and is not considered an ideal guest by immaculate housekeepers. The fluid discharge will stain some rugs but will not burn holes in floors. An average season lasts three weeks, and an average bitch enters a new one about six months after she's finished the last. A minority of bitches do not follow that time table, however. Some consider every four or five months proper, and others delight their owners by ignoring sex for twelve to fifteen months. Whatever the time lapse between seasons, it is usually SOP for a bitch until she is well past her prime.

As for the troublesome part, the owner must go to the trouble of confining the bitch, indoors and out, whether or not he plans to breed. If she lives or is exercised outdoors during her heat period, the breeze will carry her scent for amazing distances (often several miles) and male dogs will regard the fragrance as welcome news. Any dog who is free and able to walk will head for the home of the bitch. Even when locked in a dark room, she will be aware of their presence and when ripe, will make every effort to escape and join them. Ripe? At some time during her heat period—and the timing is her business—a bitch finds sex irresistible. The interval lasts from four to nine days, and it is only during these days that she will accept a male and mate. Males don't understand this and will often give the mating game a try some ten days before the bitch is officially in season.

A bitch enjoys her first season, if that's the right verb, at any time between her seventh and eighteenth months. Spaying renders her barren of seasons, of course. The operation amounts to the removal of the ovaries—safe and simple surgery—and it's the sensible solution for the dog lover who would prefer a bitch if the so-called mess and trouble of the seasons could be avoided.

The right age for spaying may never be determined. The best veterinarians are not in agreement as to age, but most are positive about a spayed bitch's future: her health and longevity will not be impaired, and any changes will be minimal, unimportant, and un-noticeable. When the owner does not plan to show or breed his bitch, spaying becomes a practical matter. Her value as a pet is not di-minished, and she remains eligible for two of the three A.K.C. sports: obedience and (if she's the right breed) field trials.

While the vets may not be able to agree, dog fanciers attend one of two schools of thought about spaying: just prior to the first heat period (guesswork), or two months after the first heat period. The "priors" believe that what a bitch never knows she'll never miss, and the "afters" contend that she should be closer to full maturity before the operation. Students of both schools of thought usually agree with the dog game's veterans, who insist that bitches, whole or spayed, are always brighter and easier to train than their litter brothers. True. Of course, there are always exceptions to prove the rule.

Last words on spaying: until now, it's been the only practical way to prevent a bitch from coming into season and going wild for love and puppies. Still, many owners of bitches continue to resist the practicality on grounds that range from the logical "I might want to breed her someday" to the weird "I want her to lead a normal life" to the irrational "It would be against her religion and mine." Cost, of course, can also be a deterrent.

The good news for those who want to own a bitch and avoid both her seasons and spaying: the solution is on its way. Any year now, and certainly by the end of this decade, at least one major pet-food company will have a contraceptive dog food on the market. A canned food with a meat base, I'm told it has been tested and proved on hundreds of bitches (many breeds, various ages) without any side effects. As long as a bitch is kept on this food, she will not come into season. Removed from it, she will come into season and resume her normal heat cycle. She can be bred, and her pups will be normal.

A chemical steroid is the secret ingredient that makes this possible. It's the canine equivalent of the Pill. When the contraceptive food becomes available, it will be found on the shelves of the usual pet-food retail outlets. The price will not be sky-high—just a few pennies more than standard foods and a few pennies less than those special foods now prescribed and sold only by veterinarians. At this stage of the prediction game, it looks as if the vets will eventually have the contraceptive in liquid (add to regular diet) and concentrated (a shot per year) forms, so in time they should be more than compensated for any loss of spaying dollars. And eventually—granted that the average dog owner accepts the contraceptive idea—we should suffer less from accidental breedings and unwanted pups.

THE RIGHT BREED: CHOICE OF, RUMINATIONS ABOUT

The dog lover must provide the right conditions for the breed of his choice. To put it another way, his life style should not conflict with the basic requirements of the beast. If that's not clear, consider these thoughts:

What about the fit? It is certainly true that a big dog can be happy almost anywhere—in the city or country, in cramped quarters or a rambling mansion. The trouble with this truism is that happiness and good health are not necessarily equivalent, as illustrated by just about any Irish Wolfhound who lives in the city. To remain in tone, this giant beast really needs about two hours of hard galloping per day. He cannot get sufficient exercise walking or trotting on the end of a leash, not even when the walk lasts all day. The only way this big hound can get enough daily exercise in the city is by chasing an electric wolf 'round and 'round a big apartment.

For our purposes a big dog is a beast weighing forty pounds or more, and his breed or mix of breeds doesn't matter. At the minimum weight, a beast needs at least one hour of running per day—and never mind what the canine authority in the supermarket told you. Ask any dog.

Running does not mean walking or trotting. Since city dogs are customarily exercised on leash and big dogs can outrun most owners, only track stars should be permitted to own beasts over forty pounds. In the city, that is. Anywhere else is okay for the big beasts as long as there is room for them to run free safely and under supervision. When the dog runs on lead or rope behind a moving station wagon, watched by his idiot owner sitting on the tail gate, he does run and he is super-vised—and he is also inhaling exhaust fumes and risking a head-on collision with another car. Owners who exercise their dogs in that manner should be arrested or avoided, whichever comes first.

As surely as the sun rises again after setting, the small- and medium-sized beasts have the best chances of staying both happy and healthy in the city. And that's why so many of the toy breeds are found in America's large municipalities, although it never seems that way on rainy days. The pint-sized beasts are ideal for apartment life but not for all the families living in apartments. Little dogs are fine for adults but not for children who aren't old enough to treat them as fragile and valuable objects.

Right breed, wrong coat? Another truism about the canine world is that the overwhelming majority of the breeds shed their coats. After achieving his adult coat, the average dog sheds it once or twice a year, depending on all facets of his life, including climate, nutrition, and health. And in all the coat-wearing breeds, a minority of the lovable beasts seem to be shedding on a continuous basis. If a dog wears a long coat, he is a pain in the neck for responsible housekeepers. And if the long coat is a double one, the same housekeeper may have to be sent away for a rest.

Shedding does not happen all at once, so that the dog is fully cloaked today and nude tomorrow. It is a matter of casting off old, dead, loose hairs, and it takes anywhere from two to four weeks. All things being equal, including proper weight and diet, the coat is back in bloom in three to eight weeks, and the amount of time is unimportant to the wearer unless he happens to be a show dog. As far as dog hairs around the house and on clothes and furniture go, smooth and short coats are not noticeable, wire-haired coats are only moderately so, and double, long, and shaggy coats very much so. Applying a comb or hard brush or both to the very-much-so coats helps contain the results of shedding. This, of course, is better known as grooming, and while once a day during shedding is customary, twice a day produces better results. Since the Chinese Crested and Mexican Hairless do not have coats, they are true nonshedders. Almost nonshedders —or perhaps it would be best to call them insignificant shedders—are the Poodle, the Bedlington Terrier, and the Portuguese Water Dog. To wit: five breeds in various sizes for dog lovers who are allergic to dog hair.

For those who are not allergic or fussy, all other breeds are open for coat consideration. There are color choices in some breeds, and just one acceptable color in others. The white and light shades display dirt at its finest, and dogs wearing those coats are not good examples for children who are expected to wash behind their ears without being reminded. Nor are the beasts ideal for city grime. Brushing will help remove it, but a bath is often needed. Either way, the light coat starts acquiring new dirt immediately. Thinking dog lovers are usually aware of a light coat's problems and perhaps that's why only four of the twenty most popular breeds (Poodle, Pekingese, Chihuahua, and Siberian Husky) have a legitimate right to wear solid white coats. All four are also permitted to wear other colors, and dogs in those colors always outnumber the solid whites.

Ideally, a coat of any color receives daily grooming. A smooth coat needs a dry, clean towel or soft brush, and short to medium coats take a hard brush. It's a hard brush again for the long coat, and a comb is a good idea to keep the hair from matting. Wire coats need plucking, a gentle art that requires a little knowledge and dexterous thumb and fingers. And then, in addition to daily grooming, weekly trimming is necessary for the average beast and occasional clipping is required for some breeds. A comb and scissors are the tools for trimming, a matter of tidying the coat and (owner's choice) keeping the whiskers flush. Clipping takes clippers and amounts to fashioning or styling a coat so that it is generally recognized as proper for kennel, field, or show. In every community, there are always a few kind souls who think that their dogs should be clipped for summer and that clipping amounts to shearing. Except on the head and tip of tail and sometimes the feet, the coat is removed right down to the skin. The idea is to keep the dog cool in warm weather. It is a crazy idea, for the dog's coat is his insulation, and without it he becomes too warm.

All the above information is to emphasize the plain fact that every dog does need to be groomed and that it takes much more time to groom some breeds than others. While daily grooming is ideal, a couple of times a week is more like it in practice, and both trimming and clipping take place as the need arises. Whatever the schedule, it is always better than no schedule—or complete neglect of coat care. Dogs do not take care of their own grooming, although many will attempt to lick and wash legs, feet, and personal parts.

Many dog lovers develop a strong liking for one or more breeds long before owning dogs. In some cases the choice of breed is so compulsive that it seems to have been prenatal. There's little sense in trying to help such people select the right breed, but for everybody else the right breed will wear the right coat, a coat that fits his owner's spare time. The only time this doesn't hold true is when the owner has spare dollars and there's a grooming parlor around the corner.

Round dog, square hole. Most of the time the right breed will be sensibly chosen for size, and coat type, and color. He has the potential of becoming the dream pet and will become just that if his owner recognizes his limited intelligence—as compared with human intelligence—and acts accordingly. Some breeds can be trained to do almost anything, and the Airedale is one of them. Others can't be coaxed to do much beyond sleeping, eating, and making love, and the Papillon is a small example. As noted in earlier chapters, many breeds were developed with double duty in mind: to be both devoted companions and skilled (but unpaid) laborers. Today only a confused duck hunter would expect his Collie (right size, right coat) to retrieve bagged ducks from water. Might as well try a Dandie Dinmont (wrong size, wrong coat). A normal duck hunter would go for a breed whose historic mission in life used to be bringing home the winged bacon from water: one of the retrievers or one of several spaniels.

Properly bred, a double-duty dog inherits the special instincts that made his breed useful and famous in the long ago. In almost all breeds those instincts must be tuned up and directed. With a little help most dogs grasp the general idea of what's expected of them and then try to improve on their performance. Training is essential, and if more owners trained or conned their beasts, then dedicated breeders would agonize less. As it is, some Shetland Sheepdogs are chased by sheep, more than a few Beagles consider the rabbit a frightening brute, St. Bernards may hate even the thought of snow, and it would be dangerous to report on the average Irish Setter's work in the field.

Let's put it this way: the double-duty dog needs help.

THE RIGHT OWNER: SELF-EVALUATION

Just as a good citizen should not abandon empty beer cans on roadsides, a good dog lover should not own a dog whose personality clashes with his. Nevertheless, good lovers continue to own the wrong breeds. Let it be said and believed that the best human satisfaction related to dog ownership is achieved when the two personalities—one human, one canine—harmonize in the pleasing manner of ham on rye. When the two personalities blend most of the time, the man does not view the beast as a difficult lunkhead and the beast accepts the man as the next best thing to a world ruled by dogs.

With quality pups it's fairly easy to predict the basic future personality by consulting the breed standard and other sources devoted to that breed's desired spirit, temperament, or personality. Chances are that this promise will hold true to a great extent, provided that the pup is not beaten, forced to watch television, or otherwise mistreated. A few breed standards do not get down to the nitty gritty of ideal temperament. In those cases, the dog lover relies on what he reads, sees, and hears about the breed. Only then should he sign the check.

It is quite possible for the right breed (size, coat, special requirement) to end up as a disappointment if a personality clash evolves. The dog game calls this the right breed–wrong owner syndrome: for example, a very active terrier and a peace-loving owner, a wary Komondor and a life-of-the-party lady, or a Rhodesian Ridgeback and a chess fan. Those personalities just don't go together.

There are dog lovers who are not right for any breed. For the most part, they are highly nervous individuals who mean well and fail to notice what is happening to the dogs in their lives. The loyal canine does not understand people to any significant degree, and in the long run the strange antics of a flighty owner will have him climbing the walls. Misanthropes shouldn't own dogs, and the same goes for nihilists. Aesthetes are wrong for most breeds, but they are often right for Skye, Yorkshire, and Silky terriers. On the other hand, atheists are right for all breeds. It's as if they have to believe in something.

"VERY GOOD WITH CHILDREN"

This phrase is the most overused and often misleading sales pitch in purebred dogdom. "Very good with babies" is a variation that is used in special situations, as when a young couple can't decide whether a dog should come before or after the first baby. A pup won't care.

It is etched in stone that a beautiful and mutual empathy exists between children and canines. That's a general truth, but the person who did the etching was probably thinking of his own little darlings or else he knew a limited number of children. The plain and horrible fact is that not all children like dogs. Whether a beast of any breed should join a family with a child who is afraid of dogs or who considers dogs so inferior that they must be mistreated is a matter for the nearest friendly psychiatrist—preferably one who is a parent and has already solved the problem in his own home. Here we are concerned with the children who inspired the words etched in stone.

It's possible to argue that all purebred dogs, and thus all breeds, are very good with children. Certainly perfect examples can be found in every breed, so a given breeder can't be sued when he advertises that his purebred beasts are VGWC. But the claim always avoids the all-important question: "Is the child good for the breed?" When you look at it that way, the roster of VGWC breeds loses members.

The worst bets are toy breeds. The spunky little beasts adore humans in any size, but they don't know their own strength and that it doesn't amount to much. Let's face it, these pint-sized relics were not designed for rough-and-tumble activity even at the level of child's play. An innocent hug from a tiny tot can fracture a pup's rib. As the object of an unintentional boot or hurt, an adult toy might defend his honor with a brief display of snip and snap. In the words of British canine authority Celia Devon-Shrumptie: Toy doggies are only good for adults, and the reverse is also true. She was a legend in her own time but not since.

Better than the toys as VGWC breeds, but only by a shade, are the small beasts in the other five groups. These breeds (up to sixteen inches) are more durable than the toys, but they also object to inconsiderate treatment and will defend their honor. Those worth thinking about twice will be found among the terriers; they're active, spirited, and fun-loving but also quick to change moods, and professionals at making unnecessary noise. As for the Beagle—long considered the ideal gift for children (availability, close coat, low price tag)—the breed has really suffered from too much popularity and quality ones aren't easy to find.

Size impresses children as well as their parents, and that's the major reason why the giant breeds are considered VGWC. The Irish Wolfhound, Scottish Deerhound, Great Pyrenees, Old English, Komondor, Bullmastiff, St. Bernard, and Newfoundland are all usually nice to children and are seldom intimidated by young extroverts. Enthusiastic hugging will not hurt one of these beasts, and it is quite difficult to push one around or to step on and damage him. None of the giants, of course, will bring happiness to economy-minded dog lovers. And while they are better bets than the toy and small breeds, VGWC only applies to children who are over ten and in good health. When a giant beast on leash decides that he wants to go in the opposite direction, it takes a very strong child to convince him that he's wrong.

Give or take a few pounds, the best bets among the VGWC breeds are in the thirty-five to seventy pound range. Quality pups in most of the breeds are not difficult to find, although caution is always a good idea with two of the most popular breeds: German Shepherd Dog and Doberman Pinscher. The foolish breeders far outnumber those who know what they're doing, and good-looking pups are too often short on temperament. In both breeds, bum breeding produces viciousness as often as shyness and fear biting. Either way, the beast cannot be trusted with a child's playmate or strangers. Even when your child and the breed are good for one another, the breed might not be so good for somebody else's child.

The very best bet as a VGWC breed? Border Collie. Hasn't changed much over the years, and it's rather difficult to find a bum one. Next best: one of the sporting breeds.

IX

Health and Happiness:
Complete Puppy Maintenance

The average healthy pup is seeing, hearing, and smelling in fine style by the end of his seventh week. He's beginning to think a little, too. His brain is adult in size, but it's quite empty. The thoughts that he stores in that warehouse during the next two months won't make or break him as a worthwhile pet. On the other hand, he'll come closer to realizing his true potential as a companion if his earliest thoughts are good ones.

The pup is ready for his new home at eight weeks, and if he's a few weeks older, it won't matter. He can handle the adjustment to the different environment as long as he's in good health, has been wormed, and has received that temporary shot. The youngster has a pretty good chance of remaining healthy for the rest of his life if his owner keeps a medical record up to date and follows the vet's advice. It is more costly than the advice offered by the man in the pet store or the dog lover down the street, but the results are always better. The most frequent visits to the vet will be made in behalf of these canine problems:

1) *Worms.* It's a rare pup who doesn't have at least round-worms in his belly, and a single worming rarely does the trick. On the pup's first visit to the vet, pack a couple of his fresh stools in a jar and take them along for an educated appraisal. If worms are present, the vet will be able to deter-

mine the type (round, hook, whip, tape?) and prescribe proper treatment. Worming is a very simple matter, but the trick lies in identifying the type of worms to be abolished.

Pups should be checked out at least every two months, although four or five months is more usual in practice—if at all. Adults who tread on solid ground should be checked every six months, but most owners gamble on once a year.

2) *Permanent shot(s)*. The temporary shot usually protects the pup through his twelfth week, but it's safest to get him to the vet prior to the last day of that week. Some vets prefer the one-shot method, and some go for two (four weeks apart). No matter what the method, the vaccine protects the pup against distemper, hepatitis, and leptospirosis.

The word *permanent* is a little misleading, since the shot is not good for the pup's lifetime. It grants protection for one year, and then it must be renewed. This renewal is called a booster shot. Since most dogs are lousy at remembering dates, responsible owners mark their calendars.

3) *Rabies*. This is the "mad dog" disease transmitted via the bite (saliva) of a rabid fox, dog, bat, rabbit, mouse, rat, squirrel, skunk, raccoon, opposum, muskrat, wildcat, or any other warm-blooded animal. It follows that a pup's chances of being bitten by a rabid animal are greater in the wild than in the city, but that doesn't mean that city pups and dogs are home free. Some states now require the vaccination against rabies, and more will in the near future.

A pup is ready for his first shot at six months. It is good for one, two, or three years, depending on the type of vaccine used. Another "permanent" shot that isn't permanent.

4) *Heartworm*. The mosquito (any species) transports this dangerous parasite from beast to beast, and all unprotected dogs are in trouble wherever and whenever the mosquito is in season. According to the experts, the insect sucks blood from a dog with heartworms and flies away to find another dog to bite. During the biting, the mosquito injects some of the first dog's blood with larvae into the new victim's blood stream. The larvae travel to the heart, lungs, large blood vessels, mature and produce more larvae, and make big trouble for the host beast.

Any dog owner who hasn't discussed heartworm with his vet should correct the oversight before the next mosquito flies into view. Loss of stamina, inactivity, labored breathing, chronic coughing, quick fatigue during play, diarrhea, and violent itching are among the many symptoms. On the other hand, a dog with heartworms can appear extremely healthy until the very day he goes into a rapid, noticeable decline.

While heartworm can be cured by extensive medication and/or surgery, it's easier, less expensive, and healthier (for the dog) to avoid the parasite in the first place. Prior to the mosquito season, the vet runs a simple blood test to determine if the pup or adult is free of heartworm. If free, the beast can be kept that way by mixing a prescribed prophylactic (tablet or liquid) into his daily ration. This practice continues until cold weather kills off the mosquito population.

FEEDING THE PUP

In all but the earlier-maturing toy breeds, a pup does his maximum growing and eating during his first ten months. The growth rate continues at a slower speed for two more months, until the pup is no longer a pup. At about one year, growth comes to a halt. The beast will not become any larger, although in the medium and big breeds his overall development will continue for another six to twelve months or even longer. Depending on the breed, certain subtle and desired changes will take place in the second year: For example, the head may become broader, the ribs may acquire more spring, and the ears may come down and look less like wings. Despite this development, the dog will need no more to eat than he did at one year—and less than he was devouring at nine or ten months—if he's healthy and close to normal canine temperature of 101.2 degrees. While we are on the subject, it's safer and simpler to use a rectal thermometer, and the dog must have been resting for at least twenty minutes if the reading is to mean anything. Take a reading right after he's been running and it will seem as if he's burning with fever.

In most breeds healthy beasts have a very low regard for table manners, and they don't play around with their food; they wolf down the meal as if there weren't a tomorrow, and then look around for more. The number of daily meals required by a pup is not an exact science and depends pretty much on one's faith in the advice offered by the pup's breeder, or veterinarian, the latest breed book, or the researchers employed by major pet-food companies. The advice varies, but that's no reason for despair. Through trial and error old hands in the dog game have devised this daily schedule, and it does satisfy. From weaning to 10 weeks, 4 meals; from 10 to 20 weeks, 3 meals; from 20 to 40 weeks, 2 meals; and from 40 to 52 weeks, 1 or 2 meals. After 40 weeks, 1 meal per day is really okay, and an owner who feels guilty and feeds in the afternoon can always slip the pup a dog biscuit in the morning. Two meals per day after 40 weeks is best for the beast who tends to either overweight or underweight. One of the meals is used as a control. By subtracting from it or adding to it, the owner can keep the beast in lean condition. After 1 year, the beast gets along on 1 meal per day.

To keep a pup from complaining, his provider should con him into accepting one meal less per day. He eliminates a given meal over a period of several days by gradually reducing its size and adding the difference to the meals that remain. All during the growth period, a pup will require more food than he will as an adult, and he usually peaks at 9 or 10 months.

NUTRITION: HOW MUCH OF WHAT

About 10 percent of America's dog owners make and mix all the food devoured by their beasts. They do a good job of this—and more power to them. Quite often the beasts are excellent examples of walking nutrition and are in far better shape than their owners. As for the other 90 percent, they raise their beasts on commercial foods, and among them the traditional best sellers are known as dry (carton or bag) and wet (can). If all the American brands of dog food (national, regional, fairly local) were gathered under one roof, more than ten thousand types would be shielded from rain, sleet, or snow.

In the beginning it is usually safe and always convenient to continue the new pup on his accustomed diet, since a responsible breeder says good-bye to a pup by sending him off with a couple of days' worth of rations. All the new owner has to do is find a source of supply and follow instructions. If and when a change in brands is desired, the pup is most likely to accept it if the switch is gradual, no more than 20 percent per day. This translates as 20 percent new brand and 80 percent old on the first day, 40 percent new and 60 percent old on the second day, 60 percent new and 40 percent old on the third day, and so forth. If the pup cannot take this diet switch in stride, he will notify the owner via loose stools or diarrhea, and the rate of changeover should be slowed. If the poor reaction persists, the provider should forget this particular new brand and seek another.

The great variety of brands means that one has a choice of a number at the retail level, but sometimes the selection is so great that confusion results. There are good brands and poor brands, and price really has nothing to do with quality. The only thing that matters is the nutritional value of the dog food. Lavish advertising, a "complete and balanced" claim, and attractive appearance and smell do not necessarily mean that a given brand provides a dog with what he needs. It's the label that counts, for it reveals whether the contents meet the canine's basic requirements.

Let's consider what a dog really needs to stay healthy and wise: protein, fat, carbohydrates, certain vitamins and minerals, and water. The guaranteed analysis on the label gives the percentages of protein, fat, and moisture (water). It's reasonable to assume that all brands supply sufficient carbohydrates and the required vitamins and minerals.

About protein: the average dog needs at least 20 percent in his daily ration, but a pup needs a little more during his first six months —at least 25 percent but no more than 27 percent. As for fat: 6 percent is the minimum for pet dogs. That leaves water. It should be available (room temperature) at all times, and dry food (kibble) is soaked in it before serving. Canned food runs about 75 percent moisture and proves that water can be expensive. Take out the water and the protein count of what's left is about triple the percentage on the label.

In addition to the analysis, an honest label also lists the ingredients—and by law the order of listing is by quantity. To be perfectly clear, there's more of the first ingredient on the list than of the second, more of the second than the third, and more of the third than any of those succeeding—including some that dogs don't need and wouldn't miss. A brand that does not include meat or meat by-products or bone meal as one of the first three ingredients just isn't worth the price.

They are all sources of animal protein and of more value to the canine than vegetable protein. A first-rate dog food meets the animal-protein qualification and also includes at least one cereal grain among the first six ingredients.

Most of the dog game's veterans put their money on dry food and mix in a little meat—canned, raw, or cooked. This brings the protein count up to the right level for pups. There are also high-protein dry foods designed specifically for pups.

Any meat is okay for canines, but pork should be cooked. Fat and vitamins are lost when meat is cooked. Any sensible pooch will devour roast beef, but fresh, raw ground beef is more nutritious for him. On the other hand, fish should always be cooked before serving. It's a great source of protein. However, when it's served raw, it's also a source of dangerous fluke disease.

Beyond finding and supplying the right food, the only important diet problem concerns quantity. If the pup is thriving on X amount of food per day this week, he will require more than X per day next week, still more the following week, and so forth until sometime in his ninth month.

Since every pup in every litter in every breed grows at his own rate—and it is impossible to predetermine that rate—the increase in weekly food allotment is pretty much a matter of commonsense, trial, and error. Most veteran fanciers start by increasing the daily quantity by 5 to 10 percent each week and keeping a weekly record of the pup's weight. Since the object is to keep the pup lean as he grows, it doesn't take long to figure out the correct percentage of food increase for new puppy pounds. Once established, this increase becomes more or less a rule of thumb; it jumps a little if the pup looks skinny rather than lean and is reduced a little if the pup is obviously round and fat.

If the chef has to be wrong, it is always better for the pup's future to err on the side of a little underfeeding. It is easier to *over*feed a pup, of course, and a majority of innocent owners are guilty of that crime. Since some owners don't know how to weigh a pup, let's look at how this is done in most places: Julie, nude or fully dressed, steps on the bathroom scales and notes that she weighs 120 pounds. Since she has a faulty memory, Julie writes this figure on a piece of paper. Now she picks up her beloved puppy, steps on the scales, and finds that the reading is 300 pounds. Julie will find it as hard to believe as anyone else, but simple subtraction proves that the puppy must weigh 180 pounds. Julie has a problem—and you will, too, if your bathroom scales are inaccurate.

Weighing the pup every few days rather than weekly is considered very important by the dog game's deepest thinkers, a minority group of scientific whizzes who relate calories per pound of food to total pounds per pup at a given age. According to this concept, a pup that is 20 pounds at 8 weeks needs about twice as many calories per day—double the amount of the same food—as another pup who attains 20 pounds at 18 weeks. Easy-to-comprehend charts are available, and there's nothing wrong with the system. The calorie count is not fixed, and it is increased or decreased with an eye to the pup's physical condition. The big trick is determining the calories in the food the pup is consuming. Most dog food manufacturers don't worry about calories, and those that do, fail to announce the count. Still, the best brands do carry a nutrient analysis on the label, and from it an informed person can figure the proper number of calories per pound. Dieticians and vets have the talent, but not all doctors.

Whatever the feeding method, the day does come when the youthful canine reaches the status of senior pup. He has reached the right weight for his body, he's burning up less energy than he did in previous months, and he no longer requires as much food every day as he did last week. If he is very intelligent, the beast will inform his master that there is too much food in the pan—and he does it by not polishing off all the goodies. The amount should be subtracted from the next day's ration. Unfortunately, most beasts have only average intelligence, and they continue to eat all that is offered. Naturally, they start piling on the fat. To correct, subtract a small amount of food every three or four days until the beast is lean.

When his weight stabilizes, the amount he's eating of a particular brand of dog food is the amount he should consume every day for the rest of his life. All his meals should be served at the same time every day or as close to that time as convenient. If a permanent change in the dinner schedule is necessary, as from morning to late afternoon, it's easier on the dog if the switch comes gradually. Feed one hour later per day until the desired dinner time has been reached.

Many a Basset Hound is too fat because his owner couldn't resist those sad eyes and felt guilty about the amount of the daily ration. The beloved pet was healthy and stayed at the right forty pounds, but his owner increased the amount, anyway. It so happens that there's a right way to do this, and it amounts to adding cooked vegetables to the dog's daily meal. This addition will add unimportant amounts of minerals and vitamins to the beast's diet, and it will fill him up without contributing to his weight. The meal will look bigger and both fool and satisfy the dog. Most cooked vegetables are okay, but avoid the cabbage family and go easy on the starches.

HOUSEBREAKING JUNIOR JUMPUP

Adult beasts that have lived a year or more in an outdoor kennel often prove to be housebroken when they start to live indoors. They might chew and damage the legs of antique chairs, rip the stuffing from pillows, and devour handy books, but they do not foul any room in the home. It is widely believed that the canine is such a clean animal by nature that he will not of his own free will desecrate his own sleeping quarters. This is true of most pooches, although some don't mind relieving themselves in the *family's* sleeping quarters.

At any rate, it is safe to assume that the canine babies will not housebreak themselves and will all require a little training. The secret of housebreaking is getting the pup to the right place at the critical times. The younger the pup, the greater the number of critical times. The pup is rushed outdoors to terra firma (or placed on paper or in a litter box) the first thing in the morning and the last thing at night. In between, he is rushed outdoors whenever he awakens from a nap, after every play session, just before and right after he eats or drinks, and whenever he gets a funny look in his eyes or keeps circling the room or sniffing at a certain spot. Once outdoors (rain or shine) he is kept there until he does his duty. If he is congratulated after each little success, it could advance the training and it always helps the relationship. If he is directed to one spot every time or most times, simple logic dictates that he will always conduct his business there when he is older and not supervised. Unfortunately, that's human logic. It has worked with some dogs, but very infrequently.

The pup that is rushed outdoors at the critical times will still have a few accidents, but the number will decrease day by day. Scolding or punishing when accidents occur won't help if the pup is under twelve weeks, and such actions often induce more accidents.

It's easy to confuse a pup. The chance of an accident during the long night is diminished if the pup is not permitted to drink for several hours preceding his bedtime.

Granted that his trainer is diligent enough to attend to his critical times before answering the phone or reading another poem, almost any pup can be housebroken within a week and often in four days. While his critical times will continue, their frequency will decrease, and he'll try to get the message across when he knows he has to go and you don't think so. Whining or barking, standing by the door, and pacing back and forth are the usual canine signs that a critical moment is at hand.

At four months most pups can refrain from bad manners for two hours during the day, but they must still get outdoors after every meal, as well as very early and very late. Once housebroken, a beast remains that way as long as he's healthy—at home, that is. There's no way of predicting his conduct in somebody else's home. He's not always the perfect houseguest.

There are oddballs, of course, and a current one is a Miniature Poodle named Junior Jumpup. He went to his new home at nine weeks and was housebroken within a week, right on schedule. And without a single accident, if you can believe lawyers. The pooch's mistress and master are lawyers and married to each other and both of them argue that JJ was a perfect beast during his first five years. Then the beloved little beast started jumping up onto the bed in the master bedroom and piddling on the spread. The lawyers resented this and tried to break JJ of his new and nasty habit, but the poodle was adamant. They hired the services of a professional dog trainer, who tried hard, but JJ wouldn't cooperate, although he did learn to walk on his hind legs and bark something that sounded like "How do you do?" Next, the desperate owners packed him off to a canine psychiatrist, who guaranteed to cure JJ of wetting his master's bed. Three weeks and several hundred dollars later, JJ came home. Since then he has never fouled the master bed, but no other bed—or chair or sofa—in the house has been safe.

Nightbreaking

This is a subdivision of housebreaking at the noise level. A night-broken pup does not howl or growl or bark or whine or scratch on doors and floors during the late and early dark hours. The first few nights in his new home a pup is sure to feel insecure when he's left alone, and he'll dedicate himself to one or more of these above antics, none very helpful to anybody trying to sleep. The pup sleeps during the following daylight hours, as if gathering strength for the next night. This deviltry lasts for several nights and in many cases for weeks. Some noisy puppies have started happy marriages on the road to Reno: "I'm going to shoot that damn pup!" he or she says at 3:00 A.M. "Over my dead body!" the spouse replies.

Nightbreaking the new pup amounts to removing his feelings of insecurity, confusion, loneliness, compulsion to raise hell, or whatever. Traditional methods are widespread but not noteworthy. It almost seems as if the great authorities have never lived in a house with a pup, for they expound at great length about keeping the light on, keeping the radio on and tuned to an all-night station, and placing a loudly ticking clock next to the pup's bed. If any of these methods has ever seemed to work, it was because the pup was kept in a sound-proof room. The baby canine doesn't know much, if anything, but he reacts like somebody who has been deserted by his nearest and dearest friends when he's left alone at night. The easy solution rests in not deserting him. Bring him right into the bedroom and park him in a designated area.

There are many dog beds on the market, but the most practical one of all is not promoted as a bed. It is the folding, portable, lightweight wire bench crate, one of the dog fancy's most useful inventions. The crate can be set up wherever desired in the bedroom as long as it is free from drafts. Making a plywood floor for the crate is a good idea, and fitting it out with bedding is even better for the dog's sleeping comfort. Just about every pet store sells canine mattresses in various sizes, shapes, and colors. The very finest idea in canine bedding is not manufactured but must be made: a pillow of mattress ticking stuffed with cedar shavings (not chips). The cedar scent keeps the dog smelling clean and also keeps him free of fleas.

Just prior to bedtime the pup goes outdoors for late evening relief. Once back in the house, he is placed in his crate and the door is shut. Chances are, he won't make any great noise or foul his nest, provided that the humans in the nearby bed do not snore so loudly that they frighten him. He will get used to snores but not the wild screams of somebody having serious nightmares. First thing in the morning, or when he is fully awake and stirring, he should go outdoors—the longer the delay, the more the likelihood that he will dirty his bed.

A crate can be used for more than nightbreaking. Once the pup becomes accustomed to it, he'll use it for his naps and retire to it whenever he wearies of human antics. As time goes on and as the needs arise, it can serve as a hospital ward, a convenient place to park the dog at party time, and a home-away-from-home in a hotel or motel room or abode of a friend. A crate is also the ideal place for a dog when he travels in a car. He's not a hazard there, and he's safe from such highway perils as bashing his head or breaking his neck when it's sudden-stop time.

Crate size depends on adult breed size. Dog fanciers probably use crates more than most dog owners, since it's the safest and most convenient way to transport beloved beasts by the numbers. Pooches are less likely to be damaged if they cannot stand. A dog should be able to rest and sit in comfort, but standing should be inconvenient for him. If it helps any—and it will if the dog is a Labrador Retriever or about that size—a proper bench crate for that breed is 20 inches wide, 24 inches long, and 26 inches high. A couple of inches under those dimensions would be absolute minimums for a Lab.

If well ventilated, metal and wooden crates are also okay. But they are more expensive and heavier; they cannot be folded and so take up more storage room.

ORIENTATION: COLLAR AND LEASH

A collar and a leash are indispensable items in a pup's life. He really should wear the former and become accustomed to the latter as soon as he's housebroken. Without the collar, he stands a fair chance of becoming lost or stolen. If he won't accept a leash and is permitted to run free, the pup is gambling with his life. Dog and man are the best of friends, but that's on a one-to-one basis. Dog and civilization are something else. That's dog against everything.

And then there's the gentle art of training the puppy to obey a few simple commands. The collar and leash are the best training tools. If he's unhappy with them or fights them, then his training becomes more difficult and advances, if at all, at a snail's pace. The trick is to fool him into accepting both the collar and the leash, one at a time and in easy stages.

Collars come in a wide range of materials, widths, weights, colors, and styles. Most are impractical and a waste of money, but they do sell like hotcakes and prove that sales appeal is more important than performance. Of the few practical collars, the best all-around one is known as a slip collar, which amounts to a length of some material with an open metal ring attached at each end. The cheapest and most useful of the slips is made of soft, washable nylon cord. When the cord is pushed through either ring, a loop (collar) results, and it fits around the pup's neck. The right size collar will just fit over the dog's head and hang a little loose on the neck. The leash is attached to the ring at the end of the loop. Thus, a tug on the leash will tighten the collar. That fact makes the slip an ideal training collar, too.

If color is important to a dog lover, the cord comes in a wide variety, but color is the least of its virtues. It is lightweight, so it won't damage the coat, and durable, so it will hold the strongest dog. If the collar catches on anything, a dog can pull it over his head or chew through it. The only drawback is a minor one: the slip collar is not expandable, and most pups outgrow one or two before their necks achieve permanent adult size. Fortunately, nylon slip collars are still on the market for under a couple of dollars.

In the world of dog leashes, the best sellers are made of chain and leather. So much for the best sellers. The best leash is the most practical and economical one, and it is made of webbed canvas. It's durable, fairly light, and doesn't wear down pup or adult or handler. And for anyone who is crazy about canvas, it is fashionable and often seen on Park Avenue.

Conning a pup into wearing the collar is easy if he is not rushed. On the first day, slip the collar around his neck a few times and play with him. Five minutes or so per session should be enough. Repeat on the second day, but increase the time of the sessions and play with him less. Ditto on the third day, and also have him wear the collar whenever he goes outdoors. On the fourth or fifth day, he won't mind wearing the collar at all times. When that happens, introduce the leash.

Again, short sessions for a couple of days. Just attach the leash to the collar. Let him play with the leash and chew on it and drag it around. Late the second day, or early the third, hang on to the other end of the leash and let the pup take you for a walk. Follow in his wake, more or less, but do try to suppress his silliest maneuvers, such as strolling in front of an oncoming truck or jumping into an open well. Keep this up for at least five or six sessions. By now he thinks, believes, or assumes that he's the master of both the leash and the giant on the other end. It's time to change his mind. He's been set up for some basic training, and he's more than ready for it if he knows his own name.

"MY NAME IS MARY," SAID THE STUD DOG

The dog game's purists insist that a pup should learn his name in a hurry, either before he's housebroken or during the process. This propaganda is believed by most dog lovers, for anyone feels less help-less if he thinks a pup knows when he's being addressed from across the room.

The second Golden Rule of the purists is that the pup's pet or kennel name—as opposed to his registered name—should be simple and preferably of one syllable. Names like Tom and Dick are easy sounds for the pup to grasp. Harry is also easy, although the purists claim that it is not. Furthermore, Harry is supposed to be more difficult to shout into the wind. Tom and Dick require less lung power.

There's nothing wrong with those rules, but they shouldn't be regarded as golden and fixed. There's really no reason for a new pup to learn his name right off the bat, and usually constant repetition of his name does the trick within a few weeks. A matter of association, or of relating the sound to himself. He's in good shape, and so is his trainer, if he responds to his name by his twelfth week or so. No sense trying to teach him the basic commands or any kind of command if he doesn't know his own name.

The number of syllables in that name are unimportant. Jo, Jojo, or Jojojo. King, King Harry, or King Harry the Terrible. As long as most members of the family can remember the chosen name and use it, the pup will gradually adopt it as his own. And as far as a male pup is concerned, Ethel is a perfectly good sound. Nor would a well-bred bitch pup object to being called Edward.

The name that is thrust upon the pup is of no concern to him. He will learn it, and it will take him no longer to learn any particular one. The only worthwhile thinking about names that has come down the pike concerns sound-alikes. A pup's training is sometimes hindered if his name sounds like a command word : viz. Syd and *sit,* Don and *down,* Ken and *kennel,* Rum and *come.*

Uttering the pup's name first rather than last helps his learning and prepares him for the simple training that the average baby beast can handle at and after his tenth week. "George, stay away from the garbage!" may not mean anything to the pup, but at least he knows somebody is talking to him. The sound of *George* in "Stay away from the garbage, George!" doesn't always rivet his attention.

Most canine authorities continue to insist that a dog should have just one name, that he should not be expected to respond to more than one. The theory is fine as far as it goes, but it doesn't go beyond puppyhood. Anyone who has shared his home and years with numerous canines—and usually several of them at a time—knows that an adult beast can handle two or three additional names with the greatest of ease, and that he picks up the extra ones without special training. You can bet your last dollar that faithful pet David knows that he's also Sugarpie when he's done something right, or Lunkhead when he's done something wrong, and Pinbrain when he won't come in out of the rain. And Mary, the famous stud dog, also accepts frequently heard swear words as his additional names.

Obviously, those authorities haven't been in touch with real life.

X

The Social Canine

The average purebred pup—if well bred—comes into the world with the potential of becoming somebody's dearly beloved and excellent pet, companion, and friend. But he cannot achieve his potential without some sort of cooperation from the somebody who is supposed to be his provider, teacher, and boss. Since he's a social animal, the pup is perfectly willing to accept family life in place of pack life, but he's not capable of learning what his boss wants him to learn without direction.

This relationship of the two social animals—man and canine—is not a fifty-fifty affair. The mortal must always go more than halfway and even further when the beast is a young pup. The more the pup is in the company of his master the faster he will adapt to his new environment and learn to do things in proper fashion. This overall socialization with the boss and other members of the family is extremely important through the pup's first four or five months, the period that pretty much molds his character or personality or whatchacallit for life. Granted that he has been trained to obey a few commands in joyous fashion by his twentieth week, it will be easy to teach him more commands at any later time. When a dog owner speaks from experience and says, "You can't teach an old dog new tricks," it's safe to assume that his pooch wasn't adequately socialized and trained as a young pup.

Any pup who goes to his new home in his eighth week should be ready to learn a command or two by his tenth or eleventh week, when he trusts the boss and is ready to try anything. Easy does it, and a wise master keeps the training sessions short and the training itself at the play level. It's really a matter of conning the pup into responding to a command. Once he gets the hang of it, incorporating the command in his daily life always helps to make sure that he doesn't forget. It's not a big deal. Once the pup learns to sit on command, for example, requiring him to sit as each of his meals is served will keep him from spilling the food in all directions.

Once he has his first command down pat—a few days or a week or two, depending more on the teacher's intelligence than the pup's limited brain power—the young canine is ready for his second command. The Golden Rule for training any dog, pup or adult, is *one command at a time.* When the boss thinks differently and tries to teach two new commands in the same training session the pup can handle the chore in his own time, and it's always a very long time; the boss must be an extremely patient person.

When the rule is followed, a pup learns each succeeding command in a shorter time span. The little beast is catching on to what's expected of him in more of a hurry, and the boss has realized his own mistakes and changed his ways. No matter how well prepared the human is—thanks to experience with previous canines or advice memorized from books—he is bound to commit errors in training. Every pup is a new adventure, and most pups haven't read a single book of advice, including this one. That's one reason why training can't be fifty-fifty and the boss must do most of the work.

A pup always comes closer to his mysterious pet potential when he knows his basic commands. There are only five of them—*come, down, heel, sit,* and *stay*—and they are called basic because they are fundamental to a happy animal-human relationship. The obedient pup or dog is less a nuisance, if at all, and sometimes he's safer, as when he obediently stays at heel in a heavy traffic zone. Also, the pooch who knows his basics has the background for learning more commands, practical or tricky, to satisfy the common sense, whim, or ego of his boss.

The basic commands are easier to teach if the boss is willing to believe—and adhere to—a few, simple guidelines. While not essential for training, they are guaranteed to help and will shorten the days, weeks, or months it would otherwise take for a pup to recognize and comply with the basic commands. To wit:

Training, Where. Anywhere, indoors or out. For control—just in case the silly pup wants to flee the scene—an enclosed space (walls, fence) is recommended. And since a pup is easily distracted, an ideal training site is devoid of attention-getters, including cheering relatives and friends.

Training, When. Any time when the pup is awake. But the very worst times are when the boss is in a rotten mood or rushed or in the mood to be doing something else.

Training Spans. A pup's attention span isn't very long, and there's no use trying to train him once he's lost interest. In the beginning, five-minute training spans are about all that can be expected. Several times a day, if possible.

Training Vocal Cords. A pup is not an army battalion, nor is he as fearless. The boss does not have to sound as loud or firm as a newly promoted colonel on the parade grounds. The baby canine hears better than the teacher, thank you, and a pleasant tone of voice that's mildly authoritative encourages the best results.

Praise and reward for minor accomplishments also help. Except for collar and leash, training a pup is rather like training a beginning child, and sometimes it's a lot easier.

Training Collar. One of the nice things about the slip collar (see Chapter IX) is that it makes the best training collar for a pup. A slight tug on the leash tightens the collar, and the act is employed as a corrective measure. The momentary tightening does not choke or hurt the pup, but he feels it and sooner or later gets the idea that the feeling means he's doing something wrong.

And so to the basic commands. While they can be taught in alphabetical order, the order really doesn't matter. *Stay* is usually the most difficult one for a pup to learn and obey, and some old-timers insist that it should climax the basic training. The pooch is primed for *Stay* by learning the other commands.

The careful reader will soon note that the *heel* command leads the short parade of basics in this book. If the pup is collar and leash oriented (Chapter IX), *heel* proves the easiest of the basic commands for the pup to learn, and it's almost sure to boost an insecure trainer's morale.

Also worthy of at least minor attention is the fact that the training tips per command on these pages are arranged under two-word commands, such as *Bozo, heel* and *Bozo, down.* Uttering the pup's name before the command word is not a law, of course, but at least the pup (if he knows his name) pays attention and might even associate the command word with himself and do something about it. Not many dog lovers think about it, so perhaps this isn't worth much thought, but a pup can be trained to heel without ever hearing the word *heel.* To make that perfectly clear, consider the case of the trained pup who heels when he hears, "Bozo, laugh!" or who sits when he hears, "Bozo, fly!" A little unorthodox, but okay for dog owners who like to be different.

What follows is designed for a pup, but it's also fine and dandy for adult beasts, either sex, any breed.

"Bozo, Heel!" With this and the other commands, there's a slight pause between the two words—just enough for each word to be distinct.

A pooch at heel stays at your side, whether you are standing, walking, or galloping. The left side is traditional, proper, and official, but it doesn't make any difference to the pup. In theory, the left side is usually better, since one's right hand is the kindly one (feeding, petting) and the left hand is reserved for correcting (via the leash). "It's a question of manners," says Vin Stiff, the friendly hermit. "A man's wife stays on his right and two steps ahead, and his dog stays on the left and even."

Place the pup at your left side, hold the leash in your left hand, utter the command, and start walking. When the pup dashes ahead or to one side, or if he lags, haul him back as gently as one plays a trout. Repeat the command and the process. When the little beast stays in position, try to keep the leash loose. He'll feel comfortable doing the right thing.

And please don't expect instant perfection. The average pup will learn how to heel more or less in several days if there are a few short training sessions on each successive day. With pups of less than six months it's really not fair to demand absolute obedience or perfect performance.

So much for training a pup to heel while you're standing or moving along. If you're lucky, the pup will start to sit at heel whenever you come to a halt. It's not that he's tired. He may think it's the right thing to do, and if he does, he's right, so praise him. It shouldn't take such a pup more than two or three training sessions of five minutes or so to learn the *sit* command. All other pups will take five to ten sessions.

"Bozo, Sit!" Another command that's easy to teach and a natural for a pup to learn as soon as he heels in proper, youthful fashion. That *heel* command is great for controlling a dog outdoors, in any public situation. But around the house the *sit* command proves far more useful; it restrains a dog from greeting visitors by placing front paws on their chests, prevents him from knocking over small children, and keeps him on the floor, as opposed to on your lap, when you are at the dinner table.

For this command, begin with the pup on your left and standing at heel. Turn a bit toward the student and utter the command. Simultaneously use your left hand to press down on his rump. If he sits, fine. Keep repeating, and don't forget to be lavish with your praise and rewards.

The hand pressure won't be enough for some pups. In that case, repeat as above, but use your right hand to tilt up the pup's head. This is done by placing the right hand under his chin. If this doesn't work after a couple of sessions, go to the leash.

The leash is held taut in the right hand. On the verbal command *sit,* pull the leash (and the pup's head) up with your right hand, and don't forget to also push down on his rump with your left hand. Your pup doesn't sit? He's too strong for you. Go to a smaller, weaker breed.

Here on our dog ranch, we used to teach the *sit* command as above, but that was many, many moons ago. Somewhere along the line, we got into the habit of requiring a pup to sit before his meal was placed in front of him. So our pups really learn the command first, while they are learning their appointed names. We find this a very convenient way to teach the command, and it always works. However, it is not the accepted method and you will not find it in the great or even the lesser training books.

"Bozo, Come!" There are many, many uses for this command, as when you want the pup to come into the house and out of the rain, to stop chasing the neighbor's cat, or to stop digging a hole in the herb garden. If you've read many training books or talked to professional dog trainers, you will find this difficult to believe: this is a very simple command to teach.

Often a pup is a natural comer and will come to you whenever you call to him as long as you make it a pleasant experience for him. And then there is the almost-natural comer, a pup who needs a little added incentive. In addition to hearing the command, this pup needs to see or hear something else. Clap your hands, roll on the floor, stand on your head, wave a porterhouse, or run away from him. To put it another way, the verbal command is accompanied by visual foolery the pup can't resist. He'll respond to something, and sooner or later you'll be able to eliminate the histrionics and rely on praise alone.

On our ranch, we use the pup's dinner dish (metal bowl) as a training tool. At mealtimes the verbal command is accompanied by the sound of the full dish being banged on the floor. That combination is very difficult for a pup to resist. It can be used before or after the *sit* command is learned.

For the stubborn pup, it's usually best to forget this command until after he's more or less learned both the *sit* and the *stay*. In this case the collar and leash are the training tools. First, put the pup on a *sit* and *stay*. Next, back off about three feet from him. Then, as you face him, give the verbal command *come*. If he does not come to you, tug on the leash. If that fails, you must haul him to you. Practice does the trick. The distance from the pup is gradually increased. Long training leashes are available, but there's no rule against adding a length of rope to a standard-length leash. Fashion is unimportant.

When you feel the pup knows the command—and never mind at what distance—try him off the leash. If he flunks, the only known remedy is to put him back on the leash and review your own behavior. Maybe you weren't lavish enough with the loving words and the tidbits.

"Bozo, Stay!" As noted earlier, this is considered the most difficult basic command for a pup to learn, and maybe it is. If a fun-loving pup reasons, he probably resents staying in position. It goes against the grain, and it's unnatural to be aware and full of vim and vigor and not

doing anything. True enough. But there are times when a pup should stay, as in *stay out of the way,* and in so doing, he serves some useful purpose for people. The pup who stays on command is as socially desirable as the darling child who is seen but not heard.

Place the pup on a *heel* and *sit.* As you sound off with "Bozo, stay!" step ahead and with your back to the dog simultaneously swing the palm of your left hand back and almost against the pup's nose. Your palm amounts to a hand signal, it says, "Stop," and in time the pup will put one and one together. When he does, you can forget the verbal command and just use the palm. At a distance, and facing him, just swing either arm in an arc toward the pup, with hand open and palm showing.

It's best to teach this command without the leash, but the collar is a help. In the beginning, the pup is almost sure to break and try to follow you. Grab him, make him sit, and try again. As with the *come* command, gradually increase your distance. If your pup learns the *stay* command within a week, he's a ball of fire.

The big trouble with this command is human expectation. We are forever overestimating the capabilities of the canine and expecting too much by way of performance. It may make sense to us when we ask a dog to stay put, but there's no evidence around to prove that the dog understands or appreciates the reason. This should lead anyone to the conclusion that it's unreasonable to expect a pup of under six months to remain on a *stay* for as long as a minute unless he is chained in position. The A.K.C. is well aware of the canine's dislike for remaining immobile, and proof of the pudding can be found in the rules and regulations pertaining to the sport of Obedience.

More on said sport up ahead (Chapter XI). For now it is only necessary to understand that only the best-trained dogs succeed in Obedience, and they must perform prescribed exercises in the approved manner. Two of the exercises or tests a pooch must not flunk if he is to win his CD and CDX degrees are the *Long Sit* and *Long Down:* respectively, one and three minutes for the CD, and three and five minutes for the CDX. True, an Obedience trial has more distractions than a backyard and Obedience dogs perform in the company of their peers, but most of the dogs are seasoned adults and polished performers, and the majority manage to pass all but the *stay* tests with flying colors. In CD only about one out of every six candidates lasts the required time spans. Many of the successful ones go on to CDX, and there, about one out of every fifteen gets over that five-minute hump.

So don't be disappointed if your pup won't obey a *stay* for thirty seconds—or less if you leave the room or go around a corner and out of sight. He'll improve as he ages. And if he becomes a normal adult, he'll stay longer on a *down* than a *sit*.

"Bozo, Down!" The purists in the dog game insist that this command should be taught right after the *sit,* but pups don't know that and the timing is of no importance to them. We have tried teaching it at various stages and have reached the conclusion that last is best. By the time a pup knows his other basic commands, he's four or five months old, has more than a dim idea of what training is all about, and can take half-hour sessions without becoming bored or stubborn. At that time of his life almost any pup can be taught the *down* in one or two sessions. Here are the easiest training methods:

Hands Method. Put the pup on a *sit*. Facing him, sink to your knees. On the command, lift his forelegs and gently lower him to the floor. Lift from his elbows or forearms, not his paws. Praise him and he'll grasp the idea sooner.

Collar-and-Leash Method. This method is preferred by most trainers, since it also teaches the pup the approved hand signal. Put him on a *sit*. Face him, with the leash in your left hand. The leash should be loose enough to form a loop between your hand and the pup's collar, with the bottom of loop about three inches above floor level.

When the scene is set, give the verbal command and step on the leash. If the pup is not double-jointed, or stronger than you are, his head will go down, followed by the rest of his body. Gobs of praise decrease the repetitions.

The leash can be held in the other hand, of course, but the left is suggested so that the right will be free to perform the appropriate hand signal. Along with the verbal command and the foot artistry, just swing the right arm up in an arc, with the hand open and the palm toward the dog in the manner of a traffic cop giving a stop signal. In time—and sometimes it's a very long time if rehearsals aren't frequent— the pooch will go down on the hand signal alone, even at a distance. Provided that he happens to be watching you.

Index-Finger Method. This will not be found in training books, probably because it is so simple or because it doesn't work with all pups. We like it because the training is so informal. When you are sitting and reading or conversing or knitting or kneading and your pup tries to climb onto your lap or otherwise intrude, just say, "Bozo, down!" and point at the rug. If this doesn't work after numerous tries, wait until next time and then tap on the floor as you give the command. Keep trying, and if you don't succeed, go to one of the other methods.

Once he understand both *sit* and *down* commands, a pup will usually stay on the latter longer. Not even the self-appointed canine psychologists know why, but a plausible explanation is that the pup is more relaxed on a *down.* He does seem to enjoy the *down,* and maybe he's bright enough to know that he isn't about to be asked to do anything strenuous. This is a very useful command around the house and often provides insurance for the future, as when that wealthy uncle who is afraid of dogs arrives unexpectedly before you can park your beast in a boarding kennel. And it can also be life insurance for the dog who rides loose in the family car. His risks are the same as those of unstrapped human passengers. On the highway the *down* keeps the dog out of trouble and also prevents him from sticking his head out an open window and exposing his eyes and nose to sharp particles in the breezes.

Once the pup has his five basic commands down pat, he can be appreciated as well as loved. The youngster is more socially acceptable and is edging closer to his pet potential. In any situation, he's no longer a pest. If he is, his owner needs a little training.

The beloved beast is now primed for more learning. He's ready to pick up new commands, either those that will help him perform certain future duties or others that will help him adjust to family life. Examples include the following:

"Bozo, Stand!" One school of thought holds that this is really a basic command, but any healthy dog knows how to stand and once he knows his *stay* command, he'll stay standing. However, if the dog is headed for the sports of show or Obedience, he must know the *stand* command and its hidden meaning.

This command really means that the dog should stand *correctly*. He assumes the proper stance for his breed, and for all but a few breeds this amounts to planting the forelegs straight down, with paws pointed straight ahead. To the rear, the hind legs are set a bit apart, with angulation (if proper) showing and hocks perpendicular to the ground. The dog is at attention, and he looks as close to his breed standard as it is possible for him to look. Not only that, but he should hold the pose.

There must be fifty different ways to teach any canine to stand correctly, but the one to be explored here will not be found in manuals or at dog-training schools. We hit on it by accident and have stayed with it because it is the easiest method for both man and beast and there are side benefits for both. The method is best for a pup, but it will also work with an older dog. And the beauty of it is that the pooch probably isn't aware that he's being taught to stand properly.

When a pup is about three months old, we place him on top of something—a dog crate, table, or box—whenever he requires our attention for such simple tasks as grooming or nail clipping or for the more difficult removal of ticks or porcupine quills. Only nonfolding crates, metal and wooden, have solid tops. Whatever the platform, the surface should be nonskid, so that the standing pup won't slip. A hard rubber, ribbed mat is dandy for the purpose. And the surface must be steady. If it shakes, the pup won't feel secure. You want him calm and cool.

Once the pup gets used to standing up in the air, you can teach him to stand properly by placing each of his paws, if necessary, on the right spots. This is done by bending over the little beast and lifting his forelegs by the elbows and his hind legs by the hocks or stifle joints. Planting his hind legs at the edge of the platform will sometimes keep them in place. The pup isn't about to back off the platform. Moving the pup's legs for him may sound idiotic, but it is far more effective than well-meant remarks, such as, "Would you mind adjusting your right foreleg a little to the left?" or "Please don't turn out your left hock. Keep it straight."

If sufficient praise is offered, a pup will learn how to stand properly and even hold the pose for half a minute. The number of times it takes to achieve this goal is unimportant, since the training is informal, always done in conjunction with something else and only when convenient. After the great day is reached, it's time to try the proper stance on the ground and to use the verbal command. For this a collar and leash are necessary.

Just walk or trot the pup at heel and sound off with, "Bozo, stand!" when you come to a halt. At that point, a tight lead is recommended. It will restrain the pup from continuing and also hold his head up. And with his head up he's more likely to stop in the proper stance.

Some children stand without slouching, and some pups stand properly. It comes naturally to them. What doesn't come naturally to a pup is standing motionless for a minute or so at a time. Still, there's nothing wrong with the pooch who stands and wiggles unless he is headed for the shows or trials.

If you use the top-of-the-crate method, it's possible to have a pup stand correctly while you groom him. But it's impossible while you attend to his nails. Complete the job, then go in for the training, and it will help the pup forget the previous unpleasantness. After a few nail-trimming sessions, you'll know just what position your pup prefers, and it will range from sitting to jumping.

Nail trimming has nothing to do with commands unless you want to use *sit* or *down* and *stay,* but it is a fact of life. A pup's nails should be checked every two or three weeks and an adult's every couple of months. The nail is trimmed back to just short of the quick, and the tools are a hand-operated pet nail clipper and file or an electric file. The last item has a rotating head and makes the job easy. If a pup gets used to having his nails clipped, he won't put up a big fuss as an adult.

Half the pet dogs in the land have foot miseries because of too-long nails. If they remain too long over a too long period, lameness can result and splayed feet are sure bets. The nail tips should never go below the pads. When your dog sends off clicks as he trots over a wood or linoleum floor, his nails need attention. The clicks are his requests, but they should be regarded as *his* commands.

"Bozo, Kennel!" This command is of local origin, and we use it to send a dog where we want him to go. In a sense it is the opposite of a *Bozo, come!* in that the dog is going somewhere and not coming toward us.

When he hears the *kennel* command, a pup or adult goes into the kennel, into his crate, or through a door or gate or other opening. In the beginning, just in case a pup doesn't know where to go, a sweep of the arm and a pointing gesture emphasize the verbal command. And when a pup is either stubborn or doesn't get the point, it is sometimes necessary to accompany him through the opening, with one hand on his collar. Used indiscriminately, as when you intend to go through the very same doorway, the command will send the dog ahead of you. We use it when we don't intend to follow or when a dog is hesitant about entering a strange building.

Animal worshippers insist that the average pet dog—whether purebred or mongrel—is capable of learning up to one hundred words, depending on his tutor. It is the sound of each word that the dog learns, of course. By associating each sound with a specific action that he's encouraged to perform, he learns his command words and becomes obedient—to at least a somewhat greater degree than before he started his enforced learning.

Well, we call it learning. A dog might call it something else, such as picking up some unnatural habits. At the command level, his only natural habit is instinctive reaction (obedience) to the tone (as opposed to the meaning) of the word. To make that perfectly clear, consider our local habitat. Those members of our canine colony who reside outdoors for one reason or another (shedding or in season, for example) welcome many midnights with excessive barking and howling. We refer to this as the Westminster Choir, and it is usually inspired by frustration, since friendly rabbits, fox, deer, and skunks come very close to the kennel fencing. The midnight choir sessions can be brief or lengthy. If brief, they last two to three minutes. If lengthy, they can continue until dawn, and the only way to prevent that is by tone of voice. If the tone is right, the words and their meaning are unimportant. Thus, "Attention! I love you!" is just as effective in quieting the choir as "Shut up, you damn fools!" or "Be quiet, you naughty dogs!" It's not the words but the tone of the shout—harsh, unhappy, ringing with condemnation—that does the trick.

And speaking of tricks—shaking hands, praying, playing dead, walking on two legs, begging, singing, and other sillies—there's time enough to teach them after the pup has more or less learned the practical commands. First things first, and commands should be more important than tricks. The secret to teaching any trick amounts to many rehearsals, abundant praise, and plenty of goodies. More advice can be found on other pages, but not in this book. Dog lovers who offend canine dignity by insisting that their pooches entertain by emulating human behavior should be willing to get down on all fours and wag their bottoms for the amusement of their pets.

XI

The Sport of Dogs

While not all dog lovers are humane, a great many do wear both hats. They are intensely interested in the welfare of all canines, and that's reason enough for their permanent war against the dog game's two money sports: racing and fighting. Thus far, it has been a losing war. The money sports continue to thrive. It's a very odd situation, for anticruelty-to-animals laws exist in every state where one or both sports flourish.

Dog racing is legal (1975) in nine states, and the promoters of the sport are optimistic about legalizing it in a dozen other states within the next few years. The Greyhound is the only breed used for racing in this country, and the few that qualify would make atrocious and untrustworthy pets. These dogs are bred for racing, and only the speediest make it to the dog tracks. The others—unfortunate beasts lacking in what proponents of the sport prefer to call competitive spirit, a polite term for *killer instinct*—are destroyed. If a dog is short on this drive, he will not run like the wind.

By way of heightening this instinct to the greatest degree, the pups are raised mean and trained on wild rabbits. Most of the racing Greyhounds are trained in three states—Texas, Kansas, and Nebraska —where wild bunnies are abundant. The taste of warm blood is the nicest thing that has ever happened to a dog in training, and it inspires him to greater speed the next time out, when he attempts to get to the rabbit ahead of the other dogs.

The speediest beasts go on to schooling tracks, crude copies of the real thing. The dogs are trained to chase a mechanical lure. A sure way to get results is to tie a rabbit to the lure and let him dangle from it by his hind legs. The live bait is moved just fast enough to keep the dogs in pursuit. Eventually, they are permitted to catch up, kill, and feast. The top beasts are promoted to dog race tracks in the cooperating states. A given dog doesn't have to win every time out, but he must place in the money often enough to keep his owner solvent and the spectators in a betting mood. The racing Greyhound who decides it's foolish to go all-out in pursuit of a mechanical lure is really asking for retirement—and usually that means an early demise. His "competitive spirit" is such that he'll go after just about anything that moves, including a kindly dog lover. A risky pet for anyone who does not wear armor.

Since racing Greyhounds do not carry jockeys on their backs, it is widely believed that dog racing is more honest than horse racing. This belief—and the big money behind the sport—may be enough to legalize dog racing from coast to coast and make it almost as popular as baseball used to be. Along the way, however, supporters will have to overcome the dedicated campaign of the Humane Society of the United States (HSUS), champion of animal rights in the world of man. "Dog racing is one of America's cruelest spectator events, largely because of the training methods, which include the chasing and tearing apart of live rabbit lures," says the HSUS.

Since those training methods are not in evidence at the race tracks, uninformed spectators are not aware of the sport's cruelties. But most would probably agree that dog fighting—the other money sport—is America's very cruelest spectator event. Of course, some might not believe that the sport exists in enlightened America.

Well, dog fighting is here (in the United States, not Canada), and it's not about to go away. Although every state has one or more laws on the books making it an illegal activity, enforcement of the laws has never been strong in any area of the nation. And where arrests have been made, the fines have always been light. It's as if law-enforcement agencies have enough trouble without adding to their woes. On the federal level the strongest action to date has been consideration by a Senate committee of a bill that would prohibit the interstate shipment of fighting dogs. A step in the right direction, but only morally. Dogfighting is a clandestine sport. Only a foolish state trooper would stop a car and try to determine whether the canine passenger is a pet or a fighter.

The official breed history of the famous coursing beast states that "The Greyhound has added another laurel to his crown," meaning racing. The ardent admirers of the favorite fighting breeds, however, aren't that proud of their sport. The big favorite is the Staffordshire Bull Terrier, followed by the Bull Terrier, Doberman Pinscher, and Alaskan Malamute. Mixed breeds and other pure breeds are used but never to any great extent. Obviously, purebreds make the best fighters, but that doesn't mean any purebred dog. The fighting dog, like the racing dog, must have the "competitive spirit," and the meanest ones come from a long line of warriors. Currently about a hundred breeders are producing most of the fighting pups, and those with the biggest potential are whelped with the killer instinct intact. This aptitude is nourished by general mistreatment, a diet that is heavy on raw meat, and such toys as declawed cats, harmless pups, chickens, rabbits, and other warm-blooded creatures. The dog who never has to be encouraged to demolish his toys is regarded as a sure bet for a fighting career, although his owner can never be sure how long that career will last.

Dogfights are rather secret affairs but only in the sense that news of them does not reach the general public. Interested parties keep in touch with what's going on through the pages of three national magazines and the mailing lists of fight promoters in various sections of the country. Fights are usually held on weekends, and four or five matches often constitute an evening's card for fifty to a hundred fans, most of them gamblers who prefer fighting dogs to fighting cocks. And several times a year the sport holds conventions, major spectacles featuring the nation's top fighting canines.

The average fight lasts anywhere from half an hour to several hours, depending on the evenness of the match and the damage one beast inflicts on another. A fight is never a pleasant sight, and it always continues until one dog turns from the fray or is physically unable to attack. He is the loser, of course, and usually the losing dog that survives the battle is in such bad shape that he must be put out of his misery. Sometimes the winner is so battered that he has to be destroyed, too.

Dogfights are held from coast to coast, but some states are more popular hosts than others. It is seldom difficult for an amateur detective to find fights in New York, New Jersey, Massachusetts, Rhode Island, California, Illinois, Texas, Florida, Georgia, North and South Carolina, and Mississippi. Most of the fights are staged in suburban and rural areas, but Chicago has been coming on strong as a big-city site. In some areas of the South, entire families attend fights. Elsewhere, the spectacles are considered "not very educational for children" and the spectators are mostly bloodthirsty, adult males.

So much for the bad news. All the other sports—major and minor—represent the good news. There is an honorable point to each of these in that the dogs use their talents to serve some useful purpose, real or imaginary. And the dogs can be trusted by both their owners and total strangers. The beasts are trained in ways acceptable to even intense critics from Sirius. If there's anything wrong with the minor sports, it's the fact that each involves only a few of the pure breeds. Thus, and no matter what the quality of their beasts, the overwhelming majority of the land's purebred owners are left out in the cold. In fairness to that majority, only the worthiest minor sports rate attention herein:

Sheepdog trials constitute the smallest of the minor sports. To compete, it is necessary to own one or more Border Collies, and training is helped if you also own a few sheep. On this side of the Atlantic most of the action is supervised by the North American Sheep Dog Society.

The Border doesn't help if you dream of going in for the more popular (but still minor) sport of sled-dog racing. Although it's okay to use other robust breeds, teams of Alaskan Malamutes and Siberian Huskies are the traditional winners over distances of up to thirty miles. Five, seven, or nine dogs constitute a team. The odd number is necessary, since the dogs work in pairs behind a single leader. There are several sled-dog clubs in the land, and many of the most important races are held under the auspices of the New England Sled Dog Club.

A little less minor but still unknown in many parts of the country is Whippet racing. The races are becoming increasingly popular in the Midwest and West, and they prove that the best beasts of a breed can be trained to race competitively without bringing basic cruelties into play. The American Whippet Club approves the races as part of the breed's improvement program; many of the racers double as show and Obedience dogs; all are A.K.C. registered, meet the specifications of the breed standard, and serve their owners as faithful pets. There aren't any parimutuel windows at Whippet races, and the owners of the speedy pooches are legitimate dog fanciers. The highest honor a beast can win is the Award of Racing Merit, a title bestowed by the national breed club. Whippet racing is regarded as a fine spectator sport for families. Even babies like to see the doggies run.

The biggest of the minor sports—and the only one run under the rules and regulations of both the A.K.C. and the C.K.C.—is the field trial. It involves more breeds than the other minors, and the only things keeping the sport from a major ranking are expense, training time, travel, and the fact that most beasts of those breeds lack the necessary talent. There are different trials and procedures for Dachshunds, Basset Hounds, Beagles, Pointing Breeds, Retriever Breeds, and Spaniels. Only the Spaniels confuse the issue: the Brittany Spaniel is a pointer, and the Irish Water Spaniel is a retriever. All the other spaniels run in the spaniel trials, where the English Springer is the dominant winner. The other Pointing Breeds: Pointer, German Shorthaired Pointer, German Wirehaired Pointer, English Setter, Gordon Setter, Irish Setter, Vizsla, Weimaraner, and Wirehaired Pointing Griffon. The other Retriever Breeds: Chesapeake Bay, Curly-Coated, Flat-Coated, Golden, and Labrador.

Dogs of the above sporting and hound breeds are the only ones entitled to wear the hard-earned title of field trial champion. If and when such a dog becomes a show champion, he is hailed as a dual champion. It follows that dogs of any other breed cannot become dual champions.

Most of the field trial action is in the United States. The A.K.C. now licenses about a thousand trials per annum, with Beagles accounting for about 40 percent of the number. In a very good year about two hundred fifty new champions are blessed. Very few of them ever get the chance to become dual champions, since few members of the field trial set are interested in show.

In comparison, the A.K.C. licenses about fourteen hundred dog shows per annum, and in an average year, about ninety-five hundred new show champs (from all the recognized breeds) make their owners happy. This makes beast showing the major sport in the dog game. Of all the sports, minor and major, it requires the least effort on the part of the owner. Or no effort at all—beyond signing checks—if the owner has money to burn and is desperate for success. Otherwise, it really doesn't take genius or unusual talent to turn one's beloved beast into a show champion, as dozens of little children prove every month.

The most important item is a good show dog, either sex, that meets the following requirements: (1) Breed: any breed recognized by the A.K.C. (2) Age: 6 months or older. (3) Proof: individual A.K.C. registration. (4) Wholeness: not spayed or castrated; a male must have both testicles in the scrotum. (5) Naturalness: appearance is unchanged, unless such changes (docking, cropping, removal of dewclaws) are okayed by the breed standard. (6) Temperament: is not vicious. (7) Disabilities: is not totally blind or deaf; is not lame.

Millions of purebreds can pass that seven-point test with flying colors, and almost all their owners will cheerfully admit that their beasts are very good ones. Every year, about a million Americans decide to prove to the world what they already know—that their purebreds are good enough to become show champions. The only way to prove this is to show such dogs in competition. The urge to have a champion in the family is a very strong one, and a smitten dog lover finds the feeling almost impossible to shake. For many, success is ambrosia, and they will continue showing other dogs. One champion is never enough.

Dog lovers who show dogs accept one another as dog fanciers, owners who know more about a breed than average owners. However, this mutual acceptance has its limitations. A Collie fancier usually counts other Collie fanciers among his friends, but they are not his equals when it comes to knowledge about the breed. This holds true whether his dog or their dogs are winning at the shows. If his dog loses and continues to lose at show after show, he begins to think that he knows more than the breed judges. When he finds a Bouvier fancier and a Tibetan Terrier fancier who agree with him about judges, the three fanciers recognize each other as the top authorities in their respective breeds. All three may be perfectly rational on non-canine subjects.

The sad truth is that many dog fanciers assume superior knowledge about their breeds or are unable to understand the printed words that represent each breed standard. What separates the men from the boys—good show dogs from otherwise good dogs—is their close resemblance to the appropriate breed standard. The closer the better, for each standard is held to be a verbal portrait of the perfect dog in the given breed. Thus a dog with two glaring faults should always win over a dog with five. The fact that he doesn't simply proves that human nature is a funny thing; a breed judge may decide that the two faults are major and the five faults are trivial. As far as anybody has been able to establish, every judge approved for a given breed is able to comprehend the standard, but some comprehend it more fully than others. The dog game has a term for an owner or judge who cannot distinguish between a really good purebred and one who is a lovable bum, and that term is *kennel blind.* If you are a kennel-blind owner, your pride and love for your beast blinds you to his weak points. If you are a kennel-blind judge, you are probably comparing other people's beasts with your memory of perfect beasts of the breed —the only perfect ones you ever saw were your own, and nobody else knew that they were perfect.

While the opinions of all breed judges are honorable, some of the honorable opinions are also silly, and that's the major reason why some of our purebred show champions are bums and the number of champs that appear in a pup's pedigree do not necessarily guarantee quality. Still, the greater the number of ancestral champs, the easier it is to sell a purebred pup and the better the chances of getting a high price for him.

The very greatest dog of his breed cannot become a show champion by remaining at home. He must compete at dog shows, although—if he thinks about it at all—it must seem like a strange sort of competition to him. All he has to do is try to look his best for a few minutes at a time while a judge studies his body and gait. The only real competition is nonphysical and in the judge's mind. He must decide who is the best dog in the ring.

The dog shows that count are known as point shows, for beasts that win are awarded points, and a beast who wins the required number of points becomes a show champion. Once he becomes a show champion, a dog can continue to compete, although the most he can win is glory for himself and fuel for his owner's ego. Trophies, too, of course, but they just take up room and collect dust. All this is true in both the United States and Canada, and a dog of a breed recognized in both countries can try for a championship title in each country. Am. & Can. Ch. Frog Hollow Millie is a Shih Tzu success story. Only careless readers will wonder why Millie can't become a dual champion.

There are two general types of point shows in A.K.C. country, and they are known as All-breed and Specialty. The former are the big ones, since all the recognized breeds may be entered. Usually a Specialty is devoted to one breed (and its varieties, if any), although there are a few for all the breeds in a given group. Sometimes, a Specialty goes it alone. At other times, it's staged under the umbrella of an All-breed. Points won at either type of show count toward a championship.

All dog shows, large or small, can be regarded as a series of eliminations that begin in the classes at the breed level. For all pooches who meet the previously explained requirements, these are the A.K.C. classes for each of the recognized breeds:

Puppy. Six to twelve months, whelped in either the United States or Canada. The young canine can't be a champion. Usually a pup starts here and picks up experience.

Novice. Six months and older, whelped in the United States or Canada. Ineligible after three wins in this class, or after winning a championship point, or after a first place in one of the following classes:

Bred-by-Exhibitor. Six months and over, whelped in the United States, not a champion. Must be owned wholly or in part by the breeder or spouse of the breeder, and must be handled by the owner or a member of the owner's immediate family.

American-bred. Six months and over, whelped in the United States by reason of an American mating, not a champion.

Open. Six months and older. Usually for dogs who have been around a while and have chalked up some championship points. Champions are welcome. The only class for dogs whelped overseas.

All the classes for a given breed are judged in the same *ring,* dog fancy parlance for a square of about thirty-five by thirty-five feet, bounded by rope and corner posts. Although both sexes are regarded as equals, they are judged separately, males first. Four awards are made in each class, and the first place winner in each gets the coveted blue ribbon and remains in the running. The elimination continues, per sex, in the following competition:

Winners Class. All the blue ribbon males from the five classes gather for the win that really counts. The victor is known as Winners Dog, and he takes home a purple ribbon and whatever championship points are up for grabs. Now the process is repeated for the blue ribbon females, and the one who gets the purple also gets championship points and the title of Winners Bitch.

The points, per sex, may or may not be the same, and in the less popular breeds, points are sometimes nonexistent. At any show, and depending upon the number of beasts present in a breed, Winners Dog and Winners Bitch can win from zero to five points. The A.K.C. has devised seven point schedules: four cover different divisions of territorial United States, and there's one each for Alaska, Hawaii, and Puerto Rico. If necessary, annual point adjustments are made. The big reason for the different schedules is the variable of breed popularity. A breed that is very popular in the East may be far less so in California and not even present in Hawaii.

No matter what the site of the A.K.C. point show, a definite point schedule prevails and the scale of points, per breed, is not debatable. It is always found up front in a show's catalog and amounts to the most popular reading matter at the show. Before a breed is judged, owners of beasts of the breed check to find out how many championship points are in the cards for the Winners Dog and Winners Bitch. To win his title of champion, a show dog must harvest a total of 15 championship points under a minimum of three different judges. Two of those wins, each under a different judge, must be *majors,* or worth 3, 4, or 5 points. The balance can be 1- and 2-point wins. Thus, no purebred can win his title in fewer than three shows (each a 5-point major), and he can win 50 points (all 1- and 2-point wins and only one major) and still lack the championship title.

The points awarded at a given show are not the same for all breeds. Generally, the more abundant the breed, the more beasts of the breed required per point. For a look at how this worked in the East and some southern and midwestern states (Point Division No. I of the A.K.C.) in 1975:

BREED	1 Point		3 Points		5 Points	
	DOGS	BITCHES	DOGS	BITCHES	DOGS	BITCHES
Pointers	2*	2	4	4	7	9
Irish Setters	6	6	24	26	66	66
Afghan Hounds	7	8	27	30	56	56
Borzois	2	2	7	9	15	18
German Shepherd Dogs	5	4	33	38	65	75
Great Danes	5	5	25	27	48	57
Pulik	2	2	4	4	7	7
Collies (Rough)	2	3	20	22	48	63
Collies (Smooth)	2	2	4	4	6	8
St. Bernards	3	3	19	17	52	55
Samoyeds	2	2	10	8	17	19
Scottish Terriers	2	2	7	7	18	22

* Number of dogs in competition.

From this sampling, it's possible to deduce that the point scale for a given breed is not always the same for each sex. The reason for this is that in some breeds—and for no particular reason—more members of one sex were entered at shows during the previous year. In the cases of major points, bitches outnumbered males in the East during 1974 in such breeds as the German Shepherd Dog, Borzoi, Great Dane and Rough Collie.

Okay. Winners Dog (WD) and Winners Bitch (WB) are the only possible collectors of championship points at the breed level. Both now proceed to the final breed class, where they compete against each other for the designation of Best of Winners (BW) and against champions of record for the title of Best of Breed (BOB) or Best of Variety of Breed (BOV), either one being the top honor at this level. Another title awarded here is Best of Opposite Sex (BOS); an honor but otherwise insignificant. The class and how it works:

Best of Breed, or Best of Variety of Breed Competition. The judge finds his BOB first, then his BW, and finally his BOS. Traditionally, BOB and BOS are champs of record, but a judge sometimes finds one or the other or both in his WD and WB; and if one of the latter two yoes BOB or BOV, he or she automatically becomes BW.

From the viewpoint of championship points, BW can be meaningless or worthwhile. Consider a show where the number of class Pointers entered and on hand provides 3 points for WD and only 1 point for WB. In this final breed class, one of them must become BW. If WD gets the nod, the win doesn't change his point total. But if WB becomes BW, she exchanges her single point for his 3 points. Now they both have 3 points.

If either of these nonchamps becomes a BOB or BOV, he or she is the only member of the breed (or variety of the breed) to survive the first levels of the great elimination. The survivor continues on to the group judging, where he (she) goes up against the best beasts of the other breeds in the division. The winner in each of the six groups goes on to the final elimination, where one beast is ultimately crowned Best in Show (BIS).

Since a nonchamp can also win points at the Group and BIS levels, time out here to consider the hypothetical case above of Sweet Pea, the Pointer bitch who goes WB for 1 point, then BOB and an automatic BW for 3 points. Onward to sporting group, where she is judged the best of the lot and is now entitled to the day's top point total among the sporting breeds. Since BW in Irish Setters was worth 4 points, Sweet Pea now exchanges her 3 for the 4. Proceed to best in show, the grand finale, where the Pointer bitch proves superior to the other five group winners and becomes BIS and everybody's sweetheart. One of the finalists was a Saluki, and back at the breed level the Saluki BW was worth 5 points. Sweet Pea has just theoretically proved that she is better than any other beast at the show. She's worth at least the 5 points. She gets them.

A class beast (WD or WB) can go on to group and best in show and pick up more championship points along the way, but it doesn't happen frequently. Still, it happens often enough to keep hope simmering in the hearts of many kennel-blind owners.

The handling of the purebreds who are trying for championship points is fairly simple. All the handler has to do is supervise the beast on the other end of the leash in action (gaiting) and nonaction (holding proper stance for breed). This does not take much training or talent on the part of man or beast, and most fanciers handle their own dogs at the shows. No matter how great their expertise, they are always rated as amateur handlers, although some give the professional handlers a run for their money. As in bruising sports, a professional hates to be outdone by an amateur, for the latter is taking bread away from him. There are about a thousand professional handlers in the United States, and all are licensed by the A.K.C. for particular breeds or all breeds. They prefer to handle winning dogs, since it's difficult to hold a client whose dog is losing most of the time. The client is always a dog fancier with several score reasons (from nervousness to lack of time) for not handling his own dog, and with the funds to hire a professional.

Those professional handlers aren't the only ones taking home money from the dog shows. There are also the breed judges, and these days about fifteen hundred of them are approved by the A.K.C. to perform in the rings at dog shows. Some judge just one breed, others are approved to judge 5, 10, or 20 breeds, and a select group of *all-rounders* are permitted to judge any and all breeds. A judge's fee for a show runs from a newcomer's small stipend (to cover expenses) to a popular all-rounder's five hundred dollars or so. Any judge, no matter what his or her number of approved breeds, is limited to arbitrating on about 25 beasts per hour and a firm maximum of 175 dogs per show. Since there are almost as many dog shows per year as active breed judges, booking a panel of top judges for a show of any size is no easy task. Proven judges are often committed to shows several years in advance.

The dog game's deepest thinkers have not been able to agree on the reasons behind the continued growth of dog shows. The sport is open to anyone who owns a registered and otherwise eligible pure-bred. Well, open to anyone who is able to walk, hold a leash, and command a little respect from his beast. And if all that's too much effort, those professional handlers are for hire and will travel. Owners who handle their own dogs to wins are generally considered to be the real sports, but those who hire others to perform the task for them seem to find just as much satisfaction in victory. Either way, many dog fanciers consider the sport an open door to social status.

That strange opinion is not so strong in Canada, where total registrations of purebreds at the C.K.C. run a little under 100,000 per annum, a figure that is just shy of being 10 percent of the annual total at the A.K.C. Despite that disparity, the C.K.C. total for point shows per annum is around 700, 50 percent of the A.K.C. total, and about 5,000 new Canadian show champions are crowned each year, a little better than 50 percent of the A.K.C. total. Obviously, Canadian dog fanciers are more avid and active, and Canada's kennel clubs have a special knack for making the owners of winning dogs very happy. The biggest dog show pay-offs in all the world are made at the United Kennel Club shows in Montreal every April; where a big $3,000 went to the BIS beast at each of the two 1975 events. A mere $1,000 went to the best pup. Group winners took home $500, and another $20,000 was divided among dogs placing in groups (second, third, and fourth), BOB and BOV beasts, and class victors. The sponsoring kennel club put up some $55,000 in prize money, enough to make all kennel clubs south of the border look like pikers.

Although Canada plays host to fewer point shows than the United States, there are twice as many types, or four. In addition to the same All-breed and Specialty shows, the C.K.C. honors the Limited Breeds (self-explanatory) and the Field Trial Conformation (held in conjunction with a field trial and limited to beasts who run in the trial). The great elimination is conducted in the A.K.C. manner, but the C.K.C. varies a little in its beginning classes. To wit:

Junior Puppy: six months to one day under nine months.
Senior Puppy: nine months to one day under twelve months.
Novice: six months and older, and never a blue ribbon winner.
Canadian-Bred: six months and older, not a champion and whelped in Canada.
Breed-by-Exhibitor: six months and older. Must be owned and handled in the ring by the breeder.
Open: six months and older.

Under C.K.C. rules and regulations, WD becomes WM, or Winners Male, and WB becomes the more polite WF, or Winners Female. The BW, BOB and BOS awards are the same as in the A.K.C., but the class is called Specials Only rather than Best of Breed. Otherwise, anyone who understands the workings of an A.K.C. point show should not be mystified by the C.K.C. version. The big difference between the two governing bodies is in championship points: it takes 5 fewer points to become a show champion in Canada. There the magic number is 10.

In the square mileage ruled by the C.K.C., WM and WF win most of their points at the breed level. Canada has different championship point schedules for each of a dozen zones: Alberta, British Columbia, Manitoba, New Brunswick, Newfoundland, Nova Scotia,

Ontario (North), Ontario (South), Prince Edward Island, Quebec, Saskatchewan, and Yukon Territory. Point ratings are the same as below the border, 0 to 5; and while the total of 10 points must be won under at least three judges, none of the wins have to be majors. Thus, two 5-point wins under different judges equal 10 points, but not a title. At least another point under a third judge is required. And along the way to his title, the beast must defeat either another member of his breed or place (win one of the four top spots) somewhere in his group, with at least five breeds competing.

Those unique conditions are necessary in Canada, for in many breeds (every zone) a dog can win a single point at 10 different shows without ever meeting competition within his own breed. As for the point scales, they are always the same for both sexes in a given breed. In Pointers (Alberta), for example, it takes 10 males for a 5-point win, and the count for bitches is the same. For the identical point total, it takes only 15 Irish Setters, 13 Afghan Hounds, 8 Borzois, 22 German Shepherd Dogs, and 10 Great Danes. Although Alberta has the toughest point schedule in Canada, dog fanciers in the United States think it's a breeze, and those with time on their hands often try to cop a C.K.C. championship for their beasts before or after achieving the A.K.C. title. All but a few A.K.C. breeds (see Chapter V) are also recognized by the C.K.C. and can be shown in Canada—and vice versa, of course. This reciprocal arrangement also goes for both amateur and professional handlers and most judges. Dog fanciers contend that the mutual respect of the A.K.C. and C.K.C. is the strongest bond between the two countries.

In both the United States and Canada, dog lovers who participate in the sport of Obedience claim that it's light-years ahead of the dog show. As far as personal satisfaction goes, that is. It's only four decades old in America, but it's already the second most popular sport in the dog game. If it is to become more popular than showing, human nature will have to change, since the beast must be well trained, very obedient. By comparison, the breed ring is child's play. No wonder showing remains more popular.

The most intelligent purebred in the United States cannot become an Obedience champion. For one thing, the title does not exist, and for another, degrees, not titles, are the goals of the sport. There are four such degrees: Companion Dog (CD), Companion Dog Excellent (CDX), Utility Dog (UD), and Tracking Dog (TD). CD, CDX, and UD must be earned in that order and they are progressively difficult. A dog can go for his TD before, during, or after his involvement with the other degrees. The beast who earns all four is rated as a UDT (Utility Dog Tracking). If he's also a show champion, he's canine proof that beauty can come with brains. "Ch. Klondike Kate of Perth UDT" would be such a beast.

Many more purebreds are eligible for Obedience than for show. One reason: A.K.C. listed (miscellaneous) breeds as well as a recognized breeds are welcome. Another, bigger reason: individual requirements for Obedience are more lenient than for show, in that a beast, either sex, does not have to be whole and can be at odds with the dictates of the appropriate breed standard. Thus, a white German Shepherd Dog is okay, and so are a spayed Papillon and a monorchid Bichon Frise, and the same goes for a Doberman Pinscher who wears a natural tail. Obviously, beasts who are eligible for show are also okay here, although they must be able to learn, think and remember.

So almost any purebred over six months who is not vicious, lame, or completely blind/or deaf can compete in the sport of Obedience, granted that he is bright enough to learn his basic commands and his owner has the talent to teach them. The big demand in Obedience is complete rapport between owner and beloved beast. Almost all Obedience dogs are handled by their owners, making this more of an amateur sport. Professional Obedience handlers are few and far between, for this is not a big money sport. And the judges, while expert and A.K.C. approved, are more on the amateur side in spirit. Unlike breed judges, they neither demand nor command high fees.

The sport's action takes place at Obedience trials. Some are staged separately, but most are held concurrently with point shows. Well, that's true of all but the TD trials, since they must be held apart on virgin, untramped territory. Unlike the attainment of the other degrees, TD is a one-shot affair and the beast succeeds or fails under the eyes of two judges. The canine candidate must follow a trail laid by a stranger for a minimum of 440 yards and top off the performance by searching for and finding a small article (glove, wallet, whatever) left by said stranger. The dog who passes the test does so without guidance from his handler, without dilly-dallying along the way, and without chasing squirrels. Aside from bestial concentration, this is really a test of scenting power, and it's rough but not impossible for the breeds that wear short muzzles (flat faces), such as the Boxer,

Bulldog and Pug. Most owners don't have the talent, time or patience to ready a beast for the TD try. Net result: in a given year fewer purebreds who earn the TD than the CD or CDX or UD.

All the other degrees are three-shot affairs, in that a successful beast must score sufficiently and properly at three different trials before he is awarded his degree, and each time out he performs under the eyes of a single judge. In a series of prescribed exercises for which he has been trained, the beloved beast shoots for a perfect score of 200. When he scores a "proper" 170 or better, he earns a "leg," and three legs amount to a degree. An improper 170 or better does not earn a leg. For a proper score, he may not earn fewer than half the allotted points in any one exercise. The action occurs in a ring, this time a rectangular area of about thirty-five by fifty feet.

For a brief look at the exercises and the scoring, per degree:

Companion Dog (CD)
1) Heel on Leash, 40 points. The leash is loose at all times and is not used to guide or correct the dog. He stays close to the handler's left side and always sits (without command) when the handler is not moving. The dog does right, left, and about face and figure eight at various speeds, as the judge directs.
2) Stand for Examination, 30 points. On command, and off leash, the dog stands on a Stay and holds it while the handler walks around him and the judge examines him.
3) Heel Free, 40 points. A repeat of the first exercise, but without the leash.
4) Recall, 30 points. On command the dog leaves a Sit and Stay, goes to the handler and sits directly in front of him, but not touching him. On the second command, dog goes to Heel and Sit.
5) Long Sit, 30 points. The dog holds a Sit and Stay for a minute in the company of other dogs who are doing the same thing. During the time span, the handler leaves the dog, faces him from across the ring, then returns to him.
6) Long Down, 30 points. Another group exercise (no more than 15 dogs per class), with the dog on a Down and Stay and holding it for three minutes. The handler's chore is as above.

That's the gist of the 200 points for the perfect score in the CD trial. In real life, perfection is a seldom thing, and it happens much more often in the backyard than at a trial. Often, the dog does something wrong, such as sitting in a sloppy manner. That can cost a few points. Too often, the handler is guilty of giving too many commands, vocally or by hand signal. That also costs points. When both dog and handler sin during a given exercise, it is the sad duty of the judge to take away points in a wholesale manner. All 40 points can go down the drain in Heel Free when a handler goes through the motions unaware of the fact that his dog is sitting and watching him, or has left the ring.

On paper the exercises seem rather simple, and training the dog to perform them is not a difficult task. At home, that is. The actual trial is something else, for there all sorts of fascinating distractions occur. The successful dog must disregard them if he is to score 170 or better. For almost any starting beast, the toughest of the CD exercises are the final two exercises, wherein the dogs are about thirty inches apart. This is pretty close for canines who have not been introduced, and the urge to say hello or engage in a little play is sometimes very strong. On the Long Sit, the dog who harvests all 30 points does so by sitting *smartly*, silently and motionless. In this case, *smartly* means squarely; eyes to the front, head up, forelegs straight and chest apart, and hind legs tucked under the quarters rather than to the side. On the Long Down, the beast who moves the most scores the fewest points. If he breaks from either the Sit or the Down, he has no chance of gaining a leg. And when one dog breaks, several others usually join him. They become losers, too.

Fortunately, there are a couple of handy ways for orienting a beloved beast to the strange sounds, sights and scents that he'll encounter at any Obedience trial. Match show trials don't count, but they are abundant, found just about everywhere, and are conducted under the formal A.K.C. rules and regulations. After a few such trials, most dogs are conditioned for the real thing. An untrained pooch, of course, isn't ready for the match trials.

And then there are the obedience schools, designed for the specific purpose of teaching owners (handlers) the easiest and best ways to train their dogs. The teaching is conducted via group method (for several handlers and their dogs at the same time). While the schools are not difficult to find, the quality varies and depends on the experience and wisdom of those in charge. Sessions are usually held once a week in the evening, and the average training course runs from eight to ten weeks, with tuition pegged at from twenty to thirty dollars. If what is learned at school is practiced at home on a daily basis, an innocent beast should be ready for his first try at a CD leg inside of three months, granted that his owner-handler has the slightest capability. If an owner who has completed the course still lacks confidence, a few match trials are in order.

Since many of the Obedience instructors have devised training methods that deviate somewhat—or entirely—from the traditional, the Obedience fans who take the sport to heart are continually going to one school or another with their dogs. This is particularly true of the fanciers who go beyond the CD. Until the beast has earned his CDX and UD degrees, they feel that the dog is rather uneducated.

Companion Dog Excellent (CDX)
1) Heel Free, 40 points. Much the same as in CD, but more demanding.
2) Drop on recall, 30 points. This is Recall with an added touch. Somewhere along the route from the starting point to the handler, the dog drops down on command or signal from his handler (who gets the okay from the judge). The dog stays down until released, or called, and then completes the exercises as in Recall.
3) Retrieve on Flat. 20 points. The handler tosses a hardwood dumbbell and the beast fetches it to hand. He sits before delivering.
4) Retrieve over High Jump, 30 points. Another retrieve of a dumbbell, but this time the dog, coming and going, takes the high jump that's set (for most breeds) at 1½ times his height.
5) Broad Jump, 20 points. The dog must clear the broad jump without touching it. The jump consists of four hurdles, set one after another and evenly spaced. They are 6 inches high and placed to cover a distance that is (for most breeds) 3 times the height of the dog. A dog gets up to a 10-foot start for the broad jump. The finish is the same as in Recall.
6) Long Sit, 30 points. Same as in CD, but goes for 3 minutes. Handlers leave the ring and go out of sight of dogs for the duration.
7) Long Down, 30 points. As in CD, but for 5 minutes. Again, the handlers leave the ring.

As in CD, three legs make a CDX, and a leg is a proper 170 or better. On the Broad Jump, the canine who takes the hurdles in fine style and then dawdles on the way back to his handler (where he makes a sloppy sit) could get 9 points. If perfect in the other exercises, his score would be 189, but not a leg. The AKC holds that 9 is less than half of 20.

Finally, the UD exercises. They may not seem very challenging on paper, but four decades of Obedience have proved that only beasts capable of concentration can overcome.

Utility Dog (UD)
1) Signal Exercise, 40 points. Really an exercise in hand signals since the handler uses signals and not verbal commands to put the dog on heel, stay, sit, come, and a finish as in Recall. Off leash, and heeling as in Heel Free.
2) Scent Discrimination–Article No. 1, 30 points. From a set of five similar articles (leather or metal) spread out about 15 feet from where the dog sits (with his back to the spreading), the dog (on command) scents and finds the one article previously touched by his handler. He picks up the article and carries it to his handler as in Retrieve on Flat in CDX.
3) Scent Discrimination–Article No. 2, 30 points. As above, but with another set of articles.
4) Directed Retrieve, 30 points. Three white work gloves are placed in different spots—right, left and center—across the ring from the dog. On command, he goes to a designated glove, picks it up, and retrieves it to handler. All accomplished briskly and minus foolishness.
5) Directed Jumping, 40 points. The dog must clear a bar jump and a high jump, both $1\frac{1}{2}$ times the beast's height. The high jump is the same as in the CDX. The bar jump is just that, a bar painted with black and white rings. The jumps are taken in the order desired by the judge and commanded by the handler. Finish as in Recall.
6) Group Examination, 30 points. The only group exercise in UD: no fewer than 6 beasts, no more than 15. They hold a stand and stay as their handlers face them from across the ring and the judge examines them (with his hands) as in the breed ring. A minimum of 3 minutes before the handlers return.

Well, that's the UD, the supreme test for the very obedient dog.

Of all the exercises, Directed Jumping is the bad news. At home, at obedience schools and at match trials, a dog can take that bar jump hundreds of times. At a formal trial, when the chips are down, the same dog often prefers to run under the bar, as if he can't resist the temptation. Sometimes a dog will do it after he has scored close to 200 on his first and second UD legs. When that happens, his handler usually assures anyone who will listen, "My dog just wanted to make sure that I'll take him to another trial."

Only silly dogs fear that they'll stay at home after copping the UD degree. Most keep right on competing in the sport of Obedience. To grasp the *how* and *why* of that, it helps to know the setup of classes at the three degree levels:

Companion Dog

Novice A Class: dogs shooting for the CD and handled by a person who has not previously handled a dog to his CD. Handler must be owner or member of owner's immediate family.

Novice B Class: dogs shooting for the CD and handled by owner or any other person.

Companion Dog Excellent

Open A Class: CD dogs trying for their CDX and handled by owner or member of owner's immediate family.

Open B Class: CD dogs trying for their CDX, as well as CDX dogs and UD dogs, handled by owner or any other person.

Utility Dog

Utility A Class: CDX dogs trying for their UD and handled by owner or member of owner's immediate family.

Utility B Class: CDX dogs trying for their UD, as well as UD dogs, handled by owner or any other person.

Utility Class: a combination of both A and B classes (above), sometimes substituted for both at Obedience trials where entries are limited.

The *how* of UD dogs continuing in the sport of Obedience is explained by Open B and Utility B (or Utility). As for the *why,* that's explained by the fact that in those classes the prizes and trophies are both more abundant and more valuable. The higher the score, the more the loot. And what's more, there are usually additional awards for the high scorers in designated breeds. This means it's possible for Sorrowful Sam UD, the only Beagle in Open B, to score a measly 174 and still take home more loot than the Afghan who chalked up an almost perfect 199 and placed first. So a UD beast doesn't have to score in the sky consistently to keep putting money in the bank and trophies on the shelf. And since any UD dog improves as he goes along and most can keep going for several years, their owners stay with the sport. Some can't shake it. Rather than waste their talents, they start breaking in new pooches for the distant future.

The sport of Obedience has been coming along very fast in the United States. It is a more satisfying sport than showing, since the handler who trains his beast witnesses the results of his labors and in the long run the canine becomes extremely obedient and comes closer to realizing his fullest pet potential. And just about every other member of the Obedience set insists that the sport is far more honest than showing. To put that another way, all the action in Obedience is out in the open, the rules are firm, and everybody knows when a dog errs. The beast's score, per exercise, depends on the judge's decision, and he (she) had better be right or the unemployment ranks will beckon. Unless standing and trotting are considered arts, show dogs do not demonstrate talent or intelligence, and it is difficult to predict the judge's decision. Does he understand the breed standard, or does his grasp of it amount to a unique misrepresentation? In the breed ring, the suspense amounts to whether the judge will select the best dog present. At an Obedience trial, the only concern is whether a very smart pooch will harvest 195 or 196 points. Let it be said that Obedience judges are more consistent than breed judges.

The sport is younger and has a longer way to go in Canada, where the annual count of C.K.C. trials is still short of 300. The C.K.C. degrees are identical to those offered by the A.K.C., and the classes, exercises, rules and regulations of both national bodies are pretty much the same, at least very, very close. Of course, only breeds recognized by the C.K.C. can compete in the Canadian trials, so (as in the sport of showing) a few A.K.C. breeds are not eligible. And Canada has a small touch of one upmanship, a championship in Obedience; the canine wonder who collects his CD, CDX, and UD degrees is confirmed as Obedience Trial Champion (O.T.Ch.). The A.K.C. hasn't followed suit to date, but you can bet that pressure for the change is in the cards. Dog fanciers do love championship titles. Such a title honors their dogs and tickles their vanity. Or is it the other way around?

Neither the A.K.C. nor the C.K.C. offers the title of Dog Fancier Champion (D.F.Ch.) to ardent, active dog lovers and owners, but that oversight doesn't keep the lovers from dreaming about copping the title for themselves. When that wonderful day comes, won't their dogs be proud?

Readers who own purebreds, have reached this page, feel inspired, and would like to become engaged (with their beloved beasts) in one or more of the official sports will be happy to learn that the governing bodies have not overlooked the higher education of dog fanciers. Both offer booklets covering the rules, regulations, and other pertinent information relating to the official sports of the dog game in the respective countries. Single copies of the following booklets are supplied gratis by the A.K.C. and for a small stipend ($.50 each) by the C.K.C.

AMERICAN KENNEL CLUB
51 Madison Avenue, New York, N.Y. 10010

Rules Applying to Registration and Dog Shows
Obedience Regulations.
Registration and Field Trial Rules (Pointing Breeds, Retrievers, Spaniels, Dachshunds)
Beagle Field Trial Rules
Basset Hound Field Trial Rules

CANADIAN KENNEL CLUB
2150 Bloor St., W., Toronto, Ont. M6S 4V7

Dog Show Rules
Obedience Trial Regulations and Standards
Tracking Test Regulations
Field Trial Rules for Beagles
Field Trial Rules for Spaniels
Field Trial Rules for Pointing Breeds
Field Trial Rules for Retrievers and Irish Water Spaniels

Select your sport and learn the rules. Field trials are for adults, and the sport can be expensive. The whole family can get into the act at dog shows, where children sometimes outshine their elders as amateur handlers. Anyone who can control a beast and guide him through his paces is old enough to handle in the breed ring. It's a fine starting place in the dog fancy for young dog lovers. If they prove adept, Obedience is the place to really test their talents. The same goes for Mom and Pop.

Of course, when the entire family gets active in the dog game, it helps to have at least one beloved beast per person.

XII

How to Speak with Authority in the Dog Game: A Glossary

Like all other games, sports, arts, crafts, hobbies, and sciences, the dog game has its own vocabulary, and it is more or less international. Dog lovers who are familiar with as few as a couple dozen canine terms are sometimes suspected of being dog fanciers, and dog fanciers who can use fifty such terms to describe a given beast can hold their own at the annual dinner of any kennel club. Some dog fanciers know just about all of the terms, and it's easy for a stranger to confuse such people with canine authorities. The way to tell the difference is to listen very carefully. A fancier who is up to his ears in doggy terms will sprinkle them into any conversation, whether the subject is beloved beasts, weather, family, politics, religion, or the economy. A genuine canine authority doesn't do that. However, he's bound to use many of these terms when he talks about dogs.

Action—movement of beast as he walks, trots, or runs
Adult—over twelve months of age
Almond eye—eye is almond-shaped
Alopecia—baldness, as in hairless breeds or as side effect of illness
Angulation—curvature of stifle (knee joint) formed by upper and lower thighs
Apple head—rounded head that is humped at center; high-domed skull
Apron—frill of hair below neck and on front of chest
Babbler—hound who sounds off when not really on trail

Balance—parts of beast's body are typically proportioned for breed

Bandy—bowlegged

Barrel—rounded rib cage

Bay—voice of a working hound

Beard—thick whiskers under jaw (e.g., Bouvier)

Belton—intermingling of colored and white coat hairs

Benched show—a show in which dogs occupy assigned positions on benches when not competing in breed rings

Birdy—canine expert on upland birds (e.g., English Setter)

BIS—Best in Show, a title awarded at dog shows

Biscuit—bread-crust color found on otherwise white breed (e.g., Samoyed)

Biscuit eater—sporting dog who dines on shot game instead of fetching

Bitch—female beast, any age

Bite—alignment of upper and lower teeth when mouth is closed: even—(also *level*), uppers and lowers meet edge to edge; overshot —upper jaw overlaps lower; scissors—outer sides of lower incisors touch inner sides of uppers; undershot—lower jaw projects beyond upper

Blanket—pattern of color over back and upper sides

Blaze—white stripe running up center of face

Blocky—a square head

Blooded—well-bred

Bloom—in prime condition (coat)

Blown—beyond bloom, poor condition of coat

Blue—blue gray

Blue merle—blue gray mixed with black

BOB—Best of Breed, a title awarded at dog shows

Bobtail—naturally tailless dog or with very short docked tail (e.g., Old English)

Bone—substance; relative size (girth) of leg bones

BOS—Best of Opposite Sex, a title awarded at dog shows

Bossy—overdeveloped up front

BOV—Best of Variety, a title awarded at dog shows

Brace—a matched pair of beasts

Breeches—trailing portion of a dog's rear under tail

Breeching—the tan on outside of thighs (e.g., Coonhound)

Breed—family of purebred dogs who are more or less uniform in looks, designed and maintained by man

Breeding—the selective mating of canines; in-, mating of closely related canines (i.e., immediate family); line-, mating of related canines (i.e., same blood lines); line-, mating of canines who are not related

Brindle—even mix of black hairs and lighter color (e.g., Cairn)
Brisket—forepart of body below chest, between forelegs
Broken color—solid color broken up by white or another color
Broken-haired—a roughed-up wire coat (e.g., Airedale)
Brood bitch—bitch used for breeding; matronly beast
Brush—bushy tail
Burr—inside of ear; formation visible within the ear cup
Butterfly nose—spotted or parti-colored nose
Buttocks—rump (hips)
BW—Best of Winners; a title awarded at dog shows
Cape—coat hairs behind shoulders (e.g., Schipperke)
Castration—removal of testicles
Catalog—publication containing the particulars and entries of a dog
    show, Obedience trial, or both
Cat foot—round and compact foot
CD—Companion Dog; an Obedience degree
CDX—Companion Dog Excellent; an Obedience degree
Ch—show champion
Character—proper looks and personality for breed
Cheeky—having prominent, rounded cheeks
Chest—forepart of body that is enclosed by ribs
China eye—clear blue eye
Chiseled head—clean-cut head
Chops—jowls; pendulous flesh of lips (e.g., Bulldog)
Clip—coat trim required in some breeds for showing
Cloddy—heavy and low-slung
Close-coupled—reasonably short from withers to hips; box-like
Cobby—close-coupled
Conformation—complete body structure as called for in breed standard
Corky—full of zip and zap
Cow-hocked—with hocks (ankles) turned in toward each other
Crank stern—screw tail
Crest—upper, arched portion of neck
Crooked front—with forelegs bent inward or outward; a fault in most
    breeds
Crook tail—malformed tail
Cropping—trimming ears (in puppyhood) so that they stand erect
Crossbreed—offspring of sire and dam of different, pure breeds
Croup—part of back directly above hind legs
Cry—music or voice of hounds
Cryptorchid—adult beast whose testicles have not descended into
    scrotum
Culotte—longer hair on backs of hind legs

Cushion—fullness of upper lip (e.g., Pekingese)

Cynologist—student of canines

Dam—female parent

Dappled—with mottled markings of secondary color

Deadgrass—dull straw or sedge color

Dewclaw—useless fifth toe found on some breeds (e.g., Briard)

Dewlap—loose, pendulous skin under throat (e.g., Bloodhound)

Dish face—concave nasal bone; poor structure

Disqualification—a specific fault or condition that makes a dog ineligible for A.K.C. or C.K.C. point shows

Distemper—most common of the canine infectious diseases

Distemper teeth—pitted or discolored teeth resulting from distemper

Docking—surgical shortening of a pup's tail

Dog—generic term for either sex, but always used to denote the male in sports

Domed—as in "domed skull": evenly rounded top of skull; convex (e.g., English Toy Spaniel)

Dominant—(characteristic) most likely to be transmitted to offspring

Double coat—coat composed of two distinct layers: top coat covers soft, dense, short undercoat (e.g., Labrador)

Down-faced—with muzzle sloping downward (e.g., Bull Terrier)

Down in pastern—with faulty pastern joints

Dropper—setter-pointer cross

Dry neck—neck with taut skin

Dual champion—beast who has won both show and field titles

Dual purpose—used for both show and field

Dudley nose—flesh-colored nose

Ears:

　bat—wide at base, rounded at tip, carried erect with orifice toward front (e.g., French Bulldog)

　button—folded forward covering orifice, with tip lying close to skull (e.g., Fox Terrier)

　drop—drooping; hanging close to cheek (e.g., American Foxhound)

　flying—sprawling all over the head (it shouldn't)

　hanging—same as drop, preferred for sporting dogs (e.g., English Setter and Irish Setter)

　prick—erect and usually pointed at tip (e.g., German Shepherd)

　semi-prick—erect with just the tip leaning forward (e.g., Collie)

　rose—small drop ear that folds over and back to reveal burr (e.g., Bulldog)

Easy keeper—beast who always has a hearty appetite

Eczema—common inflammation of the skin; can be wet or dry

Elbow—joint between forearm and upper arm

Elbows close—elbows held parallel to body as in most breeds
Elbows out—elbows turned out from body (e.g., Bulldog)
Ewe neck—neckline with concave curvature; opposite of arched
Expression—the combination of all features of head that contribute
    to beast's spirit
Faking—changing a dog's appearance by artificial means (disqualifies
    for show)
Fall—fringe of head hair overlapping face (e.g., Lhasa Apso)
Fancier—stimulated dog lover
Fault—not in conformity with standard for the breed; disqualifier
FC—Field Champion
Feathering—long fringes of hair on ears, legs, and tail (e.g., Irish Setter)
Feet E and W—toes turn out and away
Fiddle front—out at elbows, with Feet E and W
Fiddle head—long, narrow head
Field stock—bred for work in field sports
Finished—having won the desired championship or degree
Flabber mouth—self-appointed canine authority
Flag—tail on the long side (e.g., English Setter)
Flagging—inviting romance by bitch in heat; tail to one side
Flank—portion of side between last rib and hip
Flat-sided—with rib cage lacking roundness
Flea—*Ctenocephalides canis;* prefers sick to healthy dogs
Flecked—with light ticking
Flews—pendulous inner corners of upper lips
Flush—drive upland birds from cover
Flyer—magnificent beast of a breed
Fooler—dog who acts as if he's found game but hasn't
Foreface—part of face between eyes and nose; muzzle
Foul color—coat color improper for breed
Founder—brood bitch who consistently throws superior pups
Foxy—with head carrying a foxlike expression; clever
Frill—apron of fine hair decorating throat and chest
Fringes—feathering
Frogface—face with extended nose and very overshot bite
Front—forepart of a beast's body
Furnishings—desirable hair; feathering and whiskers
Furrow—indentation down center of skull to stop (e.g., Mastiff)
Gait—canine locomotion; the way a dog walks, trots and runs
Gassy—full of the old moxie; high-spirited
Gay—with exuberantly wagging tail
Gazehound—hound who is better at sighting than scenting (e.g., Grey-
    hound)

Geld—castrate

Genealogy—list of beast's progenitors

Gestation—pregnancy of bitch, a period of nine weeks

Goose rump—rump that slopes to a low-set tail (e.g., Italian Greyhound)

Grizzle—bluish gray or iron color

Group—one of six A.K.C. or C.K.C. divisions of all the breeds

Guns—marksmen who shoot the game birds at field trials

Hackle—hair on back of neck that stands upright in anger

Hackney gait—high stepping gait

Ham—muscular mass above stifle (knee) on hind leg

Handler—amateur (owner) and professional (licensed), a beast's pilot who guides the dog through his paces at show or trial

Hard-mouthed—with jaws that damage whatever is carried

Harefoot—long, narrow foot

Harlequin—white beast with irregular black or blue markings (e.g., Great Dane)

Haunch—rump

Haw—third canine eyelid; red membrane on inside corner of eye, sometimes obvious (e.g., Bloodhound)

HD—hip dysplasia; with malformed hips; a congenital defect

Heat—a bitch's season for romance

Height—measurement from ground to shoulders (withers)

Hepto—Hepatitis, dread disease of the liver

Hie on!—"Get out there and hunt, you clown!"

Hock—canine ankle

Honorable scars—marks left by wounds suffered in honest work, not in fighting

Hound glove—handy grooming glove for use on flat and smooth coats

Hound-marked—traditional white, black, and tan coloration of hound breeds (e.g., Beagle)

Hucklebone—top of hip bone

ID—identification form for dog entered at a dog show

Immortal—Judge

Impotent—a stud dog must have more than desire

Incisors—upper and lower front teeth

Interbreed—see Crossbreed

Isabella—fawn color; light bay

Jabot—fringe of longer hair between forelegs (e.g., Schipperke)

Jowls—flesh of lips and jaws

Judge—A.K.C. or C.K.C. approved mortal, either sex, for divining

Jury—owners of losing dogs who find judge incompetent

Kennel—any shelter for a beloved beast

Kennel blind—(owner or judge) fails to recognize dog's faults

Kink tail—broken tail; sharply bent

Kisses—tan spots on cheeks and over eyes (e.g., Manchester Terrier)

Klunker—cockeyed canine

Knuckling over—double-jointed carpus (wrist) throwing body weight forward

Laid back—muzzle appears pushed in, flat (e.g., French Bulldog)

Layback—angle of shoulder blade to the vertical

Lead—leash

Lean head—head with tight skin and absence of flesh (Miniature Pinscher)

Leather—ear flaps

Leg—qualifying score in Obedience trials; a proper 170 points or better

Leggy—too high on leg; legs too long for breed

Lemon—light yellow

Lepto—Leptospirosis, a very serious kidney disease

Let down: hocks—metatarsus bone (hock to foot) is short (e.g., Whippet)

Level back—topline even

Lippy—with overdone, loose lips

Litter—family of pups

Liver—deep reddish brown

Loaded—with shoulder blades shoved out from body

Locomotion—movement

Loin—portion of body between last ribs and hindquarters

Lumber—excess weight, as on a ten-pound Yorkshire Terrier

Lunkhead—stupid beast, handler, or judge

Lurcher—crossbred hound

Mad dog—rabid dog

Mane—long, profuse hair on top and sides of neck (e.g., Silky Terrier)

Mantle—dark portions of coat on shoulders, back, and sides (e.g., Chow Chow)

Mask—darker coloration on foreface (e.g., fawn Pug)

Match—informal dog show or trial

Mate—breed a dog to a bitch

Merle—blue gray with touches of black

Mismarked—with wrong coat color or color pattern for the breed

Molera—soft spot on top skull; abnormality of skull (e.g., Chihuahua)

Mongrel—offspring of nonpurebred parents

Monorchid—beast with one testicle missing from scrotum

Moulting—British for "shedding"

Music—baying of hounds on the trail

Mute—hound who is silent on the trail

Muzzle—part of head between eyes and nose; face

Muzzle band—white marking around muzzle (e.g., Boston Terrier)

Non-slip—Retriever who does his job off lead

Nose—canine's scenting power

Nurser—brood bitch; sometimes a bitch who thinks she's a mother

Neveragain—fancier who tries to swear off dogs

Occiput—upper point of skull

Oestrum—see Season

Old pie—see Founder

Open bitch—bitch receptive to being bred

Orange—light tan

OTCH—Obedience Trial Champion; Canadian title award

Otter tail—tail that is thick at root, round, and tapering (e.g., Labrador)

Out at elbows—with elbows turning out from body

Out at shoulders—with loose, jutting shoulders

Out of coat—see Blown

Overhang—pronounced brow (e.g., Japanese Spaniel)

Pacing—with legs per side moving in unison as dog gaits (e.g., Old English)

Pad—sole (cushion) of paw

Paddling—moving in a way that makes forefeet seem to slap ground

Paper foot—flat foot with thin pad

Parti-color—coat of two distinct colors

Pastern—portion of foreleg between carpus (wrist) and toes

Patella—kneecap

Peak—see Occiput

Pedigree—recorded ancestry of any beast, purebred or mongrel

Pig jaw—overshot bite

Pigmentation—coloration of nose, lips and eye rims

Pile—dense undercoat (e.g., Belgian Tervuren)

Plucking—removing dead hairs from coat with fingers

Plume—abundant feathering on tail (e.g., Lhasa Apso)

Points—credits awarded dog in competition for show championship

Pompon—rounded tuft on end of tail (e.g., Poodle in Continental clip)

Popper—beast who constantly looks to handler for directions

PRA—progressive retinal atrophy, hereditary eye disease

Prepotent sire—stud able to pass dominant virtues to offspring

Proud—with head held on high

Puppy—beast under twelve months

Purebred—dog whose sire and dam are of the same breed

Put down—groom and make ready for show

Quaint—with an oddball personality

Quality—proper breed type

Quetzal—overdressed amateur handler, either sex

Racy—slim, leggy

Rat tail—demonstrated by any Irish Water Spaniel; bare-tipped or clipped tail that looks bare

Ringer—dog who looks quite like another dog

Ring tail—tail carried up and over back with curl (e.g., Basenji)

Roach back—topline that is arched over loin (e.g., Bedlington Terrier)

Roan—fine mix of white with other colored hairs

Roman nose—high-bridged, slightly convex nose; ram's nose

Rudder—tail

Ruff—long, thick hair growth around neck (e.g., Chow Chow)

Saber tail—tail carried in a semicircle up toward tip (e.g., Komondor)

Sable—black hairs intermingled in lighter color

Saddle—black markings over back

Screw tail—short, twisted tail (and okay on a French Bulldog)

Season—bitch's time for mating; heat period

Second thigh—hindleg from stifle to hock

Self-color—solid color, sometimes with shadings

Service—stud dog's contribution to the mating act

Set—points where ears join head and tail joins body

Shedding—seasonal casting off of coat

Shelly—weak in body; with poor conformation

Short-coupled—short back

Sickle tail—tail carried out and up in a semicircle

Sidewinder—beast that advances in crablike manner with body at an angle

Sight hound—see Gazehound

Sire—male parent

Sloping shoulders—layback of shoulder blades

Smooth—short and close (coat)

Snipey—with pointed, weak muzzle

Sound—with no physical or mental defects

Spaying—surgery to prevent bitch from conceiving

Splashes—irregular markings of secondary coat color

Spring of ribs—curvature of rib cage

Stance—manner of standing

Standard—man's blueprint for the ideal dog of a breed

Stern—tail

Sternum—breast bone

Stifle—canine knee

Stilted—with choppy gait

Stop—step-up from muzzle to skull, located between the eyes; specified to some degree in many breed standards

Stud book—record of the breeding particulars of beasts of a breed

Swayback—concave topline

TD—Tracking Dog; an Obedience degree

Team—four beasts of the same breed

Thigh—hindquarter from hip to stifle (knee joint)

Throaty—with loose skin under throat

Thumb marks—black spots on pasterns (e.g., Manchester Terrier)

Ticking—small spots of dark hairs on a white coat

Timber—leg bone

Tongue—music; cry of hounds

Topknot—tuft of hair atop head (e.g., clipped Poodle)

Topline—the back from withers to tail

Trace—dark marking down the back (e.g., Pug)

Triciasis—ingrown eyelashes (may need surgery)

Tri-color—dog with black, tan, and white coat

Trim—manner of grooming; to shape hair by cutting

Tuck-up—small waist, light loin (e.g., Doberman Pinscher)

Turned-up—uptilted (foreface) (e.g., Bulldog)

Typey—beast who is true to his breed standard

UD—Utility Dog, an Obedience degree

UDT—designation for dog who has earned all four Obedience degrees

Unbenched show—opposite of Benched show; when not in actual competition, dogs are parked anywhere

Undercoat—coat closest to skin of double-coated dog

Undulator—breed judge who keeps changing his mind about type

Unfrocked—see Blown

Unthrifty—just unable to stay healthy

Upland birds—pheasant, grouse, quail, and other game birds found on dry land

Varminty—a keen expression

Vixen—a tricky bitch

WB—Winners Bitch; A.K.C. show title

WD—Winners Dog; A.K.C. show title

Weaving—crossing forefeet or hindfeet, or both, when in motion

Weedy—with not enough bone

WF—Winners Female; C.K.C. show title

Whelping—giving birth to a litter

Whelps—unweaned pups

Whip tail—stiff tail held straight out
Whiskers—long hairs on muzzle and under jaw
Withers—high point of shoulders; point from which height is measured
WM—Winners Male; C.K.C. show title
Wrinkles—loosely folded skin on face and brow (e.g., Bloodhound)
Wry mouth—improperly aligned lower jaw
Xylo—a beast who eats strange things (wood, stone, metal)
Yapper—barker who makes naise needlessly and continuously
Yeanling—Bedlington Terrier pup
Zott—bum; not worth a zott; handsome but stupid

Credits

(Affenpinscher) Courtesy of the breeder/owner Lucille E. Meystedt, photo Missy Yuhl

(Afghan Hound) Courtesy of *Dogs* magazine, photo Ken Fadem

(Airedale Terrier) Courtesy of the Airedale Terrier Club of America, Inc., photo by Ludwig

(Akita) Courtesy of the breeders/owners Nicholas and Marilyn Fiorenza

(Alaskan Malamute) Courtesy of the owner Georgia Brand, photo Richard K. LaBranche

(American Cocker Spaniel) Courtesy of the American Spaniel Club and the owner Mrs. Prescott H. Peirce, photo Bob Lapre

(American Foxhound) Courtesy of the breeder/owner Stanley D. Petter, Jr.

(American Staffordshire Terrier) Photo from Evelyn M. Shafer

(American Water Spaniel) Courtesy of the owner John H. Barth; breeder Swan Lake Kennels

(Australian Cattle Dog) Courtesy of *The National Stock Dog Magazine,* E. G. Emanuel, Registrar & Editor

(Australian Kelpie) Courtesy of the American Kennel Club

(Australian Shepherd) Courtesy of *The National Stock Dog Magazine,* E. G. Emanuel, Registrar & Editor

(Australian Terrier) Courtesy of the owner Nell N. Fox

(Basenji) Courtesy of the breeder/owner Ellen F. Scheuing

(Basset Hound) Courtesy of The Basset Hound Club of America, Inc.

(Beagle) Courtesy of the breeder Mrs. William O. Coleman, III, photo Billy E. Barnes

(Bearded Collie) Courtesy of the owner Lawrence Levy, photo Evelyn M. Shafer

(Bedlington Terrier) Photo from Evelyn M. Shafer

(Belgian Malinois) Courtesy of the breeders/owners Dr. & Mrs. Dale M. Diamond, photo William P. Gilbert

(Belgian Sheepdog) Courtesy of the Belgian Sheepdog Club of America and the owner Mrs. M. K. Maul

(Belgian Tervuren) Courtesy of the owner Francis R. Calderwood, photo by the owner

(Bernese Mountain Dog) Photo from Evelyn M. Shafer

(Bichon Frise) Courtesy of the breeders/owners William and Ida McNerney, photo Missy

(Black and Tan Coonhound) Courtesy of the breeders Don and Jackie Iden; owners James and Kathleen Corbett

(Bloodhound) Courtesy of the owner Dee Hutchinson and the Dachshund Club of America, Inc., photo Evelyn M. Shafer

(Border Collie) Courtesy of the American Kennel Club

(Border Terrier) Courtesy of Arnold Pfenninger

(Borzoi) Courtesy of the Borzoi Club of America, Inc., and the breeders O'Valley Farms, photo Tauskey

(Boston Terrier) Courtesy of the breeder/owner K. Eileen Hite, M.D., photo William P. Gilbert

(Bouvier des Flandres) Courtesy of the American Bouvier des Flandres Club and the breeder Dan Rosenberg, photo Joan Ludwig

(Boxer) Photo from Evelyn M. Shafer

(Briard) Courtesy of the Briard Club of America and breeder/owner Mary Lou Tingley, breeder Harold A. Marley and owner James C. Zaccaro, photo James C. Zaccaro

(Brittany Spaniel) Courtesy of the American Brittany Club

(Brussels Griffon) Courtesy of the breeder/owner Iris de la Torre Bueno, photo Evelyn M. Shafer

(Bulldog) Photo from Evelyn M. Shafer

(Bullmastiff) Courtesy of the American Bullmastiff Association, Inc.

(Bull Terrier) Courtesy of the Bull Terrier Club of America and the owners Carl and Ingrid Ackerman

(Cairn Terrier) Courtesy of the owner Betty Hyslop

(Canaan Dog) Courtesy of the owner Jay C. Sheaffer

(Cardigan Welsh Corgi) Courtesy of the owners Mrs. J. Bruce Morey and Charles G. Ingold, photo Martin Booth

(Cavalier King Charles Spaniel) Courtesy of the American Kennel Club

(Chesapeake Bay Retriever) Courtesy of the American Chesapeake Club

(Chihuahua) Courtesy of the Chihuahua Club of America, photo Schreick's Studio

(Chinese Crested Dog) Courtesy of the breeder/owner Anne Hermundson

(Chow Chow) Courtesy of the Chow Chow Club, Inc., and the owner Dr. Sam Draper, photo Tauskey

(Clumber Spaniel) Photo from Evelyn M. Shafer

(Collie) Courtesy of the Collie Club of America, Inc., and the owner Mrs. Dwane Shields, photo Susan Larson

(Curly-Coated Retriever) Courtesy of the owner Nancy Huntington

(Dachshund, longhaired) Courtesy of the Dachshund Club of America, Inc., photo Percy T. Jones

(Dalmatian) Courtesy of the breeders/owners Connie and Sid Gates

(Dandie Dinmont Terrier) Courtesy of the owner Mrs. W. H. Oakley, photo Tauskey

(Doberman Pinscher) Courtesy of the breeders/owners Kay Martin and Arnold S. Orlander, photo Evelyn M. Shafer

(Drever) Photo from Åke Wintzell, (c) Åke Wintzell

(English Cocker Spaniel) Courtesy of the English Cocker Spaniel Club of America, Inc., and the owner Ruth L. Cooper; breeder Rimskittle Kennels; photo Steve Poast

(English Foxhound) Photo from Freudy Photos

(English Setter) Courtesy of the breeder Clariho English Setters, photo Ray Cavanaugh

(English Springer Spaniel) Courtesy of Photos Afield, owner Larry Michnevich, photo Allen Peck

(English Toy Spaniel) Courtesy of the owner Jane E. Henderson, photo Tauskey

(Eskimo) Courtesy of the owner Adele M. Crawford, breeder Gordele Kennels

(Field Spaniel) Courtesy Photos Afield, photo Allen Peck

(Finnish Spitz) Courtesy of the breeder/owner Joan Grant

(Flat-Coated Retriever) Courtesy of the owner Grace L. Lambert

(Fox Terrier, Wirehair) Photo from Evelyn M. Shafer

(French Bulldog) Photo from Evelyn M. Shafer

(German Long-haired Pointer) Courtesy of the breeder/owner Martin Wernaart

(German Shepherd Dog) Courtesy of *Dogs* magazine, photo Ken Fadem

(German Shorthaired Pointer) Courtesy of the German Shorthaired Pointer Club of America, the breeder Walter Seagraves and the owner Donald A. Miner

(German Wirehaired Pointer) Courtesy of the German Wirehaired Pointer Club of America and the owner/breeder Jenny Farnstrom

(Giant Schnauzer) Photo from Evelyn M. Shafer

(Golden Retriever) Courtesy of *Dogs* magazine, photo Ken Fadem

(Gordon Setter) Courtesy of the Gordon Setter Club of America, Inc., and the owner Weaner, photo Dunnideer Photography

(Great Dane) Photo from Evelyn M. Shafer

(Great Pyrenees) Photo from Evelyn M. Shafer

(Greater Swiss Mountain Dog) Courtesy of the owner Alfred N. Gmur, photo Nicholas F. Gmur

(Greyhound) Courtesy of the Greyhound Club of America, photo William Brown

(Harrier) Photo from Evelyn M. Shafer

(Ibizan Hound) Courtesy of the American Kennel Club
(Irish Setter) Photo from Evelyn M. Shafer
(Irish Terrier) Courtesy of the Irish Terrier Club of America and the owners Mr. and Mrs. Frederick Sholes
(Irish Water Spaniel) Courtesy of the Irish Water Spaniel Club of America and the owner Marion Hopkins, breeders Mr. and Mrs. Robert Sparkes
(Irish Wolfhound) Courtesy of the breeder/owner Jill R. Bregy, photo Joy C. Larcom
(Italian Greyhound) Courtesy of the Italian Greyhound Club of America, Inc., and the breeder/owner Mrs. John Bloore
(Jack Russell Terrier) Courtesy of the breeder/owner Mrs. H. L. Crawford, III
(Japanese Spaniel) Courtesy of the owner Michael Pym; breeder Mrs. Eileen Haig
(Keeshond) Courtesy of the breeder/owner Alice S. Kluding
(Kerry Blue Terrier) Courtesy of the owners Mr. & Mrs. Bertram M. Tormey, photo Ken Fadem
(Komondor) Courtesy of the breeders/owners Joy and Marion J. Levy, Jr.
(Kuvasz) Courtesy of the owners Loretta S. Ouellette and Dana I. Alvi (breeder), photo Geraldine Paolillo
(Labrador Retriever) Courtesy of the owner Mrs. George Murnane, photo Joe Riser, Jr.
(Lakeland Terrier) Courtesy of the United States Lakeland Terrier Club and Mrs. John R. Loeffler, photo Larry Harton
(Lhasa Apso) Photo from Evelyn M. Shafer
(Maltese) Courtesy American Maltese Association, Inc., and the owner Marge Stuber
(Manchester Terrier) Courtesy of the American Manchester Terrier Club and the breeders Jim and Cari Manning
(Mastiff) Courtesy of the owner Edward A. Gerace, photo Walter Chandoha
(Mexican Hairless) Courtesy of the breeder/owner Anne Hermundson
(Miniature Bull Terrier) Courtesy of the breeders/owners Larry and Jackie McArthur, Photo Rich Bergman
(Miniature Pinscher) Courtesy of the Miniature Pinscher Club of America
(Miniature Schnauzer) Courtesy of the owner Muriel Ainley, photo Herbert C. Skiff
(Newfoundland) Courtesy of the Newfoundland Club of America, Inc.
(Norwegian Elkhound) Courtesy of the Norwegian Elkhound Association of America and the owner Glenna Crafts, photo by Crafts
(Norwich Terrier) Courtesy of the Norwich Terrier Club, photo Constance Larrabee
(Nova Scotia Duck Tolling Retriever) Courtesy of the breeder/owner James C. Jeffery
(Old English Sheepdog) Courtesy of Dogs magazine, photo Ken Fadem
(Otter Hound) Courtesy of the owner Hugh R. Mouat, D.V.M.
(Papillon) Courtesy of the Papillon Club of America, Inc., the breeder Pat M. Stubbs, and the owner Janis A. Stephens, photo Warlock
(Pekingese) Courtesy of the owner Mrs. Frank S. Hess
(Pembroke Welsh Corgi) Courtesy of the Pembroke Welsh Corgi Club of America, Inc., and the breeder/owner Douglas Bundock, photo Gladys Bundock
(Pharaoh Hound) Courtesy of the owner Rita Laventhall Sacks, photo S. Klein
(Pointer) Photo from Evelyn M. Shafer
(Pomeranian) Courtesy of the breeder/owner Maxwell McQuillin, photo Ludwig
(Poodle) Courtesy of the breeder/owner Mrs. Herbert H. Miller, Jr., photo Ozzie Sweet
(Portuguese Water Dog) Courtesy of the Portuguese Water Dog Club of America
(Pudelpointer) Courtesy of the breeder/owner Sigbot Winterhelt
(Pug) Courtesy of the owner Shirayne Kennels and the breeder Shirley Thomas
(Puli) Courtesy of the breeder Sylvia Curtis Owen, photo Nelson Groffman
(Rhodesian Ridgeback) Courtesy of the owner Katherine L. Fanning
(Rottweiler) Photo from Evelyn M. Shafer
(St. Bernard) Courtesy of the St. Bernard Club of America and the breeder Blanche Carey

(Saluki) Courtesy of the Saluki Club of America and the owner Mrs. Esther B. Knapp

(Samoyed) Photo from Evelyn M. Shafer

(Schipperke) Photo from Evelyn M. Shafer

(Scottish Deerhound) Courtesy of the breeders/owners Edward and Cecilia Arnold

(Scottish Terrier) Courtesy of the Scottish Terrier Club of America, and the owners Dr. and Mrs. Barry Meador, breeder Zelwyn Kennels, photo Twomey

(Sealyham Terrier) Courtesy of the breeder William M. Hitt and the owners Ray and Dianne Burnett, photo Dan Kiedrowski

(Shetland Sheepdog) Photo from Evelyn M. Shafer

(Shih Tzu) Courtesy of the breeder Kathleen Kolbert, photo Don Petrulis

(Siberian Husky) Courtesy *Dogs* magazine, photo Ken Fadem

(Silky Terrier) Courtesy of the breeder Lolita Silky Terriers and the owners, Jo Anne and Michael Piazza, and Laura Lola

(Skye Terrier) Courtesy of the Skye Terrier Club of America and the breeders/owners Mr. and Mrs. Walter Simonds, photo Ainsworth

(Soft-Coated Wheaten Terrier) Courtesy of the owner Carol A. Walek

(Spinone Italiano) Courtesy of the breeder/owner Annieta S. Mann

(Staffordshire Bull Terrier) Courtesy of the breeders/owners Ed and Sylvia Rowland

(Standard Schnauzer) Courtesy of the breeders Drehil Kennels

(Sussex Spaniel) Courtesy of the breeders/owners G. and M. Deugan

(Tahltan Bear Dog) Photo from Jim Stirling

(Tibetan Spaniel) Courtesy of the Tibetan Spaniel Club of America, Inc.

(Tibetan Terrier) Courtesy of the breeders/owners J. and G. Reif, photo Curtis A. Reif

(Toy Manchester Terrier) Photo from Evelyn M. Shafer

(Toy Poodle) Courtesy of the owner Robert A. Koeppel, breeder Joyce Peeples, photo Tauskey

(Vizsla) Courtesy of the Viszla Club of America, Inc.

(Weimaraner) Courtesy of the breeders/owners Ted and Lori Jarmie

(Welsh Springer Spaniel) Photo from Evelyn M. Shafer

(Welsh Terrier) Courtesy of the Welsh Terrier Club of America, Inc., and the breeders/owners Mr. and Mrs. James Edwardson, photo Sal Miuli

(West Highland White Terrier) Courtesy of the West Highland White Terrier Club of America and the breeders/owners Neil R. and Barbara J. Stoll

(Whippet) Courtesy of the American Whippet Club, Inc., photo Ritter

(Wirehaired Pointing Griffon) Courtesy of the breeders/owners Joseph G. and Dorothy Winter, photo Evelyn M. Shafer

(Yorkshire Terrier) Courtesy of the breeders Beerex Kennels

Index

NOTE: All breeds are indexed according to their full name and not inverted, e.g., Irish Setter, not Setter, Irish.

Kurt Unkelbach's slightly irreverent pen has helped make him America's most widely published author of canine lore and a favorite of literate dog lovers here and abroad. He confesses to having been a distinguished failure in several careers before turning to writing about the many facets of the dog game in such novels as *Love on a Leash, The Winning of Westminster,* and *Uncle Charlie's Poodle,* and such non-fiction works as *Those Lovable Retrievers, How to Bring Up Your Pet Dog,* and (with Evie Unkelbach) *The Pleasures of Dog Ownership.* He is also a biographer (*Albert Payson Terhune*), contributing editor of *Dogs,* and the unabashed author of several cat books.

Kurt and his wife Evie are well known in the dog fancy as veteran breeders, trainers and exhibitors of Walden strain Labrador Retrievers. They and their dogs dwell atop a Connecticut mountain, and their hobbies include gardening, dowsing, ornithology, and avoiding unfriendly porcupines and skunks. Other, minor canine authorities are often visible at the retreat. "We'd invite a major canine authority, but there hasn't been one in this century. If he's coming, he'd better hurry."

Kurt received the Fido Award (Gaines Dog Research Center) as "Dogdom's Writer of the Year 1975."